W9-CTG-914

THE
GREATEST
ATHLETE

(you've never heard of)

Canada's First Olympic Gold Medallist

MARK HEBSCHER

FOREWORD BY RON MACLEAN

DUNDURN
TORONTO

Cover image: Courtesy of MEARS Online Auctions
Printer: Webcom, a division of Marquis Book Printing Inc.

Library and Archives Canada Cataloguing in Publication

Hebscher, Mark, author
    The greatest athlete (you've never heard of) : Canada's first Olympic gold medallist / Mark Hebscher ; foreword by Ron MacLean.

Includes bibliographical references and index.
Issued in print and electronic formats.
ISBN 978-1-4597-4335-9 (softcover).--ISBN 978-1-4597-4336-6 (PDF).--
ISBN 978-1-4597-4337-3 (EPUB)

    1. Orton, George W., 1873-1958. 2. Runners (Sports)--Canada--Biography.
3. Athletes--Canada--Biography. 4. Runners (Sports)--United States--Biography.
5. Athletes--United States--Biography. I. MacLean, Ron, 1960-, writer of
foreword II. Title.

GV1061.15.O78H47 2019 796.42'6092 C2018-905851-X
                 C2018-905852-8

1 2 3 4 5 23 22 21 20 19

Conseil des Arts du Canada / Canada Council for the Arts

Canada

ONTARIO ARTS COUNCIL
CONSEIL DES ARTS DE L'ONTARIO
an Ontario government agency
un organisme du gouvernement de l'Ontario

We acknowledge the support of the **Canada Council for the Arts**, which last year invested $153 million to bring the arts to Canadians throughout the country, and the **Ontario Arts Council** for our publishing program. We also acknowledge the financial support of the **Government of Ontario**, through the **Ontario Book Publishing Tax Credit** and **Ontario Creates**, and the **Government of Canada**.

Nous remercions le **Conseil des arts du Canada** de son soutien. L'an dernier, le Conseil a investi 153 millions de dollars pour mettre de l'art dans la vie des Canadiennes et des Canadiens de tout le pays.

Care has been taken to trace the ownership of copyright material used in this book. The author and the publisher welcome any information enabling them to rectify any references or credits in subsequent editions.
               — *J. Kirk Howard, President*

The publisher is not responsible for websites or their content unless they are owned by the publisher.

Printed and bound in Canada.

VISIT US AT

 dundurn.com | @dundurnpress |  dundurnpress | dundurnpress

Dundurn
3 Church Street, Suite 500
Toronto, Ontario, Canada
M5E 1M2

This book is dedicated to those who never received the credit or notoriety they deserved, regardless of their profession or walk of life. The achievements of those who endeavoured to make the world a better place should not go unnoticed.

CONTENTS

FOREWORD

Back in 1990, I was seated next to my esteemed CBC colleague, Brian Williams, at the Academy of Canadian Cinema & Television Awards. We were both nominees in the Best Sportscaster category. On stage, Mark Hebscher had just opened the envelope and was about to present the winner. Brian cleared his throat in anticipation of delivering his winning acceptance speech (I often tease Brian about this). Of course, he always has the last laugh: he did win and was ever-gracious in his remarks.

But something else stood out for me that night. After Mark announced the winner, he made eye contact with Brian, then shifted his gaze to me and raised an eyebrow. There was a smile on his face and a twinkle in his eye that said to me, "It's okay, Ron, you are in the game." I never forgot that. I knew in that moment that Mark Hebscher saw beyond victory. He saw more than either the camera or the crowd was inclined to study. I knew back in 1990 that Mark could produce a book such as this.

Now, nearly three decades after that awards show, Mark has looked into something else unseen: the story of a little-known Canadian sports figure by the name of George Orton. This book is a remarkable mix of sleuthing and storytelling. And I love that it is a tale anchored in Canada, but set in Philadelphia, the cradle of democracy and the place where Orton came into his own. It's the city I associate with Thomas Paine, author of two must-read manifestos for broadcasters, *Common Sense* and *Rights of Man*.

A multitude of Canadian athletes have written great chapters of their lives in Philly: Flyer captains Bobby Clarke and Eric Lindros; Matt Stairs of Saint John, New Brunswick, who hit "The Most Memorable Home Run" in Philadelphia Phillies history; Todd MacCulloch of Winnipeg, who played basketball for the 76ers and at the same time for Team Canada at the 2000 Sydney Olympics; and Super Bowl champion Mark Rypien, who completed his last pass in the NFL as an Eagle.

But only one Canadian athlete's story bridges Canada and Philadelphia by combining the worlds of sports doctrine and sporting deeds, one story in which public issues result in the forfeit of personal prudence. It's the story of a gold medal winner, but it is also much more. It is the story of a man who did not leave his mark in Canadian sports history — until it was left to Mark to tell his story.

— Ron MacLean, host of *Hockey Night in Canada* and
the Olympics on CBC

Introduction

FIRST-TIME AUTHOR,
LONG-TIME READER

I t all started with a simple trivia question: *Who was the first Canadian to win an Olympic gold medal?*

The answer took me on a bewildering two-year odyssey.

Rendered disabled at age three, the individual in question recovered to become the most dominant athlete of his generation, despite a withered arm. As a distance runner and steeplechase champion, he was without peer. His skills in ice hockey and soccer were rarely matched. He was brilliant, too — fluent in nine languages and armed with a Ph.D. in philosophy. His revolutionary instructional books on track and field can be found in the U.S. Library of Congress. He was an innovator in the sports world, introducing the idea of placing numbers on football jerseys so spectators could identify the players. He popularized the use of a stopwatch to ensure proper pace for track athletes. He introduced ice hockey to Philadelphia, forming the first teams and creating the first league, and he was instrumental in building the first indoor arena in the city. He founded the Philadelphia Children's Playground Association, started two summer camps, coached championship track and field teams, and nurtured the Penn Relays into a world-class track meet. He taught and coached at some of the finest prep schools, was a respected and eloquent writer and poet, brought the Army-Navy football series to Philadelphia on a permanent basis, and was enshrined in seven Halls of Fame, all posthumously.

Surprisingly, the man I'm speaking of was born, raised, and educated in Canada, but nobody ever knew of him. And his story blew me away.

What follows is the story of George Washington Orton, possibly the greatest athlete you've never heard of.

1

THE BIGGEST RACE OF HIS LIFE

It is not the size nor build nor physique nor qualities of inherited ancestry that determines a track and field champion. The boy of slender build and of apparent constitutional weakness may turn out to be another George Orton, invincible in the distance runs.

— *Donald W. Hendrickson, 1909*[1]

Imagine you are three years old. You love to run and jump and play with your friends. But the doctor has just told your parents that you may never be able to walk or use your right arm again because of a terrible accident. You lie in bed, paralyzed, while your friends play outside. You dream of someday running again. Fast. Faster than all your friends. Faster than everyone in the world.

On a brutally hot July afternoon in Paris, a slender, curly-haired man with a shrunken arm is running in the Olympic 2,500-metre steeplechase. He had predicted in the newspaper that he would win the gold medal in this event, but he is in fourth place, and victory seems unlikely.

The year is 1900. George Washington Orton is the most decorated distance runner in the world, having won over 120 championships in the United States, Canada, England, France, Belgium, Holland, and Germany. At age 20, he had earned his bachelor's degree from the University of Toronto. When he was 23, he became one of the youngest to earn a Ph.D. at the University of Pennsylvania. He looks more like a scholar than a world-class

George Orton in 1893. As a student at the University of Toronto, he held the North American record for the mile-run and drew thousands of spectators to university track meets.

athlete. He is five feet six inches tall and weighs 120 pounds. He squints a lot, like he needs eyeglasses.

A week earlier, the English track and field championships had been held at Stamford Bridge, home of the London Athletic Club. In 1898, Orton won the two-mile steeplechase there, demolishing the field by 80 yards and becoming the first North American to win the coveted title. It took 24 years before an athlete from outside Great Britain won the steeplechase again.

By 1900, Orton was already a racing legend in Great Britain, and large crowds had come to see him and the other North American track and field stars in advance of the Paris Olympics.

But in the windy and damp conditions of Stamford Bridge, it was English champion Sidney Robinson who won the steeplechase that year, with Orton finishing a distant fourth. It was a painful defeat for Orton, who was in rough shape after a gut-wrenching 10-day ocean voyage from America.

He vowed to get better and defeat Robinson and the others at the upcoming Olympics.

Orton had been hired as a special correspondent by the *Philadelphia Inquirer* under the byline "George Orton — the famous Pennsylvania athlete." One of his assignments was to provide an insider's look at the Olympic track and field events and predict the winners of each discipline. He mostly chose North American athletes to win, believing them to be superior to the Europeans. And when it came time to preview the 2,500-metre steeplechase, Orton didn't beat around the bush. "Orton has more speed than the others," he wrote, "and, as he is a good jumper, he should win, if in condition."[2] It was simple and succinct. He predicted victory, but in the third person, as if he were talking about someone else.

But Orton is not in condition on this day. Not even close. He hasn't been right since leaving America nearly four weeks earlier. Forty-five minutes earlier, he had finished a close third in the 400-metre hurdles, becoming the first Canadian to win an Olympic medal, although he may not have been aware of the significance of that feat at that moment. While his opponents in the steeplechase were resting up for their big event, Orton was hurdling against the world's best.

The Olympic track and field events that year were contested on the grounds of the Racing Club of France, in the Bois de Boulogne, a huge park located in western Paris that is two and a half times the size of New York's Central Park. It may have been perfect for picnics, but it was a terrible choice as the venue for the Olympic Games.

As Orton pointed out, "The grounds are very picturesque, but not as well adapted for athletes as they might be."[3] He was being very kind. The biggest problem was the track itself. There wasn't one. The French had refused to install a cinder track in their municipal park. There was no way they were going to tear up their beautiful grass for foot racing. Instead, they laid out an irregular-sized 500-metre oval (standard size is 400 metres) on uneven grass. Orton pointed out that the track "leads around beneath the trees" and its condition was so poor that "no less than four sprinters broke down." The steeplechase course was especially brutal. Jumps consisted of authentic stone walls that couldn't be moved, thick hedges that were difficult to vault, and imposing water hazards. Even if one could successfully negotiate the water jump, a soaker would await you on the other side. The hurdles for the steeplechase were one metre high and fashioned from 30-foot-long telephone poles that had been stripped. None of the obstacles could be knocked down, unlike those in the hurdles events, which would fall fairly easily upon contact.

Conditions for the field events were hardly better. The last few yards of the running broad jump approach featured a six-inch incline. There were reports of some jumpers having to dig their own pits. As well, the venue was not spectator friendly. The Bois de Boulogne was at least a mile from any tramway and far from the nearest railroad station. "This inaccessibility affected the attendance greatly, which was disappointing considering the caliber of the runners and the importance of the events," wrote Orton.[4]

Gaining a good view of the track was another issue. Most spectators had their sightlines obstructed by a large grove of trees that made up the far end of the race course. Those who were fortunate enough to have the latest invention — binoculars — had the best view of the action.

Orton may have predicted victory in the newspaper, but he confessed two weeks later that he was anything but confident the day of the Olympic 2,500-metre steeplechase.

> No man received a worse drubbing than I in the English steeplechase championship. I must confess, while I did not

fear defeat in Paris, I knew I was against the best of the Old World and was pretty sure to be beaten. The race is sort of a dream to this day. We were all racing for the lead, and at the end of the mile we were dead to the world. A long stretch of woods was in the corner of the field and partially hid the backstretch. I was running fourth, and seemed to be out of the race, as [Sidney] Robinson was running strongly. About 300 yards from home, I seemed to realize that I was in the race for which I had come 4,000 miles.[5]

As the field headed for the treacherous water jump, Orton trailed Robinson, French champion Jacques Chastanie, and American Arthur Newton. Orton's childhood dream may have propelled him at that point. The fear of having to eat crow because of his newspaper prediction also provided the likely impetus to get a move on.

After the water, the runners would head through the trees at the far end of the backstretch and then turn for home. Nobody thought Orton had a chance, except the man with a clock in his head. You see, Orton had a near-perfect sense of pace. It was innate. He had perfected the art of running and waiting. In most of his races, Orton would conserve his energy by running perfectly timed intervals, falling behind and then finishing with a big kick, bolting past his opponents in dramatic fashion.

Most distance runners of the day did not have Orton's discipline. They ran as fast as they could for as long as they could before quitting or collapsing. Orton ran like a man with ice water coursing through his veins. Cool as can be, he would wait until the last possible moment before making his move. And most of the time, it resulted in victory.

Because he was a brilliant mathematician and had diligently studied and practised proper pacing since childhood, Orton could read a field of runners and know when to go and when to back off. When certain muscles became fatigued, he knew to change his gait and put less stress on them. He was one of the first on record to time his training intervals. He tried using a pocket watch initially, but the second hand was difficult to read and the watch too cumbersome. Orton felt that by fumbling with it, he was losing a second or two. It's possible that his withered arm made it even more difficult, and he eventually scrapped the idea. Later, he learned that British military officers were using a newfangled way to tell the time while both hands were occupied: wristwatches. Orton fashioned a primitive one with leather straps and began utilizing it, checking his intervals often. In training, he could run a mile in four minutes, 28 seconds. He paced himself with laps of 66, 68, 69, and 65 seconds. Even the most seasoned runners could not run the final lap faster than the opening lap. The fact that a teenager could do it was nothing short of amazing.

Orton always appeared relaxed during his races, without the strained look of a man gasping for air, face contorted and lungs ready to burst.

There are many photos of the legendary long-distance runner Paavo Nurmi, "the Flying Finn," carrying a stopwatch in training and in races. He also looks confident and relaxed, as if he knows he's going to win. In 1924, Nurmi, who won a record nine Olympic gold medals in track, was dubbed "the father of perfect pace."

But Orton's 100-plus victories and strict attention to time, decades before the invention of the stopwatch, should be recognized here: "The grandfather clock of perfect pace" seems like a good handle.

Back on the grass oval that Sunday in Paris, Sidney Robinson maintained his lead and was running without distress. After winning the week before in London, Robinson was poised to take the gold medal.

Orton, still running fourth, decided to make his move with an all-out sprint, urged on by some of his Penn teammates. Many in the crowd were well aware of Orton's legendary finishing kick and rose to their feet as the former Penn runner gave it the old college try.

Just then, the crowd lost sight of the runners, their views obstructed by the trees. When the runners entered the forest, Orton was fourth; when they emerged, he was in the lead!

Many were certain he had somehow lost the course and taken a short-cut. It appeared to be an optical illusion. How did he make up so much ground so quickly? As per his usual MO, Orton had timed his run perfectly, blowing past his rival Robinson with 100 yards to go. From there, he thundered down the stretch in front of the cheering crowd like a runaway freight train, flying over the final hurdle, winning handily and setting a world record: 7 minutes, 34 4/5 seconds.

Immediately upon breaking the tape, Orton raised his arms in triumph and collapsed, likely from a combination of exhaustion and elation. Robinson, the runner-up, fell right behind him five seconds later.

It was a sensational victory, as thrilling a race as anyone would see in these Olympics. Orton had erased a 20-yard deficit between him and Robinson in the final 300 yards to snatch the victory. According to the *New York Times*, the steeplechase "created a greater enthusiasm than all other events of the day."[6]

Despite suffering from what would later be diagnosed as a stomach virus, Orton had made good on his newspaper prediction. And his childhood dream had come true. In less than an hour, he had won two Olympic medals — a bronze and a gold. It would be 84 years before another Canadian, Marita Payne, would win two Olympic track medals on the same day. (Years later, Payne's fame would rise again when her son, Andrew Wiggins, became the number one pick in the National Basketball Association's 2014 draft and went on to take Rookie of the Year honours. Wiggins, and by extension his mother, Marita, are as famous in Canada as Orton is obscure.)

Orton was considered to be an American for many years after that victory, simply because he ran as a representative of the University of Pennsylvania. In his mind, the American sporting republic included Canada, but he never competed for either nation. Nevertheless, Americans took ownership of this great champion, and his Canadian heritage rarely came up. It would be more than 70 years before Orton was officially and correctly recognized as a Canadian by the International Olympic Committee.

But that didn't make him any less obscure.

When Olympic researchers made the discovery in the early 1970s, Orton's Olympic gold and bronze medals were officially removed from the U.S. total and added to the Canadian tally. This announcement was made without fanfare and without notifying any member of the Orton family. There was no press release to announce the changes, and no declaration that Orton was now a Canadian. Only a few people in Canada even knew about this discovery. Besides, Orton was already dead.

The moment he crossed the finish line on that steamy Paris Sunday in 1900, George Orton became the greatest Canadian athlete since Confederation in 1867. His sterling performance would pave the way for Canadian multi-sport stars such as Lionel Conacher and Fanny Rosenfeld, voted the greatest Canadian athletes of the first half of the 20th century. Prior to Orton, only rower Ned Hanlan and weightlifter Louis Cyr could be considered dominant 19th-century Canadian athletes, having beaten the best in the world consistently over a period of time.

★★★

Competitive rowing was a popular professional sport in the mid- to late-19th century. Winners received large cash prizes, and there was always heavy betting on the outcome.

Ned Hanlan had started out as a teenage "rum runner," rowing crates of whisky from his home on Toronto Island across the harbour for his bootlegger father. Soon, he was winning races, and from there his celebrity grew. He participated in numerous promotions, autograph sessions, and whistle-stop tours to encourage ticket sales and betting interest from the Nepean River in New South Wales, Australia, to Lachine, Quebec, and Chautauqua Lake, New York. He enjoyed meeting his adoring public and always found the time to show them how good he was on the water. Few could beat Hanlan straight-up, so he would give his opponents head starts in time or distance in order to drum up betting. Occasionally, he would give his backers fits by making it look as if he wouldn't be able to catch up. In the end, he would usually make a spirited effort to win, although there were times when he would lose on purpose just to set up a rematch and then cash in by betting on himself. Look up the word *showboat* and there's probably a picture of Hanlan next to the definition.

After he won the Centennial Regatta in Philadelphia in 1876, Hanlan returned home to marching bands and citizens lining the streets of Toronto to get a glimpse of the conquering hero. Many had bet on Hanlan to win, so the civic celebration was all the more festive. In 1880, a match race was set up on the Thames River in London, England: Hanlan versus Edward Trickett of Australia. Canadians bet over $40,000 on their native son; Australians bet over $100,000 on their man. Hanlan won easily, cementing his dubious position as Canada's greatest professional athlete.

Professionals were considered to be unsavoury characters at that time. Athletes and promoters would collude to stage events that were easy to fix in their favour. Cheating was frequent, and men like Hanlan engaged in questionable behaviour that included dodging potential challengers until the conditions were right. Usually, it was all about the money, not the athletic competition. Cries of "fix" were frequent, and the public became increasingly wary of these sporting events and the men who ran them. Following his career as a sculler, Hanlan ran a hotel and became an alderman in Toronto. He coached the University of Toronto rowing club in 1897 before taking on the same role at Columbia University in New York. Ned Hanlan died of pneumonia in 1908 at the age of 52.

Louis Cyr was the other prominent Canadian superstar prior to Orton. "The Strongest Man in the World" was widely known for his remarkable physical feats. A biblical, Samson-like character, the five-foot-eight-inch Cyr grew his hair long at his mother's suggestion. He could perform absurd exhibitions of strength. Rather than just lift more weight than his competitors, he constructed his own special events to showcase his legendary power. His specialty was the one-finger lift; he once managed 534 pounds. There was the time in Boston when he allegedly back-lifted a platform holding 18 men, generously estimated to weigh over 4,000 pounds. There is a famous photo of Cyr holding the reins of four horses, two on each side trying to run in opposite directions while their grooms cracked whips to encourage the horses to move him — to no avail.

These events would often occur during exhibitions of strength that were organized and promoted by Cyr himself. He would push a railway freight car up an incline and then dare any two men to duplicate the feat. Like Hanlan, Cyr was a showman and a capitalist, attracting large crowds by promising and delivering legendary feats of strength. He toured with a circus strongman show that featured "the French Hercules," Horace Barr, as his assistant. But Cyr was far from athletic in his later years. By the time he had reached 40, his weight had skyrocketed to over four hundred pounds. He developed chronic nephritis, a disease that affects the kidneys and was likely brought about by the constant strain of heavy lifting. He died in 1912 at the age of 48.

Cyr and Hanlan were famous wherever they went.

Orton never received the same attention, partly because he wasn't a personality like Cyr and Hanlan. He didn't have a *shtick*. The athletes the newspapers wrote about had personality.

Unfortunately, most of the 19th-century Canadian history we learned when I was in school wasn't nearly as interesting as American history. We didn't have Benjamin Franklin or Abraham Lincoln or Thomas Edison or P.T. Barnum to write home about. (No offence to Alexander Graham Bell or Laura Secord, of course.) And there wasn't a lot written about

Canadian culture: music, art, architecture, dance, literature, or even athletics. Instead, our history seemed to be about politics, industry, finance, exploration, mining, the building of the railroad, and so on. Orton's story had not been told in the history books alongside those of Hanlan and Cyr. He was never referenced as a champion athlete alongside Percy Williams, Barbara Ann Scott, and the other Canadians who reached the pinnacle of Olympic achievement.

Orton did not have an agent or a public relations person to beat the drums about his many accomplishments, although he did consider himself a publicity man in later years.

He didn't hold running exhibitions or feats of endurance (although he once put on a "fast skating" exhibition to promote an ice rink in Philadelphia). Humility is a wonderful trait and it came naturally to Orton, who rarely tooted his own horn. His newspaper prediction prior to the Olympics showed a quiet confidence along with an admirable level of sportsmanship. To make one's point in the third person, rather than shouting it from the rooftops, says a lot.

As the years went on, American superstars Babe Ruth (called shot), Muhammad Ali ("Sonny Liston will fall / in the round that I call"), and Joe Namath ("I guarantee the Jets will win the Super Bowl") all came through on their brash predictions and, as a result, achieved legendary status. In 1934, baseball pitcher Dizzy Dean predicted he and his brother Paul would combine to win 45 games for the St. Louis Cardinals. When a writer told him he shouldn't brag, Ol' Diz replied that it wasn't bragging if you could back it up. The Dean brothers went on to win 49 games that year as "the Gashouse Gang" Cardinals won the World Series.

Orton didn't have to answer to any journalists in 1900. He quietly said he was going to win, and he won. I love that he did it in such a deliciously understated Canadian way. In his book *Distance and Cross Country Running*, Orton writes extensively about the top runners of the day, of which he was one. At the conclusion of his review he added this: "Note — The reader will kindly pardon the recurrence of my name in the brief review of distance running. A survey of the lists of American champions will show that I could not do otherwise if my review were to be authentic. [Signed] George W. Orton."[7]

He didn't need to apologize, although that is certainly another endearing Canadian trait. It's in our DNA to say "I'm sorry," even if we're not.

Regardless of his birthplace, Orton felt nationality had no place in amateur sports. He believed one competed for the love of the sport rather than flag and country, and where you came from should make no difference; nor should it matter if you were amateur or professional. However, Orton did not want to see professionalism take anything, or anyone, away from amateur sports.

In 1901, he wrote in the *Philadelphia Inquirer*:

> Some of our school boys are fast and strong enough to become crack basket ballers and they are snapped up by some enterprising manager of a professional team. It also frequently happens that men are taken from amateur teams to fill the ranks of the professional leagues. All such men are ineligible for any branch of amateur athletics. It is the duty of the Amateur Athletic Union to see to it that such men do not compete as amateurs, as has very often occurred. There is no disgrace in being a professional athlete, but a distinct wrong is done to amateur athletics when professionals try to foist themselves off as amateurs.[8]

Between 1892 and 1901, Orton won a reported 121 races, from the 400-metre hurdles to the 10-mile steeplechase, and nearly every distance and discipline in between. He won a staggering 32 international and national championships during that time. His 17 U.S. national titles in track and field was a record that stood for 50 years. And that total would've been much greater, but, unlike today, some events were not run every year during Orton's prime; for example, the three-mile (5,000-metre) championship was contested only twice between 1880 and 1902, and the cross-country race took place just twice over an eight-year period (Orton won it both times, in 1897 and 1898). Orton also won the five-mile championship in 1892, but that race was never contested again.

Had Orton had the opportunity to compete in some of these cancelled or discontinued events, I am fairly certain he would be the all-time record holder for U.S. championships in track. But as far as I know, he never once mentioned these lost opportunities.[9]

Incidentally, the same would be true of his Canadian numbers. Had he been allowed to compete in all of his favourite events, Orton surely would've garnered more than seven Canadian championships. Virtually unnoticed was his incredible record for the mile run — 4:21 and four-fifths — set in 1892. No Canadian would eclipse that record on Canadian soil until 1934, when Les Wade of Montreal trimmed a fifth of a second off that time. Imagine holding a record for 42 years!

If I had accomplished any of those feats, I'm pretty sure I would have said something about it. But Orton never mentioned any of his sporting accomplishments in the many books or articles I have read. He did not refer to himself as an Olympic, world, or national champion, even though he held all those titles. He was humble and unassuming, and those qualities likely cost him well-earned accolades and recognition.

When asked about his career, he considered himself only a "fair runner" despite what the record books said. Today, an Olympic champion returns to a hero's welcome and endorsement opportunities aplenty. The day after Orton won his gold and bronze medals, the *Toronto Star* headline screamed "CANADA BEATS WHOLE WORLD."

That was misleading, though; the story had nothing to do with Orton's victory.

"IN ITS FRUIT DISPLAY AT PARIS EXPOSITION" read the sub-heading.

The following day, a smaller headline on page six of the *Star* shouted "A FAMOUS VICTORY." Underneath, the text added: "George Orton's 2,500-metre steeplechase victory at Paris Exposition was a sensational affair, as the cable-grams show."[10]

The *Star* did not mention that Orton was from Canada because the entire story was copied from the *New York Times*, which didn't mention that Orton was from Canada either, only that he ran for the University of Pennsylvania.

At the time, the *Star* was one of six daily Toronto newspapers; the *Globe*, *World*, and *Mail and Empire* were morning papers, while the *Telegram*, *News*, and a later edition of the *Globe* were published in the afternoon. The *Montreal Star* had the largest circulation in the country, followed closely by the French-language *La Presse*. None had sent a representative to the 1900 Paris Olympics.

Members of the press who did travel to France deemed fruit at the Paris Exposition to have a greater importance than the world-class athletes.

Orton's appearance in the Olympic steeplechase apparently had no chance against Northern Spy apples and Bing cherries. Consequently, there were no Canadian stories featuring quotes from the victor and perspective from the track and field correspondent. Every Olympic story that appeared in the Canadian papers originated from the *New York Times* or one of the other news services.

The Grant brothers, from St. Marys, Ontario, did not get a mention in the *St. Marys Journal*, except that they were grouped with the "other American boys" at the Olympics. George Orton may as well have been from Mars. His gold medal victory at the Olympics went unreported in Canada.

Because of this oversight, planned or otherwise, Orton's significant achievement flew under the radar for decades until it became a trivia question. Over the years there have been major errors and omissions regarding Orton's life and accomplishments. I don't understand why anyone would *not* consider him to be a Canadian through and through. Even though Orton was the first to achieve Olympic gold, others are still credited with winning that first medal, according to the *Dictionary of Canadian Biography*:

> Etienne Desmarteau is remembered for his victory at the 1904 Olympics in St Louis, Mo., when he managed a throw of 34 feet 4 inches in the 56-pound weight contest. He was long regarded as the first Canadian to have earned a gold medal, although not all experts agree. Some claim the honour belongs to George Orton, who had won the 2,500-metre steeplechase in Paris four years earlier. Orton, a Canadian by birth, was, however, wearing the colours of the United States, where he was studying. Others maintain that Desmarteau should be considered the first since George Seymour Lyon's victory in the golf competition at St Louis in 1904 ought to be disregarded, golf having been included in the Olympic Games only that one time. [Golf was brought back for the 2016 Olympics.][11]

There are 8,500 entries in the *Dictionary of Canadian Biography*. I was shocked to discover that George Orton is not one of them.

Not a word. It's as if he never set foot in Canada, much less won two Olympic medals, confirmed by the IOC in the 1970s. Meanwhile, the biographies of Desmarteau and Lyon, neither of whom were the first to win gold, *are* listed. If these so-called experts couldn't agree on Orton's status as a Canadian, where exactly were they drawing their expertise from?

I contacted the folks at the dictionary to let them know of their oversight, hoping they would take this new information under advisement and add Orton's biography to their vast collection.

They replied by email on November 14, 2017: "Please note that we are currently working on Volume XVI, which contains biographies of persons who died between 1931 and 1940. Given that George Washington Orton died in the late 1950s, it will be some time before it comes time to consider him for inclusion."[12]

I'm sure there are many Canadians worthy of inclusion, but I'll bet none of them are in the Canadian Sports Hall of Fame, the Canadian Olympic Hall of Fame, the University of Toronto Sports Hall of Fame, the Ontario Sports Hall of Fame, and the London (ON) Sports Hall of Fame. Orton made a significant contribution to society and was a positive influence on countless people. Why does he still need to be "considered" for inclusion when several reputable sources have confirmed him as a Canadian?

In November of 1983, the respected *Olympic Review* wrote of Orton: "Although official records since 1904 have always listed … Etienne Desmarteau as the first-ever Canadian Olympic gold medalist … George Orton, hitherto always known as the American winner of the 2,500-metre steeplechase in Paris in 1900, was, in fact, a Canadian."[13]

Orton was already well known in North America and Europe by 1900, so the decision made by the newspapers not to cover his exploits or those of other Canadians competing in Paris was confusing to me, especially since they had followed the careers of Hanlan and Cyr so closely.

Orton had moved from Toronto to Philadelphia at age 20 to further his education and prolong his athletic career at Penn. Why were Canadian journalists no longer interested in the subject of many of their past stories?

Perhaps they believed Orton to be a dirty American professional, interested more in money than the love of sport, and not willing to uphold the values of pure amateurism, which was considered to be a Canadian virtue. The amateur code of the time would not allow athletes to accept prize money, admission money, or any payment for coaching, teaching, or even assisting athletes. At the same time, amateurs were expected to pay all the costs associated with competing — equipment, club memberships, travel, food, lodging, and so on. That meant nearly all the amateurs of the day were men from upper-class families in big cities who could afford to pursue their sport at a private club and not have to worry about making a living at the same time. Orton, they must have figured, would fall victim to the lure of money and fame once he moved to the United States. To them, he was turning his back on his country. As a Canadian and an amateur, he was dead to them.

The more I uncovered about Orton, the more his story intrigued me. I wanted to find out how a man so multi-talented could be so overlooked by his native country. Today, most Canadians are quick to point out anyone who has any remote association with Canada — an actress who rented an apartment in Toronto for a few years before being swept away by a prince, for example. That's good enough for some. *We are going to adopt you and make you an honorary Canadian.* Yet here's an actual Canadian-born fellow who's been dead for years and still gets less respect than Rodney Dangerfield.

This injustice led me to undertake a project that would occupy the next two years of my life and strengthen my resolve to tell the story of this obscure yet remarkable man who, against long odds, achieved what very few had done before or since.

2

THE DOCUMENTARY

I lost my long-time TV job in December 2015. I won't get into it, but let's just say things worked out all right. It provided an opportunity to tell the story that had started out as a trivia question.

As a television reporter, I had learned to tell a story in the amount of time it takes to wash your hands: a few good visuals, a solid interview clip or two, and a nice stand-up in front of the camera. Boom. Some creative writing and a relevant voice-over and there's your 80 or 90 seconds.

But this documentary I was envisioning would be close to an hour — a daunting task, especially since the subject had been dead for 60 years. Orton may have been the greatest athlete I'd never heard of, but dead men tell no tales; it would be up to those who knew him or knew *of* him to fill in the blanks for me. In the pre-internet era, I wouldn't have even tried to tell a story like this on my own. But with search engines and all kinds of digital archives available, there was plenty of information to discover in order to put together a great story. It would require a tremendous amount of research, something I was not unfamiliar with, and I certainly had the time. I also didn't need to worry about anybody beating me to the story; I was pretty certain that nobody in their right mind was chasing down leads for a George Orton biography.

My plan was to scour the internet and visit libraries, historical societies, and archives. I would call and email everyone I knew who might have any insight or suggestions. I would write a script; prepare questions; determine shooting locations; gather photos, newspaper clippings, and documents; delve into Orton's family history; find relatives, friends, and other key interviewees; ask all the right questions; dig doggedly for answers; and use my experience and enthusiasm to create a compelling documentary that everyone, not just Canadians, would want to see. Easy, right?

I even paid for a subscription to Ancestry, one of those websites that traces your family back hundreds of years. The first thing they ask you is the name of the family member you want to search for. Oh, he's not a family member. Is that okay? When I entered "George Orton," I suddenly felt as if I were his real great-grandson. I was trying to find out as much as I could about my great-grandfather, the one I never knew. Oh, I had heard stories, but you're never sure how much to believe about your relatives, right? What is truth and what is legend can easily become one and the same, especially when relatives tend to embellish the stories over the years. But what if you found out that your great-grandfather was the first Canadian to win an Olympic gold medal and nobody else knew about it? That's the way I was feeling. This man was now my surrogate great *zaida*.

When the time came to pitch the documentary idea to several broadcasters, I was pretty confident. I figured at least one executive would love the story, green-light the project, and finance the whole production so that it could be released in time for Canada's sesquicentennial celebration in 2017 (which turned out to be pretty lame). After all, who wouldn't love a story about an obscure Canadian who overcame incredible odds to win the first Olympic gold medal for this country? Especially someone with such an American-sounding name.

Yet the response to my pitch was underwhelming, to say the least. The needle didn't move at all. *Don't call us, we'll call you.* I was crushed. If the George Orton story was ever to be told, I would have to tell it alone. There would be no co-production with a big crew and a unit manager and a travel budget. It would be me and my VISA card.

When my wife was informed of this slight deviation in plans, she wondered aloud when I was going to get a real job and stop fantasizing about becoming a documentary filmmaker. But I couldn't stop now. There was a story to tell, and damn it, I needed to do this.

A big challenge was the acquisition of pictures and other visuals. When you write a book, all you need are a bunch of photos if the subject matter is biographical, and maybe a map or a pie chart. But a documentary film requires tons of visuals to accompany the narrative, and where was I going to get those? Nobody wants to see talking heads all the time, so those shots must be covered with film, video, photos, newspaper and magazine articles, and other documents.

I had one visual.

One photo.

Did I mention how challenging this was going to be?

George Orton's only living relative — a granddaughter, whose birth name was Constance Ulerich — would've been born in the early 1940s. I didn't know if she was alive, but her name didn't show up in any obituaries, so that was a good sign. I discovered she had been married at least three times and it appeared as if she had changed her name after each marriage. There may have been some hyphenated versions of her surname over the years, as well, and she might've gone back to her maiden name for a time. A real needle in a haystack.

Constance hadn't been heard from since the 1990s, when she was a professor at Mills College in Oakland, California. I had contacted the folks there many months before, looking for any information as to her whereabouts. My hope was that she was (a) alive and (b) lucid. I would hate to find out that, after all this searching, she had no stories to tell and no memories of anybody, much less her famous grandfather, my famous surrogate great-grandfather.

I had even considered hiring a private investigator to help in the search. Maybe get him or her to do some door-knocking around Oakland and see if anything came up. Without the only living descendant of George Orton, it would be difficult for me to properly and completely tell the story of his remarkable life. While I waited, I wrote down what I knew.

George Washington Orton was born in Strathroy, Ontario, on January 10, 1873, five and a half years after Confederation. Strathroy is an off-the-beaten-trail kind of town. Home to about 20,000 residents, it's located several miles off the 402 highway, about a half-hour west of London, and less than an hour from the border towns of Sarnia, Ontario, and Port Huron, Michigan. Like most of southwestern Ontario, Strathroy is surrounded by flat farm country and lots of it. Turkey- and chicken-processing plants sit alongside fields of corn and tobacco. If you want to stay at the best hotel in town, it'll set you back $80 — Canadian, of course.

There is no disputing that Orton was born in Strathroy, but a few things I had read didn't make sense. For example, the photo that accompanied the original newspaper article about Orton in the *Strathroy Age Dispatch* was that of a handsome blond-haired fellow with a regal nose. He looked to be in his early 20s in the photo and is wearing a track outfit with a "P" on the chest. Orton had attended the University of Pennsylvania and ran track there, so that made sense. I cross-checked the picture with a couple of other sources and it matched up. To my knowledge, there was no other photo available, so I had no reason to believe that this was *not* a picture of George Orton, especially since it had been in circulation for years.

George's father, Oliver Henry Orton, was born in 1843 in the eastern Ontario town of Lancaster, which sits on the St. Lawrence River at the Ontario-Quebec border. He was of Scottish descent. His father, also named Oliver, had been born in Bennington, Vermont, in 1794 and moved to the Ottawa area when he was a child. Young Oliver was raised in the Presbyterian faith; whether he subscribed to its tenets is unknown. His mother, Flora, was raised Roman Catholic, but despite her leanings, Oliver followed his father's faith and, at age 18, was an apprenticed wheelwright and a practising Presbyterian.

Young Oliver was living with a Roman Catholic family, the McDonells, in Lochiel, near his birthplace of Lancaster, when he met Mary Ann Irvine.

Mary Ann was born in Quebec City in 1846, the daughter of Samuel and Elizabeth Irvine, both of whom were born in Ireland. Mary Ann was the youngest of four children. She and Oliver were married in 1868.

It's possible that members of the Orton family had, at one time, been named "Horton," and vice versa. Oliver Henry Orton was once listed in property records as Oliver Henry HORTON. It may not have been a typographical error. French-speaking people do not use the "h" sound. Hockey is pronounced "ockey." Henry is pronounced "On-ree." Horton could have been pronounced and thought to be "Orton." There are many people from Quebec and Eastern Canada who inadvertently add an "H" sound to words that begin with vowels. Therefore, Orton could be pronounced "Horton." Think about that the next time you get a coffee from that famous chain named after the hockey player. Had the chain been known as "Tim Ortons," perhaps George's name wouldn't be so obscure in Canada. Even in the Toronto city directory in the 1890s, next to the listing for Orton, it reads, in parentheses, See also "Horton."

George was the third of six Orton children. His older brother, Samuel Oliver, was born in Winchester in 1869. Next, sister Mary Louisa (Minnie) was born in Cornwall in 1871. The family then moved west to Strathroy, where George was born in 1873. Sister Helena was born in Strathroy in 1875, and then the two youngest, Irvine in 1878 and Maude in 1880, were born in Winchester.

George's father seemed to be a bit of a wanderer; he rarely kept the family in the same place for more than five years. The move to Strathroy, just before George was born, came about when Oliver got a job as a carriage maker. This may have been facilitated by Mary Ann's family, who lived in the area. Her brother Thomas Irvine had been married in Strathroy in May of 1871, and Oliver and Mary Ann were witnesses. Maybe they liked it there. Thomas was listed as a grocer in the 1871 Strathroy census.

On a snowy February evening in 1874, disaster nearly struck the Orton family down. Oliver was a passenger on the Great Western Railway train as it headed west, past London and into Komoka, the last stop before reaching Strathroy. The train's steam-powered engines were fuelled by burning coal, and a fire broke out in one of the cars. Oliver was in the car nearest the engine and was overcome by smoke. He leaped from the moving car into the darkness below, shattering a kneecap and breaking an ankle in the fall. He then risked his own life by dragging three or four others off the tracks and to safety, according to eyewitnesses.

Oliver Orton was a hero that night, but the physical damages he suffered in the fall would keep him out of work for at least six months, as reported by the *Globe*.[1] The Ortons stayed in Strathroy and managed to make ends meet despite Oliver's injuries.

Eventually, they moved back to Winchester. The 1881 Ontario Census noted that the family of eight lived in West Winchester. The family farmed while Oliver was still plying his trade as a carriage maker. In 1885, O.H. Orton is listed as the owner at Concession 6, Lot 4, in West Winchester. It was a large tract of land, right along the Boyne Road at the eastern tip of the village, next to the Beach foundry, which had been destroyed by fire on July 12, 1884 (sadly, the owners had no insurance).[2]

Oliver likely had a training track on the property for testing his wagons, sulkies, and carriages. "I was around horses my whole life," said George Orton in a 1942 interview, "and my father was a great harness racing man."[3]

It is believed that the Orton family stayed on the farm in Winchester until around 1889, when they moved to Toronto.

Today, it's easy to find out where someone attended school, paid taxes, went to church, or received immunization. Uncovering similar information from the late 19th century is hit or miss, or at least it was for me — mostly the latter. The recording and filing of information was, to put it lightly, inconsistent. If you weren't home when the census people arrived, you may not have been counted. You could cross the border from the United States into Canada and vice versa with near impunity. Government documents were not always necessary. School records from the Winchester Public School were not available from the 1880s because the school had burned down — twice. Orton never offered up any information about this period of his life. He was very vague when it came to childhood memories and where they took place. He never revealed which schools he attended prior to the University of Toronto. It's possible that, with six children, the Orton home, or Oliver's workshop, may have been the proverbial one-room schoolhouse. It's obvious the Orton family put a premium on education, but coming from such humble roots, perhaps it was best for George not to mention where or how he grew up.

It's not clear when, but somebody mistakenly reported that Orton had attended Guelph Collegiate Institute in Ontario prior to attending university. Others later included that tidbit as part of their biographical sketch of Orton, and eventually, somebody lobbied for Orton to be in the Guelph Hall of Fame. It seems there was a man named George Turner Orton, a local doctor and politician. He may have been the George Orton who attended Guelph. Or it could've been a Richard Howitt Orton, who was from Guelph and attended the University of Toronto at the same time as George Washington Orton. It had been reported that Orton once won a footrace in Guelph, but that may have been the only time he visited that fine city. Perhaps when he won that race, the people of Guelph thought he was a local boy.

This was yet another example of mistaken identity that had burrowed its way into Orton's real life story. Too many mistakes had been made. As Sergeant Joe Friday always said on *Dragnet*, "Just the facts, ma'am. Just the facts."

After several months of research, I had discovered bits and pieces about Orton's life, but not enough to produce a documentary. Then one day in late June, everything changed.

I had asked Google to alert me if any information came available online with "George Orton" in the title or text. And there it was: the names of the inductees for the Philadelphia Sports Hall of Fame. One of them was George Washington Orton. Imagine that! They say timing is everything, and this news could not have come at a better time. It's as if the Hall of Fame knew somebody out there was thinking of Orton. What a huge break.

One of the other upcoming inductees to the Hall was Jimmy Watson, an excellent defenceman for the Philadelphia Flyers of the National Hockey League when they won two Stanley Cup championships in 1974 and 1975. Watson was born in Smithers, British Columbia, and played junior hockey in Calgary, Alberta. Other former Flyers would be attending the dinner and ceremony in a few months' time, all of them Canadian-born and raised. I wondered if any knew of Orton's accomplishments or even recognized the name.

I needed to be there with cameras rolling to record the event in early November. It would become a key part of the documentary. But I couldn't do it all by myself. I needed a partner. Someone who trusted me, believed in the story, and was willing to invest some money in exchange for a 50 percent ownership stake in the film. That person would be able to pay for cameras, travel, accommodation, editing, and all the other stuff. I could concentrate on the creative side.

With that, I needed to improve my photography skills, so I purchased a 2016 iPhone 6S Plus with a 4K camera and took some lessons on how to shoot with it. You never know when you'll need another camera, and since I was working on a shoestring budget, I had to take on many roles and be prepared for any eventuality.

Arriving home late one night in July, I checked my computer for email messages. I noticed a familiar name. "Re: George Washington Orton," read the subject line. But the email was from someone named Connie Meaney, not a name that was familiar to me. At first I thought she was the mother of my son's friend, Cam, who had the same last name. It took me a second to realize that *Connie* was short for *Constance*, and that got me very excited.

Orton's only living descendant was retired in San Francisco with her third husband, Ray Meaney. She was 74 years old.

I wrote back and told her of my plan to shoot a documentary about her grandfather. She was delighted and said she would help me in any way she could. I asked if she happened to have any pictures of George, perhaps some other memorabilia that she could show us. She replied that she had a couple of big boxes of stuff in her garage but hadn't looked at it in 20 years. I asked if, by chance, there might be any medals in there. She said there might be. It had been so long since she'd looked at it.

I was so excited I was literally shaking. This was the break I needed; the needle had been found in the haystack. Connie Meaney could transform this project from a good story into a great one. I immediately wanted to inquire about Orton's Olympic gold medal, but instead I bit my tongue. After searching for Connie for months, I didn't want to immediately screw up the relationship.

Getting to meet the granddaughter of my subject was going to be very cool. I asked if she could wait until I got to San Francisco with a camera crew before she opened those boxes. I envisioned a close-up shot of a dusty old crate that hadn't been opened in years. When the lid was lifted, there would be a jewellery box, and inside, a shiny gold medal. The money shot! Then, I thought about broadcaster Geraldo Rivera and that TV show where, after much hype, he opened gangster Al Capone's vault, hoping to find treasures. Instead, the big reveal was a big dud. The vault was empty. I asked Connie if she might go through the boxes in advance and let me know if there were any medals. That way there would be no surprises. The last thing I needed was to travel 3,000 miles for a box full of nothing. Besides, we could always "pretend" that she was opening the box for the first time when we went to shoot the scene in San Francisco.

I sent Connie a copy of the newspaper article from Strathroy so she could see what had been written about Orton. Within a few minutes she had emailed back. "That's NOT a picture of my grandfather."

Wait, what?

Usually, when a person is misidentified in print, someone in the know points out the mistake to an editor, who does some fact-checking. If warranted, an apology, correction, or retraction is printed and the mistake is rectified. But if nobody knew what George Orton looked like in the first place, how would they know the wrong picture had been published? And if that wasn't a photo of George in the article, who was the impostor?

According to Connie, the blond fellow in the picture was George's younger brother, Connie's great-uncle Irvine Orton. Irvine ran track at Penn a few years after his brother, and somebody obviously thought he was George. A check of the Penn track team photo of 1904–5 shows a blond-haired Irvine Orton in the second row. He bears little physical resemblance to his older brother, with the exception of his diminutive stature.

So here was a famous athlete with an American-sounding name who resided in the United States but was born and raised in Canada — George

Someone mistook Irvine Orton (second row, third from left) for his brother George and sent the wrong photo to Canadian researchers in the 1970s. Irvine ran track for the University of Pennsylvania in 1904–5 and later became a dentist.

GEORGE W. ORTON.

George Orton as captain of the Penn track team, 1897. Note how he keeps his weak arm and hand behind him, away from the camera.

Washington Orton. It would be like an American family naming their son Pierre Elliot Orton. I could see how it might be confusing.

Orton also has, post-mortem, the misfortune of still being misidentified as his brother. The photo next to George's name on several websites, including Wikipedia and the London Sports Hall of Fame, is still that same one of Irvine Orton.

Despite being rediscovered as a Canadian in the 1970s, Orton did not enter the Canadian Olympic Hall of Fame until 1996. In the interim, 65 track and field athletes were inducted before Orton was honoured as a Canadian Olympian (the first ever). Even as late as the summer of 2018, the Canadian Olympic website (olympic.ca) had no picture associated with George Orton's biography. Now tell me, which is more disrespectful to an Olympic champion and his family — the wrong picture or no picture at all? The Olympic Hall of Fame dropped the baton on that one.

Despite all his accomplishments, and now his induction into the Philadelphia Hall of Fame, Orton was still a nobody in his home country. He had been snubbed, overlooked, and misidentified on several occasions. What else had been omitted from the Orton story? And what else did he accomplish that we don't know about?

I would soon find out.

The official Canadian Olympic website still does not have a photo next to the name of Canada's first Olympic champion — pity!

3

THE BOY WHO NEVER WALKED

When he was three years old, George Orton was climbing an apple tree when he fell and landed on his head.

Someone fetched the local doctor. Without the benefit of X-rays (which would not be invented until 1895), he made an educated guess that George had suffered a fractured skull. It turned out that a blood clot had developed on the young boy's brain, and the doctor feared he would never walk again. Young George had suffered partial paralysis, which would greatly affect his motor skills and muscular coordination. He was unable to stand fully upright and required assistance just to get up. He could barely walk, much less run, and seemed destined to be a "cripple" for the rest of his life. He had to be carried almost everywhere — the modern wheelchair had not yet been invented and would not be mass produced until 1933.

The fall and subsequent blood clot had caused another problem: a deformed right arm and hand. The arm was shrunken and weak. It would never develop properly; George would use his left hand for everything. "Each day I practised with dumbbells and Indian clubs," he recalled. "At first, my right hand fingers were too weak to hold a club so I used to strap it to my wrist."[1]

In time, his right arm and shoulder became stronger, but the wrist, hand, and fingers were unable to perform with any dexterity. The nerves had been permanently damaged. It was, for lack of a better term, a "dead arm."

Orton seemed evasive when asked, in 1905, about his childhood and the accident that left him disabled. "At the age of eight," said Orton, "I seemed to come suddenly out of a dream. From that day onward, I was always wanting to run."[2]

In a foreword written by James E. Sullivan for Orton's book *Distance and Cross Country Running*, he says that Orton had fully recovered from his paralysis by the age of 12. During and after his recovery, George paid close attention to those who could run. As much as a young boy was able, he looked at running from a technical point of view, studying images of the great runners of the day. His dream was to run faster than anyone else, so he studied their technique — the ease of their gait and the length of their stride.

He discovered that each runner was different. Some swung their arms a certain way, others hardly used their arms at all. Some ran on their toes, others drove off their heels. Some held their heads high, others leaned forward. Given the opportunity, what kind of runner would George Orton become?

Once the blood clot had fully absorbed and George had slowly regained his strength and mobility, he couldn't sit still. He went from being able to stand fully upright to walking to jogging to running and jumping. Before long, the "cripple" was running everywhere and became known locally as "the boy who never walked."

There were plenty of opportunities for a young boy to compete in athletics. On weekends and holidays in the summer, nearly every community held an athletic meet of some sort, usually as part of a carnival, a county fair, or a church picnic. Organizers would include events such as the boot race on the program. That's a game in which competitors toss their shoes into a big pile and then, on the starter's gun, run shoeless toward the pile, find their own pair, lace them up (no slip-ons allowed), and then run 50 or so yards to the finish line. Any drooping laces or mismatched shoes would get you disqualified. The sack race and three-legged race were also very popular.

These events fostered a spirit of goodwill in the community and occasionally provided moments of hilarity when contestants fell down or tripped over each other. When it was time for the trained athletes to compete, things got serious. The program would include several competitions — weight throwing, ball throwing, tug of war, and, of course, track and field events that required running and jumping.

Oliver Orton couldn't help but notice the ease with which his son had been beating other teenagers, so he entered George in a local meet where he would run against grown men in an open competition. To the astonishment of everyone, including George, he won the half-mile race. He had discovered his true calling in life. "I found other boys could beat me at the sprints, but as soon as the race became long, I killed off all my adherents. This taught me that distance running was evidently my forte and I practised this continually," said Orton.[3]

As he grew stronger, George took a crack at other sports with great enthusiasm. He found success and enjoyment in playing hockey in the winter and soccer and lacrosse once the snow had melted. He played these sports at the highest levels, often against much older boys and men. What he lacked in size and strength he made up for with intelligence, grit, and the incredible will not just to succeed but to triumph in the face of adversity.

To make up for his deformed right arm, Orton developed a left-handed shot in lacrosse and hockey that was as hard and as accurate as anyone with two good arms. Orton would use his right hand to hold the end of the stick while the strong left hand could slide up and down the shaft and do all the manoeuvring as well as provide the necessary power. More often than not, he played one-handed, and remarkably well. When he was 14, Orton was good enough to play on an intermediate lacrosse team made up of much older boys. Even though he was by far the smallest and lightest player on the team, he was also the fastest. Orton was also an excellent midfielder on one of the top association football (soccer) teams in the province of Ontario at the age of 16. He could run all day and had the stamina to outpace most of his opponents (and teammates) on the soccer pitch.

In baseball, there is the rare athlete who can do everything exceptionally. He is known as a "five tool" player. He can hit for average, hit for power, run the bases well, field elegantly, and throw powerfully and accurately. Hall of Famer Willie Mays is one of the most famous examples of this type of player.

George Orton could be considered a five tool performer, except his five qualities would be different: He was a man of high moral character. He was academically brilliant. He was a dominant athlete. He was humble and unassuming. And he had an exceptional work ethic.

Willie Mays was regarded for his outstanding skills as a baseball player only. That's all he will be remembered for. The same is true of most elite athletes: They are judged by their accomplishments on the field or in the arena. That's what defines them.

The scholar-athlete is cut from a different cloth. Education is more important than athletics, but the two can be combined to produce exceptionally well-rounded people.

Missouri high-school basketball player Bill Bradley turned down 75 athletic scholarships to attend Princeton University in New Jersey, which did not offer scholarships. He won an Olympic gold medal in 1964 and was the collegiate player of the year in 1965. He then became a Rhodes Scholar and attended Oxford University before he ever played in the NBA with the New York Knicks. After winning two NBA titles, Bradley switched hats and entered politics. Soon, he was elected as the Democratic senator for the state of New Jersey, where he served for 18 years. He also ran unsuccessfully for president in 2000. Not bad for a sharpshooter from Missouri who wanted to get a solid education.

Football lineman Peter Dyakowski was attending high school in Vancouver in the early 2000s when he won a scholarship to Louisiana State University. He made the Southeastern Conference (SEC) academic honour roll twice, won numerous community service awards, and appeared on the wildly popular TV show *Jeopardy!*, where he finished third. His dry sense of humour and Mensa-level IQ combined with his athletic abilities made him very desirable. In 2012, he was named "Canada's Smartest Person" by winning a popular TV quiz show that aired on CBC Television. Not only was he considered Canada's smartest person, he was a three-time East Division All-Star with the Hamilton Ti-Cats. Peter is also the default number one draft choice of any team that wants to win a trivia contest.

I was fortunate enough to be his teammate in 2011 on what was supposed to be an all-star trivia team. The pressure was enormous, especially for Dyakowski, who was expected to answer every question correctly and without hesitation. He didn't, but he got most of the questions right and we won.

Byron "Whizzer" White was an All-American running back at the University of Colorado and runner-up for the Heisman Trophy in 1937. Despite being drafted fourth overall by Pittsburgh in 1938, he planned on attending Oxford University as a Rhodes Scholar. Instead, he was allowed to delay his start, and he led the NFL in rushing in 1938. He attended Oxford and then Yale Law School, and when the Second World War broke out, he enlisted in the U.S. Navy and became an intelligence officer. Later, he was appointed U.S. deputy attorney general by John F. Kennedy and then nominated as a Supreme Court justice, where he served for 31 years. He was as proficient on the bench as he was on the gridiron.

In 1890, the Orton family moved to 89 1/2 Beaconsfield Avenue, in the West End of Toronto, near Queen and Dufferin Streets. It was and still is a working-class neighbourhood.

Oliver Orton had been hired by Massey Manufacturing, farm equipment manufacturers and one of the largest employers in the city at the time. It seems he began as a clerk in the foundry, but under his name in the Toronto City Directory in 1890, it says "trav," which I assume meant travelling salesman.

George Orton began his studies at the University of Toronto in the fall of 1890 at the age of 17. He was so intelligent that he was placed in the *second*-year arts program at the school's University College. Orton was fluent in English and French, so it was no surprise to discover that he had no trouble easing his way into the main languages of the Old World. Orton could understand a dozen languages, including Indian Sanskrit and an Algonquin dialect from Quebec and Eastern Canada known as Montagnais. He was said to be fluent in nine languages — a remarkable accomplishment. He was also brilliant at calculus and possessed the powers of near-perfect recall.

Few knew about Orton's athletic potential that first year, as he had injured his knee playing soccer the previous summer and had not yet fully recovered.

In 1891, the Orton family was still living on Beaconsfield and Oliver was now a salesman for the newly formed Massey-Harris Limited, which was a short walk from his home. Also nearby was the brand new West End YMCA and Great Hall, at the southeast corner of Dovercourt Road and Queen Street West. This is where George spent the majority of his time when he wasn't attending classes. Dr. James Naismith had just invented basketball at the YMCA in Springfield, Massachusetts, and some of the early basketball games in Toronto were played in the new gymnasium at the West End YMCA. The facility also included a swimming pool and bowling alleys. Upstairs, the Great Hall had a seating capacity of up to 1,000 for live shows, lectures, and other events. For George, the crown jewel of the building was the new elevated circular wooden running track. This was his home away from home. His knee was feeling better, and the constant training had made it stronger than ever.

The original West End YMCA was relocated to Dovercourt Road and College Street in 1912 and remains there to this day. The Great Hall is now an upscale banquet and conference facility, but the original wooden track where Orton trained still remains in one of the rooms, Longboat Hall.

Canadian runner Tom Longboat, who won the 1907 Boston Marathon, trained there and represented the West End YMCA in the early 1900s.

On July 18, 1891, Orton ran his first real race at the Queen's Own Rifles athletic meet in Toronto. He won the half-mile in 2:07 and took the mile in 4:56 and three-fifths. It was the first time he had ever run a mile in competition, and he did it while wearing his football suit and lacrosse shoes. On August 11, Orton won the mile on the grounds of the St. Catharines Amateur Athletic Association. Representing the Varsity Football Club, he won in four minutes, 41 and one-half seconds, trimming nearly 16 seconds off his personal best. On September 26, at the Rosedale Grounds in Toronto, the 18-year-old was entered for the first time against the world's best in the Toronto Amateur Athletic Association championships. Another first for Orton: He would wear spiked shoes and run on a cinder track. The *Globe* was there to report on the race.

> Orton is only a boy, but a surprisingly fast one for a mile. It had been given out by those who knew that he would come pretty close to winning the race notwithstanding the fact that he had to go against W.B. George, who made the Canadian record of 4 min 29 4-5 sec. here a year ago....

On the back stretch in the second lap, George pushed up to the front, and when the crowd saw Orton pull out to pass, they cheered loudly. The little fair-haired lacrosse club representative was undoubtedly of sterling quality and on he went to the heels of Reid, who was only a yard behind George. The men traveled along in this order until about 300 yards from the finish, when Orton turned out to pass Reid. The crowd went fairly wild as they saw the boy gaining inch by inch on the record-breaker, and when he had cleared Reid and kept on after George in a plucky, determined manner their shouts could have been heard a mile away. George is a great runner for that distance, however, and Orton had to be satisfied with second place, but the performance was exceedingly creditable. Should he continue in his present progressive form he will yet be a world-beater.[4]

After reading that account, I wondered if anyone had known much about Orton's background. Likely not or they would've written about the obstacles he had overcome as a child. To go from where he once was to the top of the racing game certainly was impressive for a teenager in his maiden championship race. His story would've made for a great Hollywood script, except Hollywood wasn't much more than a couple of adobe huts back then. Movie making was in the embryonic stage, and Thomas Edison wasn't accepting any movie scripts. Besides, the story was just developing. Orton was only a second-year university student, but he was the talk of the U of T campus in the fall of 1891.

Every Varsity boy will be delighted with the performance of our representative at the annual meeting of the Toronto Amateur Athletic Association in Rosedale.... G.W. Orton ('93) ran second to one of the best mile runners in the world, pushing George right to the tape for first place, and beating the Canadian mile record ... for a youth of seventeen, [he was actually 18] who, three months before, did not know he could run, it is a surprising performance.

There is every prospect that in a short time our Varsity boy will hold his own with the best that can be brought against him. It is not only on the race course that young Orton has won laurels. In the class lists he is placed first in his year in Spanish and Italian, with a fair stand in German, French and English. A thoroughly modest and amiable fellow, *The Varsity* congratulates him heartily, and hopes to do so on many future occasions.[5]

Orton's victorious ways would continue in 1891–92. On October 10, he won the mile at the University of Toronto games. He duplicated his feat at the McGill University games in Montreal on October 23 in meet record time, and he took the half-mile race as well. On November 10, at the Rosedale lacrosse grounds, Orton handily won the cross-country race and, according to *The Varsity*, "did not seem the least bit fatigued by his effort as he flew in with his easy and graceful stride."[6]

The winter of 1891–92 saw organized hockey make its debut at the University of Toronto. The first Varsity hockey club was formed the previous winter, but there wasn't a decent place for the team to practise. A makeshift rink was constructed inside the residence enclosure, at quite an expense, but it was too small and always out of condition.

The *Varsity* lamented the lack of a decent facility for an institution of over a thousand students: "At present, our sports virtually terminate with the coming of the snow. Such would not be the case were a suitable rink provided."[7]

The squad that was formed, of which Orton was a member, was known as a residence team. They played games whenever and wherever they could, weather permitting, usually outdoors at the Toronto Granite Club.

The University of Toronto didn't exactly provide a welcoming athletic environment at that time. There wasn't a gymnasium on campus to help in the training and development of the undergraduates, except for Moss Hall, which had a few horizontal bars, some Indian clubs, and a ladder. Outside, Orton didn't have a cinder track to train on, even though he had run the fastest mile in North America that season. It wasn't until 1893 that a new gymnasium was built at the university.

In the fall of 1892, Orton began his final year at U of T. He had moved into a rooming house at 179 Dovercourt Road, just around the corner from the house on Beaconsfield. Oliver decided to move the rest of the family to the East End of Toronto, to 536 Ontario Street in an area known as Cabbagetown. The house was directly across the street from the Winchester Public School, north of Carlton Street and east of Sherbourne Street.

As a travelling salesman for Massey-Harris, Oliver seemed to take the word *travelling* quite literally, moving Mary Ann and the family frequently. The following year, 1893, they rented a house at 498 Ontario Street, two blocks away. In 1898, they moved six blocks north and west to 222 Bleecker Street, just above Wellesley Street.

Minnie Orton, George's older sister, was still living at home at the age of 27. She was employed as a clerk for a lawyer and politician named Emerson Coatsworth, who would go on to become the mayor of Toronto from 1906 to 1907. Twenty-year-old Irvine Orton was listed as a student, as was 18-year-old Maude.

In 1899, the Ortons moved once again, this time a few blocks south to 168 Bleecker Street. The following year, 1900, it was back to Ontario Street; the address this time was 678, farther north, above St. James Street. The family stayed there for three years and then moved to 59 Homewood Avenue, which is between Sherbourne and Jarvis Streets, south of Wellesley. By this time, Minnie was a saleslady and Maude was a telephone operator. The family lived on Homewood for two years before moving yet again. In 1905, their residence was 166 1/2 Brunswick Avenue, far from Cabbagetown and centrally located between Bathurst and Spadina, south of Bloor.

At this time, Maude was a saleslady for the W.A. Murray Department store on King Street East. While working there, she met a man named William Hague, who, like her father, listed his occupation as a traveller. They were married in Toronto on September 7, 1907, but had no children. Maude died suddenly of a thyroid condition on February 25, 1913. She was just 32.

Toronto was growing at a rapid pace during the 1890s. The first electric streetcar had been introduced in the summer of 1892. Within two years, the horse-drawn streetcar would disappear from city streets. The age of technology had arrived.

Construction had also begun on a new city hall at the corner of Queen and Bay Streets. Toronto was by far Canada's fastest growing city. Its population had swelled to 181,000, second only to Montreal's 219,000. Nearly one-third of the city's residents had been born in England, Ireland, or

Scotland. Protestants made up an overwhelming majority of Toronto's population, led by Anglicans and Methodists. Followers of Catholicism accounted for just 15 percent of the population. Long-standing cultural and religious bonds allowed the citizens to maintain standards and tastes that would make "Toronto the Good" a desirable place to live, work, and prosper.[8]

While the rest of the Orton clan was still living in the East End, George continued to work out at the West End YMCA. On the track, he was virtually unbeatable at any distance. When he wasn't racing, he was getting straight A's in history, modern languages, calculus, English, and philosophy, epitomizing the scholar-athlete ideal at the University of Toronto. At one track meet, he won the 440-yard dash, the 880-yard dash, the mile, the two mile, and the mile relay. He represented the university at intercollegiate meets and wore the colours of the Toronto Lacrosse Club at the big-time championships against the world's best.

The university did not pay for any expenses incurred by an athlete, but the Toronto Lacrosse Club did. The same was true for the Balmy Beach Club, the Toronto Canoe Club, the Argonaut Rowing Club, the Parkdale Club, the Rod and Gun Club, and other sports organizations in Toronto and throughout the country. As long as you could prove that the expenses were legitimate, you wouldn't be considered a professional, which was a dirty word in those days of pure amateurism, especially in staunchly conservative Toronto.

On September 24, 1892, a warm and hazy Saturday at the Montreal AAA grounds, over 3,000 fans turned up for the Canadian Amateur Athletic Association track and field championships. The Canadian and American record holder and defending champion, A.B. George, was the favourite for the mile, but a lot of folks thought young George Orton was good enough to beat him, especially after running a close second the year before. Former world record holder Tommy Conneff, a New Yorker by way of Ireland, and American Ernie Hjertberg made the field that much tougher. The *Globe* reported on the race:

> Orton ran a magnificent mile, beating Hjertberg, the second man, by over 50 yards in 4 minutes 21 and four-fifths seconds, thereby smashing the Canadian record of 4:27 and two-fifths made by A.B. George. Orton finished strong, and there is no doubt that if he had been

pushed for the last 300 yards, he would have beaten the
American record of 4:21 and two-fifths.[9]

Had Orton known he was that close to the American record, he likely
would've broken it. However, the stopwatch had not yet been invented. Still,
considering the elite competition stacked against the 19-year-old Orton
that day, winning by 50 yards seemed inconceivable. Ernie Hjertberg, the
runner-up, was a wonderful distance runner who became a top trainer at the
New York Athletic Club and later immigrated to Sweden, where he coached
their Olympic team at the 1912 Olympics in Stockholm. A.B. George was
the current world record holder, while Tommy Conneff was the former
world record holder and is considered to be, like Orton, one of the greatest
distance runners in history. Conneff was seven years older than Orton, and
in 1895 he would set the world amateur record again: four minutes, 15 and
three-fifths seconds.

Conneff and Orton would wage some tremendous battles on the cinder
track over the years. In the span of 361 days, Orton had shaved nearly six
seconds off the Canadian mile record. In doing so, he had obliterated a field
of world-class runners and won the hearts of hundreds of students at the
University of Toronto, as well as thousands more who saw him run or read
about his exploits in the newspapers.

A week after the triumph in Montreal, Orton won two huge races at the
U.S. championships at the New York Athletic Club. He not only won the
mile but also crushed the field in the four-mile run. If his performance in
Montreal didn't impress the Americans, this one definitely did. The plucky
little Canadian kid with the shrivelled arm was the real deal.

When asked about Orton's performance, Tommy Conneff could not
hold back.

It is now admitted beyond question that this young
Canadian, who by the way is only nineteen years old, is
about one of the best runners to be found in the world.
The fact of the matter is that the boy is a wonder. Even the
best judges cannot fathom his ability or find out how fast
he can run or what distance he can stay, for the reason that
he has won all his races so far, with so much ease that one

can only conjecture his true form if drawn out in a race. In my opinion, if the boy enjoys health and turns out all right next spring, the world's amateur record of 4 minutes 18 and two-fifths seconds will be at his mercy.[10]

What a marvellous testimonial! Orton was now a legitimate world-class runner. Conneff's endorsement of Orton was fortuitous for the University of Toronto as well. The school was thrilled that one of their undergraduates had been recognized as one of the best in the world, and it took full advantage, leveraging Orton's popularity by promoting his appearances at their athletic meets. The teen sensation from Strathroy was now a major attraction: a marquee name for the annual Varsity Games and any other meet that wanted to draw top competition. Teams from McGill, Queens, Royal Military College, and Trinity College were quick to sign up, knowing Orton would be a big draw. The October 21 edition of the *Globe* could not have been more effusive in its praise of Orton: "An unusual interest will attach to the sports this year from the fact that this will be the first opportunity the Toronto public will have of seeing Mr. George W. Orton, Varsity's famous runner, on the track since his great performance at the meet of the N.Y.A.C. in New York, where he easily distanced the heretofore invincibles of the great athletic clubs of that city."[11]

Despite a cool and windy late October day, over 2,000 fans shoehorned into the Rosedale Grounds to see the teenage champion run against other schoolboys. Orton was entered in four events: the quarter-mile, half-mile, mile, and mile relay. He won them all.

The half-mile was the most exciting race of the day as Orton nipped his buddy Dick Grant at the wire by less than six inches in a four-way blanket finish. The *Globe* provided a harbinger in their coverage the next day, referring to Orton as "the champion of America." Perhaps they meant that Canada was part of America. When asked about it years later, Orton pointed out a few subtle differences between the two nations, including Canadians' love of soccer.

At Toronto University, where I was an undergraduate, we had all the sports played in our American colleges with the addition of Association football. That college is noted for its hard students, but though every sport was really supported by those who played it, I have known six football teams to represent Toronto University the same day, elevens playing in the Senior College League, the Intermediate and the Junior Football League at both the Association and Rugby games.[12]

It's hard to believe today, but soccer and rugby football were more popular than ice hockey while Orton was attending U of T. From the September 3, 1892, edition of the *Globe*: "Association football holds a position amongst Toronto University athletics second to none. It may confidently be affirmed that it holds the foremost place in respect to the interest taken in it, as compared with any other sport."[13]

Orton played for the Varsity team in the Senior College League and was a member of several all-star teams in Toronto, including a Canadian championship squad that lost to the powerful Fall River East Enders of Massachusetts, the American Cup champions of 1892. While studying at Penn, Orton founded what is believed to be the first all-American soccer team at the Belmont Cricket Club. At the time, there were several English, Irish, and Scottish soccer teams in the United States, but none that carried

University of Toronto Gymnasium Club, circa 1891. Orton is seated on the floor, fourth from left. He was influential in the construction of the school's first gym and cinder track in 1893.

strictly Americans (some of whom were Canadians). In 1910, at the age of 37, Orton was still at it. He started at centre-half for the Philadelphia all-stars against the New York all-stars at Haverford, Pennsylvania. A decade later, he suited up for the Merion Cricket Club. He played competitively until he was into his 60s, and only a recurring knee injury prevented him from playing longer.

By the time Orton had graduated from the University of Toronto in the spring of 1893, there was nothing more to be achieved in his native country. Having successfully represented the university and the Toronto Lacrosse Club, and with no prospects for athletic advancement, he accepted an offer to attend Penn as a graduate student. What the scholarship offer entailed is unclear, but the arrangement at Penn would allow Orton to work toward his master's and Ph.D. while advancing his athletic career, with the full support and encouragement of the university. He would have four years of athletic eligibility to represent Penn at intercollegiate meets.

Three days after his arrival in Philadelphia, Orton reported to the track team for his first practice. As the Canadian record holder for the mile, Orton was a known commodity. He was asked to try the two-mile steeplechase. He tried it and liked it. Two weeks later he was entered as Penn's representative at the championships in New York. In defeating a top field of steeplechasers, Orton also earned a much-coveted varsity letter. It is believed that no athlete since has won a P at Penn after only two weeks at the institution.[14] Folks at Penn knew they had a keeper.

Later that fall, Orton was invited to compete at the World Track and Field Championships in Chicago. That city was hosting the World's Fair of 1893, and track and field was a big draw. In advance of the championships, the *Chicago Tribune* featured the first major profile of Orton, saying, "He stands five feet six inches in height and weighs about one hundred and twenty pounds. He has the appearance of being a delicate youth; when quite young he was anything but a robust child."[15]

The race everyone wanted to see was the mile, pitting Orton against archrival Tommy Conneff. *Globe* correspondent Trainer Warwick reported that it was "one of the finest races I have ever witnessed."[16]

Orton said in a 1953 interview that the Conneff race in Chicago was the most exciting race he had ever been a part of:

> We had a windstorm. The gale was so bad they had to use planks to hold down the hurdles. In the first quarter, I led Conneff, but in the second quarter I let him go to the front. The wind hit us with terrific force. I'll never forget that back stretch. I felt I just had to win. I saw Conneff running out so I tried to change my gait. I'll never forget Conneff's face when I pulled up alongside him. We were running side by side, like a team. The finish was just ahead. Finally, I managed to pull away from him.

When Conneff realized he could not catch Orton, he collapsed on the grass, and they had to carry him home.[17] Orton won easily, in four minutes, 27 seconds. He gained many new admirers that day. The *Akron Daily Herald* wrote, "Canada possesses a phenomenal distance runner in the person of George W. Orton of Toronto, who has proved in many a hard fought race that he had the speed and endurance of the wild deer."[18]

A few weeks later, at the New Jersey Athletic Club in Bayonne, Orton won the two-mile steeplechase by a remarkable 52 seconds. That same day, he was entered in the 10-mile run, which involved 40 laps around the Bayonne cinder track. Trailing E.C. Carter by a full lap, Orton quit after 22 laps, exhausted. Carter would win by five-and-a-quarter laps.

It was becoming obvious to Orton and others that distance running was quite popular at the collegiate level, and he felt that organized cross-country races should be run between colleges and universities. In 1894, he proposed in letters to all institutions of higher learning in the East that an annual meet be set up. Of all the schools contacted, only Cornell took Orton up on his offer. The other schools declined, believing the only reason Orton wanted to start an intercollegiate cross-country meet was so he could win it every year. It wasn't far-fetched. Orton had beaten the best long-distance runners in the world, so why would any college kid think he could beat him in cross country? Orton may have originally come up with the idea for altruistic reasons, but the naysayers were right: He won the cross-country race in each of its first four years.

The popularity of these meets became so great that the Amateur Athletic Union (AAU) decided to bring the cross-country race back after a five-year hiatus. They designed a course at the Morris Park horse racing track in New York for the 1897 U.S. National Cross Country Championships. It was just over six miles in length and featured forty-three jumps, four of which were water jumps. In April of 1897, Orton smashed a field of 57 runners, winning by over 100 yards! It was the turning point for the sport, and the day Orton fell in love with cross-country. In fact, for his work in raising the profile of the sport, Orton was given the title "the father of cross-country running" by the *Philadelphia Bulletin*. He was certainly the sport's greatest booster.[19]

> Cross-Country running is the most pleasurable form of distance work. If possible it is best to get a number to run together, led by a man who has sense enough not to get them racing. Then, about a mile or a mile and a half from home, on the return, the men can be lined up and allowed to race the remainder of the distance. If one wishes to try out the men, it is best to do so by handicaps, or by dividing the men into two or more packs, according to their speed. A very great deal of the pleasure in this work will depend upon the leader, and it is essential that this position should be given to a man who will watch his pack and run at such a speed that, although there is no loafing, the run will not be a race.[20]

In Canada, many newspapers continued to update their readers on Orton's progress against the world's finest. Every time he ran a strong race, and even when he didn't, his time was reported, and occasionally, a race recap and description were included in the story. Rarely, however, were Orton's Canadian roots mentioned. He was George Orton of the University of Pennsylvania. Eventually, Canadian coverage of his exploits disappeared — and a piece of Canadian history was lost.

A DIRTY PRO

George Orton was becoming a big man on the University of Pennsylvania campus. As a veritable distance-running machine, his accomplishments were well documented in newspapers all over the northeastern United States at the same time attention in Canada was dwindling. In some circles, he was no longer considered to be a Canadian since moving over to the Philistines and taking up residence there. According to the *Ottawa Evening Journal*, he was a talented and desirable Canadian who was being used to help prop up the Americans:

> The New York Athletic Club is making an effort to corral Geo. W. Orton, the Toronto runner, who is now attending the University of Pennsylvania, and recently defeated the crack Conneff. They want Orton to be on the N.Y.A.C. team that will compete in the coming international games with the London Athletic Club. At the present time,

the N.Y.A.C. has Geo. R. Gray, of Coldwater, Ont., the champion shot putter. While the pursuit of such men as Gray and Orton by a club like the N.Y.A.C. speaks well of Canadian athleticism, it is hardly palatable to think that native born Canadians should be the means of defeating a British team in an international contest, and it is not at all likely that the American papers will take the trouble to point out the presence of Canadians on their team.[1]

Even though he was a Canadian citizen, and the North American champion, Orton was "not eligible to run in the [Canadian] championship mile on account of his residence in Philadelphia," according to the July 8, 1895, edition of the *Globe*. A number of influential writers, editors, and amateur officials in the late 19th century represented the views of the majority of sports people in Toronto and Ontario. They were, for the most part, well-respected citizens. If they thought Orton and other Canadians had gone over to the "dark side," they were going to be treated differently. Nationalism was important for a country that wasn't even 30 years old. There were strict rules to protect the honour of Canadians. If you weren't a resident, you couldn't compete for the Canadian championship.

George Orton in training, 1895. He won a record 17 U.S. National championships in track, and seven Canadian championships. Orton never represented the United States or Canada in international competition during his career, as that practice did not begin until 1908.

The leading sportswriter in the country during this era was Toronto's Henry J.P. Good, who had worked for virtually every newspaper in the 1880s and '90s. He was the first full-time sportswriter in Canada. At that time, there were no bylines attached to a newspaper story, so no one writer received credit for the published story; it was a collaborative effort. Good, however, had a well-known style, and besides, his byline was attached to many magazine articles, so people knew whose work they were reading. His columns nearly always had to do with stories of great Canadian victories abroad. Once the publicity man for world-famous Canadian sculler Ned Hanlan, Good knew how to write a story filled with nationalistic references that would be gobbled up by his hungry Canadian readers.

Good was also the former president of the Canadian Lacrosse Association. When Orton, the Toronto Lacrosse Club's star runner, left to go to the United States, it was Good who complained the loudest. He was a staunch supporter of amateurism and felt professionalism was ruining sport. The irony here was his past association with Hanlan, who epitomized the "dirty professional" that Good was now railing against. Although it would be impossible to prevent Orton and other Canadians from moving to the United States, Good was tired of losing these great athletes and urged Canadian officials to make it more desirable for an athlete to stay in, and compete for, Canada. His pleas, like those of Orton's, fell on deaf ears. The Canadian authorities wanted nothing to do with Orton if he was going to earn a living in the United States.

Dr. Bruce Kidd, 1964 Olympian and vice-president of the U of T, commented about this to me during the filming of the documentary:

> I know Canadians of my grandmother's generation prided themselves and preached to us that she was a proud United Empire Loyalist and when I went to the United States to race, she would say that God is helping you punish those Americans for what they did in 1776. It's very hard to put yourself in the spirit of those times, but there was a fierce anti-Americanism in many parts of Canada, and especially in the industrial heartland of Ontario.[2]

Orton in 1896. Despite being born and raised in Canada, he could not run in his home country's championships. Many thought of him as a dirty American professional.

Competing against the Americans was one thing. Competing *with* the Americans was different. George Orton may have been Canadian-born, but once he put on the uniform of the New York Athletic Club, all bets were off and that *P* word reared its ugly head again. At the time, the difference between professionals and amateurs was either considerable or minimal, depending on where you came from. In the United States, the two often competed together, with separate records listed for the amateurs and professionals. In Canada, the battle lines were clearly drawn between the two biggest cities.

As Dr. Kidd explained, "There was a serious divide between the two, and Toronto newspapers such as the *Globe* and the *Telegram* were fiercely partisan for amateur athletes and would not spare the condemnation of those who turned pro, whether in the United States or Canada."[3]

The *Toronto Star* felt the same way. Besides pointing out that an American victory at the Canadian championships that day would be aided by Orton and George Gray, both Canadians, the editorial made the newspaper's position on amateurism crystal clear: "Canada may not be able to compete on the track with the American sprinters, but when the Canadian athlete is a true and pure amateur, without a trace of Professionalism about him, in this one respect he differs widely from the American."[4]

I showed that quote to Professor Emeritus Bob Barney, the founder of Western University's International Centre for Olympic Studies in London, Ontario. His reply was:

> The view on professionalism in Canada at that time, especially with regard to track and field athletes, there was a different view entirely held by the people in Montreal from the people in Toronto, and this fellow [the author] was echoing what was certainly prevalent in Toronto: a purism of athleticism. And the difference between the two, Montreal and Toronto, was, in Toronto's case, they viewed any athlete who participated in a contest in which a professional also competed, that *contaminated* that individual. He was a professional. In Montreal, that was not true. The athlete could participate with a professional in an event and not sacrifice his amateur status, and that was actually the subject of a great war between the two, the Federation in Montreal and the Association in Toronto.[5]

Dr. Bruce Kidd agreed: "Montrealers, or 'Westmounters,' were more liberal, and were much more willing to cross that divide, to contemplate amateurs playing on the same team as professionals, for example, or amateurs playing against professionals. And of course, Western Canada was much more liberal, by a long shot."[6]

In an attempt to clear up any misconceptions, the Amateur Athletic Association of Canada decided to add a clause to its bylaws in 1897 to ensure there was no grey area when it came to making the distinction between amateur and professional. According to association secretary G.M. Higinbotham:

> If it is the opinion of the Executive Committee … that an athlete has in any way been charged with professionalism, the Secretary shall be instructed to write to the party so charged, enclosing him an affidavit, setting forth the definition of an amateur, which he shall swear to as having observed and return the same within 10 days; otherwise, the party so charged shall be disqualified, and notified to that effect by the Secretary.[7]

Canadian athletes had to be extremely careful in those days. Losing your amateur status would affect your reputation and cause the public to have misgivings about you. If an athlete accepted a meal and didn't pay for it, he might have to defend himself against charges of professionalism. Toronto's Tom Flanagan, who managed the famous Canadian distance runner Tom Longboat for a time, was well aware of this policy. His brother was John Flanagan, three-time Olympic gold medallist in the hammer throw. He was supposedly an amateur.

> My brother John … always got train fare, full expenses and $150 when [he] came to a meet in Canada from New York. Down there, they lived at the New York A.C. and signed chits. At the end of the year, they were presented with a bill for what they had consumed the past twelve months. They threw the bill into the waste basket and forgot about it. But they had fulfilled the amateur requirements. The bill had been sent.[8]

By 1897, Orton had graduated from Penn and was the director of physical education at the Eastburn Academy in Philadelphia (formerly the

North Broad Street Select School) when trouble came calling. Orton had to face accusations that he openly and willfully advertised his new position for a "consideration." He was charged with professionalism and suspended by the AAU. Some felt his recent victory in the cross-country race at Fairmount Park in Philadelphia should be rescinded.

These were serious charges and Orton defended himself vigorously. The AAU carried out an extensive investigation to determine Orton's fate. On December 21, they determined that a verdict of not guilty was in order. Orton was reinstated immediately, and his reputation remained intact.[9]

Had the decision gone the other way, Orton could have been banned from competing, possibly for life. Professional athletes were not held in the same high regard as they are today. The most famous charge of professionalism in sports centred around Oklahoma-born Jim Thorpe, who was part Black Hawk, part Sac and Fox. Thorpe was a star college football player who, in 1912, won the decathlon and pentathlon at the Stockholm Olympics, becoming the first Native American to win an Olympic gold medal. Sweden's King Gustav V was so impressed with Thorpe's performance that, upon congratulating him, he remarked "Sir, you are the greatest athlete in the world," to which Thorpe reputedly replied, "Thanks, King."

In January 1913, a story broke in the *Worcester* (Mass.) *Telegram* claiming Thorpe had played two summers of semi-professional baseball while attending Carlisle University in 1909 and 1910. College athletes frequently played in these summer baseball leagues for a few dollars, but they used pseudonyms so as not to be identified. Thorpe had naively used his real name when signing up and was caught. In a letter of apology he wrote to AAU president James Sullivan, Thorpe admitted that he received money and that he was "simply an Indian schoolboy and did not know all about such things." Thorpe went on to say, "I did not know that I was doing wrong, because I was doing what I knew several other college men had done, except that they did not use their own names."[10]

The AAU stripped Thorpe of his amateur status, which forced the International Olympic Committee to ban him from further competition. They also took away his two gold medals, since he had competed as a professional. Unknown to Thorpe at the time, the IOC rules stated that any disqualification must take place within 30 days of the violation. The ban was imposed several months after the Olympics and should not have been allowed. Not until 1982 did the IOC restore both Thorpe's amateur status and his two Olympic medals.

In an odd twist, Thorpe's career took a turn for the better once he was declared a professional. He played six seasons of major-league baseball from 1913 to 1919, mostly with the New York Giants. His salary of $6,500 in 1913 (which included a $500 signing bonus) was seven times that of the average American worker. It was a poor investment for the Giants. Hall of Fame manager John McGraw had little room for Thorpe and used him in only 19 games that year. In the fall of 1915, Thorpe began playing professional football, earning $250 per game to suit up with the Canton, Ohio, Bulldogs. Crowds in Canton had been around 1,200 for football games before Thorpe's arrival. In his first game, the Bulldogs drew over 8,000 fans for a game against archrival Massillon, Ohio, and Thorpe was the star, drop-kicking field goals from 38 and 45 yards. Professional football had its first big gate attraction, and soon teams began popping up all over Ohio, with Dayton, Columbus, Youngstown, and Akron fielding teams to take advantage of Thorpe's popularity.[11]

Despite the adulation, racism followed Thorpe wherever he went. Indigenous people were considered to be second- or even third-class citizens. To many, Thorpe represented the stereotypical Native, and the newspapers helped the public form these opinions. From the *Winnipeg Tribune* in 1913:

> Jim Thorpe may be a taciturn Indian and all of that, but the redskin is always there whenever there is an opportunity to make a dollar. He has sold to a couple of moving picture concerns the right to make moving pictures of his upcoming wedding to the Cherokee maiden whom he will make his wife at Carlisle about the middle of next month.[12]

Sportswriter Lou Marsh of the *Toronto Star* occasionally penned racist comments about the athletes he covered, especially the great Indigenous runner Tom Longboat. Longboat was Onondaga, from the Six Nations reserve in Ohsweken, Ontario, near Brantford, and was the subject of many of Marsh's tirades. Marsh was never at a loss for critical words when it came to Longboat, calling him "the original dummy ... Wily ... unreliable ... as hard to train as a leopard."[13]

Despite these musings (and other, more racist ones not fit to print), Marsh was revered as Canada's greatest sportswriter. Soon after his death in 1936, the *Star* began sponsoring the Lou Marsh Award, which is given annually to Canada's top athlete. Ironically, the first winner of the award was black — Dr. Phil Edwards, a middle-distance runner who won five Olympic bronze medals for Canada. Born in Guyana, a nation that did not have an Olympic team, Edwards was raised in New York and attended New York University. He was unable to represent the United States at the 1928 Olympics but was told he could compete for Canada, as he was considered a British subject. Representing Canada, Edwards won a bronze medal in the 4 × 400 relay at the 1928 Amsterdam Games. After graduating from NYU, he enrolled at McGill University Medical School in Montreal, where he captained the track team. In 1932, at Los Angeles, he entered three events and won bronze in all three: the 800 metres, 1,500 metres, and 4 × 400-metre relay. At the 1936 Berlin Olympics, his last as a competitor, Edwards took the bronze medal in the 800-metre race.

Before returning home, the Canadian team checked into a London, England, hotel that was owned by Canadians. As one story goes, 50 or 60 angry Canadian athletes gathered in front of the hotel with their suitcases, ready to leave. Edwards had been refused service because he was black. It's not clear whether the matter was settled by Canadian officials or if the team took their business elsewhere. Edwards went on to become a captain in the Canadian Army and an expert in the field of tropical diseases. He died in Montreal in 1971 at the age of 63. To this day, the Phil A. Edwards Memorial Trophy is given annually to Canada's top track athlete.

His Indigenous heritage aside, Jim Thorpe was no more than a high-paid benchwarmer on the powerful New York Giants. McGraw's men were the class of the National League in those days. They won the pennant in 1911, 1912, and 1913, only to lose the World Series each year. The 1913 squad had loads of talent, led by Hall of Fame pitchers Christy Mathewson and Rube Marquard. They won 101 games versus just 51 losses. The roster also included two wonderful players known more for their gaffes than their great plays.

Fred Merkle, as a 19-year-old rookie in 1908, failed to touch second base on what would have been a game-winning hit against the Chicago Cubs in the ninth inning of a hotly contested game in the thick of the pennant race. He was declared out and the winning run was nullified. The game was called because of darkness after the New York fans stormed the field at the Polo Grounds, thinking they had won. The umpires could not clear the field, and the game was declared a tie and had to be replayed. The Cubs won the makeup game and ended up winning the pennant and the World Series, and Merkle's blunder became part of baseball legend, even though he went on to have a fine career. After that 1908 adventure, Merkle appeared in five World Series without winning a title, unable to avenge the gaffe.

The other Giants player who got a bad rap was a fine centrefielder named Fred Snodgrass, who dropped a routine fly ball leading off the 10th inning of the final game of the 1912 World Series against the Boston Red Sox. Despite making a spectacular game-saving catch on the next play, Snodgrass could not prevent the Red Sox from winning the World Series, and he took the blame for the loss in the newspapers. One opportunistic and sadistic manufacturer of women's furs even marketed a product known as a "Snodgrass Muff." Giants manager John McGraw not only didn't blame Snodgrass for the loss, he raised his salary by $1,000 for 1913.

Jim Thorpe never had more than 300 at-bats in a season and finished his major-league career with a modest .252 batting average. After baseball, he played eight seasons for six different teams in the National Football League, retiring at the age of 41 in 1928. Thorpe also barnstormed with a basketball team, the World Famous Indians of LaRue (Ohio), for two seasons.[14] Thorpe died in 1953, just after being honoured as the greatest athlete of the first half-century by the Associated Press. He was certainly the greatest athlete I had ever heard of. Who knows what would've happened had he not become a professional all those years ago.

George Orton was eventually exonerated of all charges of professionalism by the AAU and remained an amateur. Although he was living and working in Philadelphia, he still held true to his Canadian roots and felt very strongly about developing and advancing Canadian talent for the entire world to see. "One of the things that I admire about George Orton," recalled Dr. Bruce Kidd, "is at some point he wrote to the amateur authorities of the day, saying

'We have outstanding athletes here in Canada. Why don't you put together a team and send them abroad to represent Canada?'"[15]

Had the authorities considered his request, Canadians would've enjoyed following the adventures of homegrown athletes as they competed at the Olympics and other international events. Just because there were no national teams didn't mean folks in Canada wouldn't be rooting for their countrymen as they took on the world's finest athletes on the big stage. Instead, the Canadian authorities resisted, forcing many athletes to leave and become reluctant Americans. In the United States, these athletes were encouraged and supported by an enthusiastic sporting republic that loved winning above all else.

In addition to Orton, the Grant brothers, Dick and Alex, and Ronald McDonald were the four Canadians who competed in Paris in 1900. But Canada could have been represented by several more world-class athletes. Unfortunately, the country was late to the Olympic party and Canadians would know little to nothing of Orton, the Grants, and McDonald. Not until the 1908 London Games would Canada field an international team of athletes. Those Games were originally scheduled for Rome, Italy, but the devastation caused by the eruption of Mount Vesuvius in 1906 forced the IOC to change locations for financial reasons. Canada did send a strong team to London, winning three gold, three silver, and 10 bronze medals.

The first Canadian Olympic star was Bobby Kerr of Hamilton, Ontario. He won gold in the 200 metres and bronze in the 100 metres in 1908. The fans in London considered Kerr to be a representative of the British Empire, since he had been born in Northern Ireland before moving to Canada. The support he received, at home and abroad, was heartwarming. Had George Orton and company received similar support eight years earlier, things might have turned out differently.

5

YOUR HUMBLE NARRATOR

In the early 1980s, I hosted a nightly two-hour sports talk show on AM radio station 590/CKEY in Toronto. It was a decade or so prior to the boom in sports talk radio. There was no cellphone technology and certainly no internet. On Friday nights I would open the phone lines for trivia, and callers would try to stump me with questions. If the caller could stump me, I would fire back a question from the sport of their choice. If they answered correctly, they would win my undying respect, plus a gift — a watch, a pair of sneakers, or perhaps a VHS copy of *The Best of Johnny Carson*. Whatever we had in the prize vault. The phone lines would light up like a Christmas tree. People wanted to talk sports, and I was in my glory. I was the king of sports trivia and wore the mantle with pride. It was the one thing I was better at than everyone else. I was a full-on sports geek as a kid and it would serve me well.

I grew up in Willowdale, a suburban Toronto neighbourhood, in the 1960s and '70s. Willowdale was part of what's now known as North York, and my family lived in the Yonge and Steeles area. My parents, Sylvia and Sid, had both enjoyed playing sports when they were younger. My mom was a pretty good baseball player in her day, and my dad played hockey until he suffered a badly broken ankle in his mid-20s. My mom's brother, my uncle Paul Finstein, had a profound influence on my love of sports. He was a great athlete in high school at Bathurst Heights Collegiate and a co-captain of the football team.

In the summers, my folks would take all of us — my uncle and my brothers, Stephen and Barry — to Triple-A baseball games at Maple Leaf Stadium, down by Lake Ontario. And once a season, usually around Christmastime, Sid would score tickets to see the Maple Leafs play at Maple Leaf Gardens. We would get dressed up and go to Bassel's restaurant at the corner of Yonge and Gerrard for dinner before the game. I could never enjoy those meals though, because I had butterflies the size of buzzards in my stomach. Just knowing I would be seeing my heroes, the Maple Leafs, at the shrine of hockey was enough to make me a nervous wreck.

On Saturdays, we would always watch our beloved Maple Leafs on *Hockey Night in Canada* on the CBC. For many years, the game would start at 8:00 p.m., but it wouldn't come on TV until 8:30. We had to watch *The Saint* with Roger Moore instead of the hockey game. Eventually, the powers that be realized that showing the entire game would be a good way to build a solid audience. My dad always said the reason they didn't show the whole game on TV was simple: Everybody would stay home and watch instead of buying tickets to the game.

Football was also big in the Hebscher household. Sundays in the fall and winter, we would watch the NFL's Cleveland Browns play on WBEN-TV, Channel 4 out of Buffalo, New York. We were always Buffalo Bills fans, but when O.J. Simpson was drafted by the Bills, we became HUGE supporters. At that time, O.J. was known only as a great football player. Little did we know. In the early 1970s, *Monday Night Football* with Howard Cosell was a must-see.

By contrast, the Canadian Football League games were not always available on TV. The Toronto Argonauts games were mostly blacked out on local TV in the '70s, and that archaic blackout rule made many of us lose interest in the league. The blackout was in effect for reasons similar to what my dad had explained about hockey: You had to buy tickets if you wanted to see the game. There was no local TV coverage available within 75 miles.

I was also a big baseball fan, having watched the *Game of the Week* every Saturday on NBC since I was in diapers. The Maple Leafs Triple-A baseball team had moved to Louisville, Kentucky, after the 1967 season, and there was a void that needed to be filled. When the expansion Toronto Blue Jays came along in 1977, I was in my glory. I attended that very first game at a snowy Exhibition Stadium and fell in love immediately with the Jays. Their games were on TV occasionally, but what really got me hooked was the radio coverage of the team: Every game was broadcast on radio, and I remember staying up late with my brother Stephen, listening to faraway broadcasts with Tom Cheek and Early Wynn from Oakland, Anaheim, Seattle, and Kansas City.

NBA basketball was available occasionally on TV as well, although it was many years before the birth of the Toronto Raptors. The Buffalo Braves played a handful of games in Toronto, featuring the likes of Bob McAdoo, Ernie DiGregorio, and Randy Smith, but soon they moved to San Diego and became the Clippers. U.S. college basketball was shown occasionally.

Soccer was for immigrants from Britain, Italy, and Portugal. It was never on TV. Golf and tennis were shown on the weekends. Five- and 10-pin bowling was big. My maternal grandfather, Irv Finstein, was a very good 10-pin bowler, and for a number of years I had my own bowling ball and played in a Thursday night league.

As a boy, I would wait anxiously for the *Toronto Star*, the afternoon newspaper, to arrive at our doorstep and then devour the sports section. Occasionally, I would get the *Globe and Mail* or *Toronto Telegram* (and later, the *Sun*) and any out-of-town newspaper I could scrounge up. Hotel lobbies were the best places to find discarded newspapers. The Royal York Hotel in Toronto had not only a huge lobby but also a barber shop downstairs that always had newspapers (and *Playboy* magazines) lying around. Across the street, at Union Station, trains from all over North America would arrive, and that meant the chances were good that a copy of the *New York Times* or the *Boston Globe* or even the *New Orleans Times-Picayune* might be sitting around once the porters got through with it. Failing that, there was always the deli, the shoeshine stand, or the bus station.

While most kids my age wanted toy guns or car racing sets for birthday presents, I asked my parents for a subscription to *Sports Illustrated* when I was eight years old. For my ninth birthday, they got me a subscription to the *Sporting News*, which had box scores from every baseball game played, even though they were two weeks old. I took on a paper route at the age of 10 and delivered the *Globe and Mail* every morning for one reason only: to be able to read the baseball box scores before anybody else. As soon as baseball season ended, I quit the job.

Track and field was something that was of interest to me only during the Olympics. Occasionally we would watch the famous Penn Relays or the Millrose Games on *ABC's Wide World of Sports*. My dad and my uncle Paul would take me to track meets at Toronto's Varsity Stadium, where I would watch the great distance runners Bill Crothers and Bruce Kidd and sprinter Harry Jerome. In the schoolyard, I could not run fast and I could not jump high. The first time I tried the hurdles, I fell flat on my face. I never dreamed of winning a race. I was happy just to not finish last.

As you can probably tell, sport was the only thing that mattered to me. Playing it. Watching it. Reading about it. I never had an interest in a girl — unless she could name every player on the Maple Leafs and knew what the infield fly rule was all about. There's a great scene in the 1982 Barry Levinson movie *Diner* where Steve Guttenberg's character, Eddie, a Baltimore Colts football fanatic, is planning to marry Elyse. First, though, she has to pass a difficult football quiz that Eddie has devised featuring 140 questions: short answer, multiple choice, true or false. If she fails to get 65 percent of the questions on the quiz, Eddie will call the wedding off. It's a scene that I identified with. If there's something that interests you THAT much, why wouldn't you want to share it with someone who shows a similar level of passion?

All through high school, people would ask what I wanted to do when I graduated, and I always said I wanted to be a sportscaster. Since there were only about six sportscasting jobs available in all of Toronto, and I wasn't going to get one anytime soon, my parents suggested that perhaps sportswriting might be worth a try. My mother thought that any kind of writing was a noble profession, and she was a voracious reader herself. Besides, I could picture myself wearing a fedora with a little card that said "Press" sticking out of the hat band.

But my marks at Newtonbrook Secondary School were not good enough to get me into the journalism program at Carleton University in Ottawa, or any other school for that matter. One needed a degree in journalism in order to work as a writer for a newspaper, and that wasn't going to happen for me. I had also applied to Humber College in Toronto, which offered a course in radio broadcasting. Right up my alley. You didn't even need to have great marks to get in. Nevertheless, they flat-out rejected me. I never did forgive Humber for that snub. Not until both of my sons ended up attending Humber in a strange and ironic twist.

As a last resort, I applied to Conestoga College in Kitchener, Ontario, an hour west of Toronto, to study radio-TV arts. I believe you needed a 60 percent average in high school with no felony convictions in order to gain entry into the course. That was me. As long as the cheque for the tuition cleared, I was in.

After a few months at Conestoga, I got my first job in broadcasting. It was as a country music disc jockey at a local station (even though I knew nothing of that musical genre — I was a rock 'n' roll kind of guy). When the boss at the radio station asked if I had ever cued up a record, I said, "of course," even though I hadn't.

The radio gig meant I could skip classes at school because, really, who wanted to listen to an instructor teach radio out of a textbook when I was already working in the industry? I took on a couple of other gigs in radio and eventually dropped out of school. My big break came when I caught on at 1430/CKFH radio, owned by the legendary broadcaster Foster Hewitt (hence the *FH* in the call letters). The station had the broadcast rights to the Blue Jays and the Maple Leafs. It also had a nightly sports talk show hosted by Bob McCown, who was nice enough to hire me as his producer after I begged him for a job every day for two weeks straight.

One night, Bob handed me a phone number to call while he was on the air. "Ask for the champ," Bob said. I dialed, and a man at the other end picked up. I introduced myself. His voice sounded familiar. It was Muhammad Ali. I thought I had died and gone to heaven. "Just a minute, Mr. Ali, I'll put you on the air with Bob," I said. "Call me Champ," he replied. "All my friends do, and Mark, you are now my friend." The man known the world over as "the Greatest" wanted to be my friend. Life couldn't be better for this 20-year-old.

After seven years on radio, I was offered a job as the co-anchor of *Sportsline* on Global TV in Toronto. This was in 1984. At that time, TV sportscasts were one-man shows. Satellite technology was just becoming popular, but the late-night sportscasts still showed highlights from games that were 24 hours old. *Sportsline* was revolutionary. Jim Tatti and I delivered a lightning-quick 30-minute highlight show. It was as if you were watching a couple of sports fans sitting around commenting on the games. The ratings were huge and we enjoyed cult status for over a decade. Other shows tried to copy our format and style. None came close.

It was during this period that I really learned to tell stories as a reporter. *Sportsline* covered all the big events: the Stanley Cup playoffs, the World Series, the Super Bowl, the Grey Cup, the NBA Championship. I knew how to work with camera operators and field producers to craft a great story with solid interviews, vivid pictures, and compelling sound. In subsequent years, I polished my play-by-play skills by doing football and hockey. I interviewed thousands of players, managers, coaches, fans, writers, broadcasters, and everyday people. When I moved over to news, I interviewed politicians, teachers, cops, firefighters, activists, lawyers, judges, doctors, and business owners.

With the introduction of the internet, fact-checking became even more important. The need to get information corroborated by independent sources was imperative. Back in Orton's day, newspapermen were revered as tellers of the truth and rarely were questioned about the facts. A good story was a good story, and Orton had provided them with reams of good copy during his years at the University of Toronto. Unfortunately for Orton, the Canadian scribes weren't interested in following a champion athlete who was leaving for the United States. Little did they know of the stories they'd be missing out on.

6

PHILADELPHIA FREEDOM

Dr. George W. Orton, who ran under the colors of the University of Pennsylvania, won more national championships than any other American athlete.... Orton competed from 1892 to 1903. During that time he won the one mile American championship six times; cross-country American championship twice; the two mile steeplechase eight times and ten mile American championship once. In addition he won the intercollegiate championship twice, the English championship in 1898, the European 1,500 metre and one mile championships, and the two mile steeplechase in Paris in 1900. He stands as the premier American athlete of all times having seventeen National championships to his credit.[1]

— *William H. Rocap, sports editor*

Although George Orton was well respected in Philadelphia, it took 93 years from the time that article was published until he was elected to the Philly Hall of Fame. The induction ceremonies would take place during the first week of November. I still didn't have a business partner for the documentary, and it was nearly October. With nine months having elapsed, all my research was complete, and the time had come to start shooting interviews. A friend told me about a producer who might be interested in the Orton story. I met him at a coffee shop and gave him the pitch. It took about 30 seconds for him to agree to put up the costs of production in exchange for a 50 percent stake in the film. He loved the story and couldn't wait to get going. Let's call this producer "Mister X."

I had set up a shooting schedule that consisted of two days in Philadelphia followed by two days in San Francisco. The key interviewees would be those who had actually heard of Orton before and could speak to his time in Philadelphia: Mark Frazier Lloyd, the head archivist at the University of Pennsylvania; Dave Johnson, the director of the famous Penn Relays, which Orton had managed for several years; Steve Dolan, the Penn track coach (Orton had coached the track team at Penn for many years), who was going to make the acceptance speech on behalf of Orton at the induction ceremonies; and Ken Avallon, the director of the Philadelphia Sports Hall of Fame, which was finally honouring this man. In San Francisco, Connie Meaney, Orton's granddaughter, would be my only interview, and I was secretly hoping she had found that Olympic gold medal and other cool stuff that would help paint a better picture of her mysterious grandfather. After that, I would go home, watch all the interviews, write copious notes, and begin to shape the story.

Mister X would make all the travel and hotel arrangements and ensure I had a top-notch shooter in Philly and another in San Francisco. Once I had returned, we would set up times to shoot more interviews in Ontario and then book editing and post-production facilities when the time came to put the whole thing together. I was nervous and excited.

My wife drove me to the airport and shot the first video for the documentary — me walking away from the camera, pulling my suitcase toward the airport terminal doors. The discovery adventure would begin in the City of Brotherly Love.

Mister X had booked me into the Microtel Inn and Suites near the Philly airport, so when I disembarked at 6:00 p.m. on November 1, I immediately hopped on a shuttle bus to the hotel. I was hoping to meet my cameraman and go over the plan for the next two days of shooting. His name was Nick, and I knew nothing about him except Mister X said he was driving from Niagara Falls, New York, to Philly and would be there that night. On a good day, that trip takes six and a half hours by car. Nick texted me around 9:00 p.m. to say he was still a few hours away, so I texted him back and told him I would see him in the morning and that I wanted to leave by eight o'clock.

If someone asked you to pick out the cameraman in a crowded room, it would be pretty difficult unless the guy actually had a camera with him. As I scanned the hotel's breakfast buffet the next morning, I could not see anyone who might resemble Nick, and there was nobody slinging a big camera over his shoulder. Nobody made eye contact with me. No nod. No wink. No "Hey, are you Mark?" I checked with the front desk and they said Nick had arrived late the night before. I wanted to get going by eight because there were going to be transportation issues and we had to get downtown; SEPTA, the Southeastern Pennsylvania Transit Authority, was on strike, and it would be commuter hell out there on the streets of Philadelphia.

So I grabbed a coffee and waited for Nick to show up. If he didn't appear by eight, I would phone the room and roust him out of bed. Not the best way to start a producer-cameraman relationship, but I had to let him know who was boss. After a while, the buffet was emptying out, and over in the corner sat one guy who had been looking at his phone the whole time. I didn't know what his deal was, but I got the feeling he might be my guy. "Hey, are you Nick?" I asked. He didn't even look up from his phone. "No, I'm George Orton."

Nick was around 40 years old, tall and bald with glasses. He looked a little dishevelled, like he had just slept in his clothes. (That's not at all unusual for cameramen, at least the ones I've worked with.) Nick told me he was from Florida but hadn't spent much time there lately. He had been editing a project in Niagara Falls when Mister X hired him to be my shooter. I told him what our schedule was for the next couple of days and filled him in on the Orton story.

Apparently Mister X hadn't told Nick much about the documentary. That raised a bit of a red flag with me. Besides knowing Orton's name, maybe Nick figured he didn't have to do anything except take the lens cap off the camera before hitting the record button. He acted shocked when I told him he was going to be our driver, too. I guess he thought Mister X had rented a car for this shoot. No such luck.

Nick's 1997 Honda Accord, with 260,000 miles on it, and nearly as many dents and scratches, was literally held together with chicken wire, Bondo, and duct tape. It was Nick's car and home, filled with clothes, camera

The author with Mark Frazier Lloyd (left). He provided extensive photos, articles, and correspondence from the University of Pennsylvania archives and was a great storyteller.

equipment, lights, microphones, tripods, cables, batteries, fast-food wrappers, and the like. The car looked as if it hadn't been cleaned since the year of the small potato. Maybe never.

We made our way into downtown Philly to meet up with Mark Frazier Lloyd, who knew more about George Orton than anyone. He is the director of the University Archives and Records Center at Penn, having started there in 1984. When I first reached out to inform him that I was doing a documentary on Orton and wanted an interview, he gave me the old Price Is Right battle cry: "Come on down!"

When Nick and I arrived at his office, the George Orton file was already out. Mark hadn't looked at the file in years, but when he opened it, the memories came flooding back. Orton was an absolute superstar at Penn, both athletically and academically. He had edited and authored a popular book, *A History of Athletics at Pennsylvania, 1873–1896*, and had been written up in several newspaper and magazine articles. There were letters and photos in the file, which were especially interesting because this was the first time I had seen a picture of the "real" George and not his brother. Mark had also pulled out a few yearbooks from the mid-1890s, and there he was — curly hair, semi-permanent squint that could've been called a scowl, and a withered right arm that he kept away from the camera, angling his body so he led with his left shoulder and the viewer wouldn't notice the deformity.

Nick the cameraman was doing a great job. Mark was pointing out various articles and letters that Nick had to get shots of while the interview was being conducted. Sometimes Nick would shoot the same article from different angles so it would be easier to edit later. In the end, if you didn't know better, you'd think we had shot the scene with three cameras instead of just one. We would record several takes where Mark had to repeat what he had just said and point to the article he was holding so Nick could get a close-up. One newspaper columnist had been particularly impressed with Orton, and Mark just had to read the article out loud while the camera was rolling.

> His success has been tremendous. His handling of the Penn Relay Carnival makes it the greatest event of its sort held anywhere in the world, perhaps the greatest in all history so far as annual affairs are concerned. He embraces athletics in all its stages, from the wee hero of the grammar school to the cream of the college athletes. It has also widened until now, and is international in scope, the premier of its kind in all the world.[2]

When Orton first arrived at the University of Pennsylvania, he was hardly a country bumpkin. He had raced and won in New York, Boston, and Chicago, as well as in Canada. He was the Canadian one-mile champion and had graduated from the University of Toronto with double honours in modern languages. He was wise beyond his 20 years and considerably more mature than many of his classmates and teammates. In 1893, he was working toward his master's and, after receiving his M.A. in 1894, began studying for his doctorate in philosophy.

On the track, he helped take Penn from an also-ran to a strong contender. His record in 1894, at age 21, was staggering: 30 starts, 22 wins, four second-place and three third-place finishes. The following season, he captained the track team and won the mile at the very first Penn Relays. But his greatest feat took place at the New Jersey Athletic Club grounds at Bergen Point on May 30, 1895. In front of 5,000 enthusiastic supporters, Orton stayed with Tommy Conneff, and the two went shoulder to shoulder over the final lap, just like their meeting at the Chicago World's Fair two years earlier. From the *Philadelphia Times*:

Conneff started the third quarter at a rattling pace, with Orton five yards behind. Try as he would, the ex-champion could not shake off the Canadian.... they ran in this order up to the stretch, where Orton, with a magnificent burst of speed, passed the New York man and beat him out by four yards.... The stirring finish was too much for the spectators and they tore down the fence encircling the track and swarmed over the field to the finish line. Orton received an ovation and was carried off the track on the shoulders of his friends.[3]

In 1896, Orton was again captain of the Penn track team, but his new coach was his old nemesis, the legendary Mike Murphy, who had coached at Yale, Michigan, and Villanova, as well as the Detroit Athletic Club and the powerful New York Athletic Club. Prior to that, he trained heavyweight boxing champion John L. Sullivan.

Murphy was considered track and field royalty, and he was the perfect coach for Orton. The first time Orton ran for Penn against Yale, Murphy tried to set a trap. The coach entered a couple of Yale sprinters in the mile race, not expecting them to finish, but hoping their jackrabbit start would get Orton to chase them. Orton was dog-tired when the sprinters eventually faded and left the track, grinning merrily. He knew he had been set up but vowed not to let the other runners pass. Orton's winning time of 4:23.4 set a meet record that lasted for 12 years. Murphy was impressed — so much so that he left Yale to coach the likes of Orton and sprinter Alvin Kraenzlein, a future four-time gold medallist in Paris.

Orton and Murphy had a similar approach to running. The *Washington Post*, in a 1913 article, called Murphy "the father of American track athletics." He was said to have revolutionized the training methods of athletes and reduced it to a science. Among the many innovative techniques Murphy developed was the crouching start for sprinters. His coaching combined with Orton's running and the numerous talents of Kraenzlein and others vaulted Penn to the top of the track and field world.

The more we learned about Orton's popularity in Philadelphia, the more unknown he seemed to be in Canada (if that was even possible). We had spent a couple of hours with Mark Frazier Lloyd before he came upon a letter that would clearly illustrate Orton's obscurity in his country of birth. It was from the University of Western Ontario (now Western University). Canada would be hosting its first Olympics in Montreal in 1976, and researchers wanted to find out more about Canada's past Olympic champions. The letter was dated November 26, 1975, and addressed to the University of Pennsylvania Alumni Association.

> Dear Sir: One of your long ago alumni, Dr. George Orton, won a gold medal in the 1900 Olympics. Could you possibly send me a picture of this man, and any other relevant material you may possess.... In addition, it is rumoured that Orton came from a small town about 40 miles from here [London, ON], although as of yet, I have not been able to verify that fact.
>
> Glynn Leyshon, Ph.D., Assistant Dean[4]

Somebody at Penn, when asked to retrieve a photo of George Orton in 1975, had mistakenly sent a picture of the 1904–5 Penn track team, which included Irvine Orton. Seventy-five years had elapsed since Orton had won Canada's first Olympic gold medal, yet nobody knew what he looked like. Prior to 1972, The Olympic Record Book listed Orton as an American, but some stellar work by Olympic researchers uncovered the truth: He was Canadian by birth. All post-1972 editions of The Olympic Record Book have listed Orton as being from Canada, but that hasn't made him any less obscure. It took the Canadian Sports Hall of Fame until 1977 to induct him. The decision by the Canadian Olympic Hall of Fame to wait until 1996 to induct Orton is inexcusable.

We thanked Mark Frazier Lloyd for a great session at the Penn archives. He then directed us to nearby Franklin Field, where we had scheduled some interviews on the track. Nick carried the camera, a tripod, a reflector board, a power pack with an extra battery, and the camera bag stuffed full of cables, microphones, and whatnot. I carried my European handbag and my iPhone, which would double as a second camera for this shoot. I also

The author with Dave Johnson, director of the Penn Relays, at iconic Franklin Field, Philadelphia. Johnson was largely responsible for getting Orton inducted into the Philadelphia Sports Hall of Fame, 58 years after his death.

had to make sure I had a free hand so I could hold all the doors for Nick. He was younger, stronger, and bigger than me. But hey, never let it be said that I didn't pull my weight on a shoot.

Our walk to Franklin Field took us right through the Penn campus. It didn't look like downtown Philadelphia at all. For all we knew, it could've been Cambridge, Massachusetts, or New Haven, Connecticut, or Princeton, New Jersey. Tree-lined walkways featured sculptures and interesting architecture — buildings that had housed some of the great minds in American history. Franklin Field itself was even more beautiful than I had imagined, even though I had seen it on TV numerous times. The stadium was built specifically for the Penn Relays; it is the oldest stadium in the United States that functions as both a football field and a track and field stadium. It was also the first stadium to install a scoreboard.

We met Dave Johnson, the director of the Penn Relays, there. The Penn Relays is the oldest and most prestigious track and field event in the world. George Orton managed the Relays from 1919 to 1925 and won the mile and the mile relay at the inaugural event in 1895. It was known as the Penn Relay Carnival in the early years, and Orton was one of its star attractions.

The 1920 games, which Orton managed, were considered by the *New York Times* to be a fine spectacle:

> A crowd of 30,000, the greatest gathering that has ever attended a Penn relay carnival, turned out for the closing day's competition of this history making athletic attraction. From noon until the program was well under way, the spectators came in droves, by auto, surface car and subway. By the time the schoolboys were called to the line for the first event, the spacious wooden stand was filled and through the entrance gates there poured a steady stream of humanity. The bleachers seat 25,000 and they were jammed. Standees watched in rows of three and four deep from the railed-off section outside the track proper, while from the windows of Weightman Hall, the Penn Gymnasium, hundreds of necks craned for a glimpse of the happenings below on the track and field. The gathering presented a picturesque spectacle, the women's finery blending harmoniously under the rays of a strong and warmth-instilled sun in the row upon row of humanity seated in pyramid fashion.[5]

Charles Clegg was responsible for handing out the prizes at the Penn Relays for nearly 60 years. At the first event, he drove to Franklin Field in a horse-drawn wagon loaded with silver wreaths. The winners were brought to the wagon, and Clegg placed the wreaths on their heads. Fifty-five years later he reminisced for the *Philadelphia Inquirer*:

> It was back in 1904 or 1905 when George Orton ran the five-mile relay. Penn's team was not overly good and George was the anchor man. The Princeton man was almost a lap ahead when George started. No one expected Penn to have a chance. But George so measured his time that he cut a fifth off each lap and finished about two feet ahead.[6]

With the spirit of George Orton watching over us at his old stomping grounds, Franklin Field, Nick and I had a great day to shoot video — a high blue sky, temperature about 22 degrees Celsius (72 degrees Fahrenheit), no wind, and the full co-operation of the Penn Athletics Department. November in Philadelphia could not have been more beautiful. On the track were sprinters, hurdlers, and runners working out in the glorious sunshine while the Quaker varsity football team practised on the gridiron. It made for a terrific atmosphere.

Dave Johnson showed us a beautiful plaque attached to the grandstand at Franklin Field commemorating the Penn Relays. It was donated by the Steinbrenner family, owners of the New York Yankees. George Steinbrenner, who bought the Yankees in 1973, competed at the Penn Relays in 1952 as a hurdler while attending Williams College in Massachusetts. His father, Henry George Steinbrenner, was the captain of the track team at the Massachusetts Institute of Technology (MIT) and won the hurdles at the Penn Relays in 1927. Orton is featured prominently on the plaque and the medals that are awarded each year.

The design for the plaque and medallion was created by Canadian sculptor, physician, and educator Dr. R. Tait McKenzie.

McKenzie grew up with James Naismith, the inventor of basketball, in Almonte, Ontario, near Ottawa. Even though Naismith was five years older than McKenzie, he was only two years ahead of him at McGill University in Montreal. (Naismith was 21 years old when he graduated high school.) The two played sports together for a number of years, and then Naismith became McGill's first athletic director while McKenzie was the school's top gymnast and later a respected physician and surgeon. He became the first director of physical training at McGill. It was there where he developed innovative physical education programs, including those for wounded soldiers. Later, when the First World War broke out, McKenzie went to England to enlist in the Canadian Army in 1915. After encountering some red tape, he joined the Royal Army Medical Corps. When the Brits discovered he had authored the textbook on rehabilitation they were using, they put him in charge of the entire program.[7]

Although the challenges of his job didn't allow much time for hobbies, McKenzie began to dabble in art. His tremendous knowledge of anatomy and physical education allowed him to create his first sculpture. It was called *The Sprinter* — homage to the human form of a well-conditioned athlete.

Orton won Canada's first gold medal in the 2,500-metre steeplechase in 1900. Only one other North American has won an Olympic gold in steeplechase. Here, Ross Wilson (left) and Nick Tuck of Penn attack the difficult water jump.

McKenzie's design for the Penn Relays plaque and medallion shows the founder of the University of Pennsylvania, Benjamin Franklin, sitting in a chair holding a laurel sprig. Four nude runners stand facing him, the last holding a relay baton. The third runner resembles the form of George Washington Orton. Orton was instrumental in getting McKenzie hired at Penn as the director of physical education in 1904. Years later, McKenzie would immortalize his friend in bronze. According to Dave Johnson, McKenzie was hired specifically to oversee the interior design of Weightman Hall, the field house that became home to the finest gymnasium in the country.

McKenzie also helped Orton establish the Philadelphia Children's Playground Association in 1905. It was McKenzie who designed the famous Olympic medallion, *The Joy of Effort*, for the 1912 Stockholm Olympics. He won a bronze medal for Canada in the art competition at the 1932 Los Angeles Olympics. He died in Philadelphia in 1938 at the age of 71.

Orton made All-American all four seasons at Penn. This was when Penn Athletics was in the midst of a comeback, and Orton was a big draw while competing for the Quakers on the intercollegiate level against such power-houses as Yale, Harvard, and Princeton. He was a three-time All-American in the one-mile run, three-time All-American in the steeplechase, All-American in the two-mile run, and two-time intercollegiate champion in the one-mile. He captained the Penn track team for two seasons, during which time he was studying for his Ph.D. As Dave Johnson pointed out, "Orton's contributions to Penn go well beyond what he accomplished on the track."[8]

Nick and I had an opportunity to shoot some great video in Philadelphia. We were given full access at Franklin Field, and we took full advantage. Orton won his gold medal in the 2,500-metre steeplechase, an event that is no longer contested. That's why his world record still stands to this day. I wanted to get a sense, for the documentary, of how difficult it would've been for him to hurdle those obstacles, especially the water jump. I set up my iPhone on a low tripod at the end of the water jump, about six inches off the ground, and began recording in slow motion. Nick's camera was shooting from farther away and at a wider angle. In editing, I could cut back and forth between the two angles.

We asked Nick Tuck, Penn's top steeplechaser, and Ross Wilson if they wouldn't mind taking a few runs at the water jump for the cameras. When they approached the obstacle, which is three feet high, they jumped on top of it and then vaulted toward the shallower water at the end of the jump, right where my camera was stationed. The two landed with a splash and then kept on running, out of camera range. I stopped the recording and hit rewind. The shot was perfect. You see from ground level as Nick and Ross step on the vault, fly through the air toward the camera, and splash up a slow-motion shower. Months later, in the editing room, I was still patting myself on the back for that one.

THE FATHER OF PHILLY HOCKEY

> Canadians in the 19th century came to believe themselves
> possessed of a unique "northern character," due to
> the long harsh winters that only those of hardy body
> and mind could survive. This hardiness was claimed as
> a Canadian trait, and sports such as ice hockey were
> asserted as characteristically Canadian. Outside the arena,
> Canadians express the National characteristics of being
> peaceful, orderly and polite. Inside, they scream their
> lungs out at hockey games, cheering the speed, ferocity
> and violence, making hockey an ambiguous symbol
> of Canada.[1]
>
> — *Toronto Star*

Ice hockey was becoming popular in pockets of the United States when
Orton was at Penn in the mid-1890s. As far as he could tell, though, there
were no hockey players in Philadelphia. The city did not have a rink of any
kind, unless Centennial Lake or the nearby Schuylkill River in West Philly
had frozen over. And the only people who had skates and sticks seemed to
be the Canadians who were attending Penn. Orton had played hockey every
winter and wanted to introduce the great game to Penn and to Philadelphia.
He decided to form the "Canadian Club" at the university and was elected
its president.

The objectives of the Canadian Club's constitution were:

1. To bring together the Canadians in the University.

2. To welcome, advise and help Canadians upon entering.

3. To mutually aid each other while in the University and after [college] life.

4. To keep the merits and advantages of the University before the Canadian public and to foster their interest in the same.[2]

With that, 25 students became members of the first Canadian Club, and Orton had enough talent to start a hockey team at Penn *and* uphold the constitution. Practices began on Centennial Lake in December 1896. Orton was team captain.

HOCKEY TEAM OF THE UNIVERSITY OF PENNSYLVANIA

The Father of Philadelphia Hockey, Orton (top row, second from right) organized the first team at Penn in 1897. Stanley Willett is seated on the far right. Orton later started the first hockey league and was instrumental in having the first indoor arena built in Philadelphia.

At first, folks in Philly thought ice hockey was a fad, but the students seemed to love it, and Penn had a good team. A 20-year-old from Chambly, Quebec, named Stanley Willett was the Quakers' best player. He had recently played for the Stanley Cup–champion Montreal Victorias.

There were only a few indoor arenas in the United States at that time. The Ice Palace, at Lexington and 107th Streets in New York, opened on December 14, 1894. Two weeks later, the North Avenue Ice Palace in Baltimore hosted the first indoor game played in the United States on December 26. Johns Hopkins University took on the Baltimore Athletic Club before 2,500 spectators. Prior to the game, the public was invited to skate on the new rink. Electric lights were to have illuminated the building, but a winter storm caused problems and gas lights were used instead. The rink threw its doors open at half-past seven o'clock, and soon the smooth surface of the ice was crowded with skaters. At half-past eight, the game began. According to the *Baltimore American*, the rules of hockey were simple: "Everybody knows how to play hockey, or 'shinney.' The players use a stick with a crook at one end, and each side endeavors to knock a block of wood, a couple of inches square, to goal."[3]

Ah yes! The square wooden puck. It was often made of cherrywood and sometimes covered in rubber cut from a ball. The original puck was a clump of frozen horse manure known as a "road apple," so this was certainly a step up in consistency if nothing else. Pretty soon, they did away with the wood altogether, and a vulcanized rubber disc, made popular by the Montreal Victorias, became the norm in the late 1890s.[4] Hockey was becoming so popular in the United States that the newspapers were compelled to post the rules in such a way that was easy to explain. This, from the Lincoln, Nebraska, *Evening Call*, was especially catchy:

> Hockey is a variation of the old Scotch game of shinty. It gets its name from the pleasing custom the players practice of whacking their opponents over the shins if these worthies are indiscreet enough to attempt to strike at the ball when they are off side. The well known warning cry of "Shinney on your own side!" from a player on one team is usually the fore-runner of black and blue shins in the opposing aggregation. Shinney is played on the ice in the open air, and the opposing teams are made up of two

> disorderly mobs of unlimited numbers of player who use
> little system and have but a single object in view — the
> driving of the ball across the goal line or between the goal
> posts of the opposing team.[5]

Changes to the sport were inevitable as hockey evolved from the disorderly game of shinny to a more finesse-based sport where a premium was placed on skating and passing.

Equipment was changing as well, from pucks and sticks to the hockey goals themselves. During the 19th century, hockey goals were just two rocks placed six or eight feet apart on the ice. Soon, the hockey goal had evolved into a couple of vertical steel posts drilled into the ice, with a horizontal bar across the top.

Often, there were arguments as to whether a goal had actually been scored. Goal judges stood alongside the goal line and waved a flag if they believed the puck had gone between the posts and under the bar. These umpires were not always unbiased arbiters; often they were affiliated with one of the teams. George Orton was, for many years, an official during games in which his own team was playing. This was common practice in those days of seven-on-seven hockey and the source of much anguish for supporters of the game. There had been a great deal of lively and heated discussion as to how to prevent goal disputes from muddying up the game. One man came up with a novel idea: goal nets.

Francis Nelson, sports editor of the *Toronto Globe*, had visited Australia in 1899. He had seen fishermen come back from a day on the water with hundreds of fish trapped in their nets. Nelson was convinced that attaching nets to hockey goals would resolve all disputes. He arranged to have two large fishing nets brought back to Canada. Since there were no artificial rinks in Toronto (not until 1912), Nelson had the nets shipped to his friend Bill Hewitt, sports editor of the *Montreal Herald*. Hewitt, whose son Foster would popularize the phrase "he shoots, he scores" as the first hockey broadcaster, arranged to have these nets attached to the goals for a game between the Montreal Victorias and the Montreal Shamrocks. The experiment was a smashing success; the nets held the pucks, and the dignity of the officials was preserved. Soon, hockey goals with nets attached were approved for play by the Ontario Hockey Association and other leagues.[6]

There were many more opportunities for Canadians to play competitive hockey in U.S. arenas in the 1890s and early 20th century. Pittsburgh's Schenley Park Casino rink was built in 1895. The famous St. Nicholas Arena was built by the elite society of New York in March of 1896. It measured 80 feet by 180 feet and hosted college and amateur games until it was destroyed by fire in 1918. New York's third artificial rink of the era, the Brooklyn Ice Palace, opened in October of 1896. It measured 85 by 155 feet. That same year, what was reputed to be the largest sheet of artificial ice opened in Washington, D.C. The massive Convention Hall measured an incredible 155 by 205 feet. That's five feet longer and 70 feet wider than the standard National Hockey League rink of today. No wonder the games featured seven skaters a side in those days.

Pretty soon, indoor arenas were popping up in cities like St. Louis, Philadelphia, San Francisco, Boston, Cleveland, Chicago, New Haven, Syracuse, San Diego, St. Louis, Portland, Seattle, and Spokane. Canada lagged far behind when it came to artificial ice rinks. As late as 1920, there were only four artificial rinks in the entire country.

As the manager, travelling secretary, and captain for the University of Pennsylvania Quakers hockey team, Orton had made arrangements for his squad to play games in the new arenas in Baltimore, Washington, and New York during that first season. The Quakers had held daily practices on Philadelphia's Centennial Lake in January and February and were ready to take on all comers.

On Friday, February 19, 1897, in their third game of the season, Penn faced off against the University of Maryland at Baltimore's North Avenue Ice Palace. The *Philadelphia Inquirer* called it a "snappy game." The headline read: MR. POND SMASHED MR. GEORGE ORTON AND THE GAME BREAKS UP IN A ROW. The *Baltimore Sun* had a complete game story: "The play had been somewhat rough from the start, but now it became desperate," the paper said. "The men did not confine themselves to body checking, but brought arms and hands into play. Several fouls occurred in quick succession, but they escaped the notice of Referee H.G. Penniman."[7]

In the midst of a 2–2 tie, Orton had apparently gotten under the skin of one William Pond and a skirmish broke out. The two fell over a bench, and the referee said Pond had struck Orton in the face. Pond claimed he had only used his elbow and forearm to push Orton away. The referee ordered Pond off the ice, much to the chagrin of the Maryland players, who supported their teammate. When Pond refused to leave the ice after five minutes, Penniman awarded the game to Penn by forfeit.

The crowd became enraged, and a policeman had to escort Penniman off the ice, while the band played a two-step. The *Sun* article suggested that Penniman, in calling Maryland for numerous offside infractions, had given the distinct impression that he was favouring Penn.

Pond was somewhat famous in Baltimore. His older brother, Arlie Pond, was a star pitcher with the Baltimore Orioles, having won 16 games in 1896.[8] Perhaps Orton said or did something to antagonize Pond. That wasn't Orton's style, but he may have been somewhat cranky after a long week on the road. Six days earlier he was beaten by a whisker at the tape by Ernie Hjertberg in the two-mile steeplechase at New York's Madison Square Garden. That was the second incarnation of the legendary Garden; the original, built by P.T. Barnum, was the first to have an artificial ice surface in 1879. In 1890, a new Madison Square Garden was built on the same site, at East 26th and Madison Avenue. It did not feature artificial ice but did host indoor college football games, bicycle races, boxing, the famous Westminster Kennel Club Dog Show, and, of course, track meets.

The Penn hockey team was clearly better than their opponents during the 1897 season, largely due to their Canadian content. After winning by forfeit against Maryland, the Quakers went on to defeat Johns Hopkins 3–2 the following night and then travelled to New York for the first intercollegiate game between Penn and Columbia on Friday February 26. Over a thousand students crammed into St. Nicholas Arena, as reported by the publication *The Amateur Athlete*:

> The Quakers won, due principally to the brilliant individual playing of the four Canadians in the persons of Agnew, Phymester, Willet and Orton. What Orton lacked in the use of an arm, which is crippled and entirely useless, he made up in the agility of his legs and other arm.[9]

Few were aware that Orton had a deformed arm when he was running track, but it soon became evident that he was playing hockey and lacrosse with a severe handicap. It did not go unnoticed. The *Brooklyn Daily Eagle* marvelled at his abilities, saying, "Orton, the Pennsylvania long distance runner, is a remarkable athlete considering that he has a withered arm and could use only one arm in handling a hockey stick."[10] The *Pittsburgh Press* wrote, "George Orton, the former University of Pennsylvania athlete, has a withered arm. It did not stop him playing hockey. He became quite adept, using the stick in one hand."[11]

By now, there was a surge of interest in Philadelphia ice hockey, but participation was totally dependent on the elements. Orton lobbied hard to have an indoor rink constructed, and in December 1897, the West Park Ice Palace at 52nd and Jefferson opened for business. The Penn hockey team, though, was in limbo by this time as Orton's college eligibility had run out and Penn did not commit to keeping the hockey team going.

Orton wanted to keep hockey in the forefront and was committed to institutionalizing the sport in Philadelphia. With that, he formed the Quaker City Hockey Club and the Hockey League of Philadelphia in late 1897. Teams that first season included Haverford College, Philadelphia Dental School, Wayne, and Quaker City. Orton was elected president of the league, and he also captained the Quaker City team. There was never a mention of conflict of interest. Everybody knew that Orton was "Mr. Hockey" in Philly, and without his efforts, the game never would have taken off.

A schedule was set up, rivalries were formed, and Quaker City won the first championship, thanks to Orton and Willett. The following season, Haverford could not field a team, but Penn, with the support and sponsorship of the university, entered the league.

By this time, Philadelphians were flocking to the new Ice Palace to pleasure skate, watch hockey, and witness skating exhibitions. Orton was a tremendous skater, and to spur interest, he put on a "fast skating" exhibition in January of 1899. The newspapers trumpeted the event, with Orton hailed as "the famous University athlete." At the time, Orton could *run* a mile in about four minutes and 20 seconds, but that was on a quarter-mile oval. The Ice Palace was considerably smaller, with much tighter turns. In front of a delighted crowd of about 800, Orton skated the mile in 3 minutes, 59.1 seconds.[12]

Even though Orton's heart was in the right place when it came to hockey, the Quaker City squad was considerably more talented than the other teams in the Hockey League of Philadelphia. Quaker City won all their games quite easily, and Orton won the scoring title. In one memorable game against Baltimore, Orton scored five goals and added four assists in a 12–1 rout. After that, he went looking for better competition as Quaker City was clearly the best team outside of New York City. Orton applied for membership into the American Amateur Hockey League, which was based in New York. The AAHL consisted mostly of Canadian-born players, but there were several skilled Americans in the loop. Teams included the Brooklyn Crescents, Brooklyn Skating Club, New York Athletic Club (of which Orton was a member as a track athlete), New York Hockey Club, and St. Nicholas Hockey Club. The team from Montclair, New Jersey, had disbanded, so Quaker City took their place for the 1900–1 season.

American-based teams were not eligible for the Stanley Cup in the days prior to the formation of professional hockey leagues. The Cup was awarded to Canada's top amateur team through a series of challenge games and league play. Nevertheless, teams competing for the Stanley Cup would always take up a challenge from their counterparts in the AAHL and would win most of the time. The AAHL was a good, competitive league, but definitely a notch below its Canadian counterpart, the Canadian Amateur Hockey League (formerly the Amateur Hockey Association of Canada). Orton was Quaker City's team captain and leading scorer, managing eight goals in 11 games that year. One of his teammates was a 19-year-old named William Clothier, who would go on to win the 1906 U.S. Open tennis championship.

Clothier was one of several top-flight tennis players who skated in the AAHL. Seven-time U.S. Open champ William Larned was the captain of the St. Nicholas team. One of his teammates was four-time U.S. Open singles winner Robert Wrenn, who also played a mean game of doubles. Wrenn and Malcolm Chace won the 1895 U.S. Open and were runners-up the following year.

Chace had been introduced to ice hockey during the summer of 1894 while playing tennis tournaments in Canada. "You may be able to beat us in tennis," said one of his clay court victims, "but come back in the winter and we'll show you how hockey is played." Chace knew nothing of this Canadian game. The American equivalent to ice hockey at that time was ice polo or roller polo, played on roller skates with a ball and a thin stick. The English version of the game was known as bandy. "The Canadian hockey stick is longer and larger, with a thick body," wrote the *Chicago Tribune.*

"The ball is a block of rubber, an inch long and with a diameter of two and a half inches. It is elusive and not capable of nearly such scientific strokes as the American ball of rubber."[13]

The president of the Ontario Hockey Association, a Mr. Houston, invited Chace and fellow tennis player Arthur Foote of Yale to assemble a team to visit Canada that following winter for a series of games. Chace organized a squad of skaters, several of whom were outstanding tennis players. They included the aforementioned Larned, of Cornell, and Wrenn, of Harvard, as well as Wrenn's teammate Fred Hovey, a three-time U.S. Open champ. During the Christmas holidays of 1894–1895, the American squad played games in Toronto, Hamilton, Ottawa, Kingston, and Montreal. Despite being badly defeated in all their matches, they gained valuable experience and quickly learned the rules and intricacies of the Canadian game.

Returning to the United States, Chace formed the first collegiate team at Yale, and soon squads in Baltimore were formed at Johns Hopkins University, the University of Maryland, and the Baltimore Athletic Club. When Yale faced off against Johns Hopkins on a cold, rainy February 1, 1896, at the North Park Ice Palace in Baltimore, it marked the first inter-collegiate ice hockey game in the United States. The game ended in a 2–2 tie, but two weeks later, in the rematch, Yale prevailed 2–1. Chace scored both goals, including the first game-winning goal in U.S. college hockey history. Chace died at the age of 80 in 1955. "He was credited with being the father of hockey in the United States," wrote the *Providence Journal* in his obituary.[14]

Chace is enshrined in the International Tennis Hall of Fame but not the U.S. Hockey Hall of Fame.

The 1900–1 season was a tough one for Orton's Quaker City team in the AAHL. To begin with, their uniform colours were maroon with white stripes and looked virtually identical to the ones worn by the Brooklyn Crescents, who had seniority in the league. When the teams met on January 4, 1901, at the Claremont rink in Brooklyn, it was tough to tell your teammate from the opponent. "The lack of teamwork on both sides was evident," as pointed out by the *Brooklyn Daily Eagle*, "with the players afraid to make rapid passes." The article goes on to mention that, even though it was the first game of the season for both clubs, Quaker City was at a distinct disadvantage. "The Crescents have had the Brooklyn Skating Club team to practice against," wrote the *Daily Eagle*, "while the Quakers can find no team in the vicinity of their home rink strong enough to make them play hard." It was also the first time the Quakers had played in a game with goal cages, having previously used the old-time posts. Orton scored the only goal for Quaker City and was hailed as "the best man on the Quaker team, with an excellent left handed shot." Brooklyn, led by Canadians Bill Dobby and Bob Wall, beat Quaker City 5–1.[15]

Unfortunately for Quaker City, that was their only season in the AAHL. It had nothing to do with the team's lack of success on the ice, even though they won just two of 11 games. Their home rink, the Ice Palace, burned to the ground on March 24, 1901. It would not be rebuilt, and that spelled the end of organized hockey for a number of years in Philadelphia.

George Orton had always wanted to bring hockey back. By 1916, he had the political influence and name recognition to do so. Orton had been Philadelphia's athletic commissioner a decade earlier and originated the Philadelphia Children's Playground Association for the purpose of building up the health of local kids. He was also elected as the first president of the mid-Atlantic region of the Amateur Athletic Union. Now, it was time to form another hockey league, and so the Philadelphia Hockey Association was born.

The city had agreed to build an artificial ice rink, the Winter Palace, at 39th and Market Streets. There was no roof on the facility, so the ice surface was covered by a giant tent. Several teams joined the PHA, including two each from the Merion Cricket Club and the Philadelphia Cricket Club and a team called the Wanderers, which featured the greatest hockey player in the country, Hobey Baker, a Philadelphia native.

Baker had been a star at Princeton earlier in the decade but returned to Philadelphia before heading off to the First World War. Baker was killed in France when his airplane crashed. He was 26 years old. Today, the Hobey Baker Award is presented annually to the top collegiate hockey player in the United States.

Competition in the PHA was strong, and interest in the sport was growing rapidly. Just as hockey was about to really take off, though, fate dealt Orton and company a crippling blow: A severe winter storm tore down the immense tent that covered the ice surface at the Winter Palace. It could not be fixed and the hockey season was abandoned.

Undaunted, Orton immediately began beating the drums for construction of a new, permanent ice rink. The original Ice Palace had burned down in 1901 after less than four years of existence. The progress of Philadelphia hockey had been retarded without the availability of a proper rink, and with virtually every other major city having at least one indoor arena, it was time for Philadelphia to join the 20th century. The war would put a temporary hold on any plans, but Orton, along with hundreds of Penn students and alumni, signed a petition in January of 1917 calling for the university to resurrect the hockey program. Nothing would be considered until after the war, but Orton had laid the groundwork for a new arena and the imminent return of hockey. Again.[16]

When the Great War ended in 1918, Orton immediately requested the university resume its sponsorship of the hockey team and, after securing their promise, went out and pestered local businessmen to help build a brand new arena on Walnut between 45th and 46th Streets. Many turned Orton down, telling him that Philadelphia would never be a hockey town. But Orton was relentless. His tenacious fundraising along with his enthusiasm for hockey got the job done.

Once Penn had agreed to support hockey again, Orton volunteered to take on significant responsibilities. He became the unpaid director of athletics at the university, doing everything from writing press releases to coaching the hockey team to arranging for a full schedule of road games for the 1919–20 season until the new arena was completed. He had been hired by the city to manage the arena and book all the events there.

On February 14, 1920, the Philadelphia Ice Palace and Auditorium celebrated its grand opening. The ice surface was huge: 220 feet by 101 feet. There were 4,000 seats with unobstructed views, 1,500 of which were located in the balcony. The skate room could hold 3,000 pairs of skates and 4,000 coats.[17] Ironically, Orton's Penn team was not scheduled for opening night. Yale beat Princeton 4–0 before a capacity crowd of over 4,000. The only complaint about the new Ice Palace concerned the entrance to the building. There was only one, and it could not accommodate thousands of patrons trying to enter or exit at the same time.

The following November, Orton presided over a meeting to organize the new Intercollegiate Ice Hockey League, which included teams from Dartmouth, Harvard, Yale, Princeton, Columbia, Penn, and Cornell. The delegates agreed to adopt the rules of Canadian intercollegiate hockey, with six-man teams instead of seven a side. Orton had invited Yale and Princeton, as well as Penn, to play their home games at his new arena. Princeton, New Jersey, is only 45 miles from Philly, but New Haven, Connecticut, is some 180 miles away. With the Yale rink incapable of producing good ice that year, the Bulldogs welcomed the opportunity to play their home games at the Ice Palace, especially after an extended road trip through Canada to begin the season.

By taking on the dual role of volunteer hockey coach and manager at Penn, Orton was spreading himself too thin. He was also managing the Penn Relays and coaching the Penn track team. This made him incapable of focusing on the hockey program, and after three unsuccessful seasons at the helm, Orton hired a new coach, Frank "Coddy" Winters. Even though he became a member of the U.S. Hockey Hall of Fame, Winters could not coax enough victories out of the Penn varsity and left after one season.

Determined not to let Penn fall on hard times again, Orton hired one of the most prominent hockey and lacrosse coaches in North America, Eddie Powers, to take over that dual role with the Quakers. Powers, from Toronto, had coached the Westminster club of Boston to the U.S. amateur hockey title the previous season. Over 100 players attended his first practice, hoping to win a spot on the team. But the enthusiasm was short-lived and the dual coaching role took its toll on Powers, who lasted two seasons at Penn before leaving to coach in the National Hockey League. With the Toronto St. Patricks, Powers coached future Hall of Famers Jack Adams, Babe Dye, and Hap Day. He spent two seasons there before the team was sold to Conn Smythe and eventually rechristened the Toronto Maple Leafs. Powers coached in the minor leagues and worked for the Leafs organization for many years as the head of their farm system. He died suddenly in 1943 at the age of 54. The Eddie Powers Memorial Trophy has been awarded annually to the top scorer in the Ontario Hockey League since 1946.

Orton may have had a hand in the hiring of another coach destined to have a prestigious trophy named in his honour. In 1920, former Penn football player John L. Heisman was recruited to coach the Quaker varsity team after 16 successful years at Georgia Tech. It was Heisman who had Tech run up a 222–0 score over Cumberland College in 1916 — the most lopsided victory in football history. He insisted that he wanted to get even for Cumberland's 22–0 win over Georgia Tech in baseball because Cumberland had used professional players. (Heisman was also the baseball coach at Tech.) Heisman had resigned from Tech in 1919 after a very public divorce. His wife, Evelyn, decided to stay in her home town of Atlanta, so Heisman took the job at Penn to avoid any social embarrassment. He and Orton had sat on various college football committees, and both were quite famous in the sporting world. Both were progressive thinkers. It was Orton who had vigorously supported the numbering of players during a football rules committee meeting, as reported by the *New York Tribune* on February 1, 1914:

> I am very much in favor of numbering the players. It would do much to popularize the sport further. I think the idea that some football men have that it would tend to give away the plays is bunk, for the numbers would be on the backs of the players. In all our games I think the spectator should be considered. Numbering is done in many branches of athletics, and has always proved beneficial to the games and a help to those watching. It seems to me a rather narrow idea of sport in general; to make the generalization that sport is for the players and for them alone. What would college football be without the spectators? I am afraid that at least 50 per cent of those playing it would not play it at all if it were not for the prominence given the game in various ways. Number the players by all means.[18]

The football team at Dartmouth University was thought to be the first to use uniform numbers. Washington and Jefferson University had used them with great success; so had the University of Chicago. Track athletes had been numbered for years. Most agreed with placing numbers on uniforms. Hobey Baker was in favour. Sort of. Besides his prowess on the ice, Baker was captain of the Princeton football team. He said,

> I cannot say I like the idea for it seems to me it brings a sort of a professional and business element into a sport already

too much that way. There is no getting around the fact that it would make the game more interesting to the casual observer and easier for the reporters, and of course, these outsiders, if you will permit me to use the word, have to be considered! In my mind it is consideration for outsiders against the element of professionalism it brings in, and I think consideration for the outsider wins; in other words, I am in favor of numbering the men.[19]

While Orton coached the hockey team at Penn, Heisman took over the newly numbered football squad in 1920. Over three seasons at Penn, Heisman's teams won 16, lost 10, and tied two. In December of 1936, at the age of 66, John L. Heisman died of pneumonia. The iconic Heisman Memorial Trophy has been awarded annually to the top collegiate football player in the United States ever since his death.

Orton's final season behind the hockey bench at Penn was 1921–22. Sixty players tried out for the Quakers, and Orton kept 15 of them. He was helped along by the team's manager, William MacIntosh, and assistant manager, Howard Butcher III, Class of '23. Butcher was a pretty fair soccer player but wasn't much of a hockey player, according to his son, Howard Butcher IV, aged 81:

Pop went up to Hanover, New Hampshire, with the team for a game at Dartmouth. A number of players partied pretty hard the night before the game, and weren't in shape to play. Coach Orton was furious, and he had to dragoon Pop into playing. Dartmouth played their games outdoors on Occom Pond near the school campus and there were no boards or anything so when the puck was shot out of play, you had to go and get it because they didn't always have another puck nearby. Coach told Pop that whenever Penn got tired, he should shoot the puck so far into the snowbank that it would take a while to find it, and give the players a break. That's how he saved the team's bacon. I don't recall if Penn won that day, but it sure made for a great story.

Ironically, Butcher III was largely responsible for Philadelphia's next great ice rink, according to his son.

> He loved Penn more than anything but our mother. Attending the school and being involved in sports was the highlight of his youth and he was very loyal to Penn and very generous. There was already a dormitory named after him thanks to a generous donation, and when he raised enough money for a new rink, including a 3 million dollar personal donation, he wanted to make sure it was named after his college class. The Class of 1923 rink was opened in 1972, and has been the home of Pennsylvania hockey ever since.[20]

Orton let go of the coaching reins in 1922 but continued to play hockey at a high level for many years. On January 11, 1929, a day after his 56th birthday (the newspapers claimed he was 62), Orton laced up the blades and started at left wing for the Penn Athletic Club as they took on the team he founded in 1898, Quaker City. A different team, the Philadelphia Quakers, entered the National Hockey League for one season, 1930–31.

Not to be confused with the University of Pennsylvania Quakers, this moribund team was known in a previous life as the Pittsburgh Pirates before their financially strapped owners moved them to Philadelphia. In their lone NHL season, the Quakers set a record for futility by winning just four of their 44 games. They were forced to suspend operations after the 1931 season, never to be heard from again.

In the ensuing years, diehard Philadelphia hockey fans would have to settle for the University team, the Quakers, or the minor leagues. The rink had been renamed the Philadelphia Arena and played host to a number of teams: the Arrows, the Ramblers, the Comets, the Falcons, and the Rockets. Occasionally it hosted basketball games, including the odd appearance by the NBAs Philadelphia 76ers. In 1983, the arena met the same fate as the original Ice Palace. It was destroyed by fire.

When the NHL added six teams in 1967, they must've forgotten all about the ill-fated Quakers because Philadelphia was awarded an expansion team, the Flyers. They would reward their long-suffering fans with consecutive Stanley Cup victories in the mid-1970s. A tip of the cap should go to George Orton. His persistence, tenacity, and unbridled enthusiasm for the sport of hockey was unmatched. He taught Philadelphians how the game should be played, officiated, and observed. Philadelphia may never have become the great hockey city it is today were it not for Orton. Flyers fans should be most thankful.

FAMILY LIFE

During the course of his athletic and academic pursuits at Penn, Orton met a young lady named Edith Wayne Martin. How they met is unknown, but Orton was a big man on campus and Edith was a beautiful young woman.

Edith was 19 in 1894, while George was 21. She lived with her parents, Robert Martin and Laura Eugenie Martin, and her three younger siblings, Charles, Robert Jr., and Helen. The family lived at 332 South 43rd Street, a mile and a half from the Penn campus in an area known as Spruce Hill. Robert Martin worked for L. Martin and company, one of the nation's largest printers.

George and Edith were married in Montreal, at St. James Methodist Church. The date was August 28, 1898. When I mentioned this fact to Connie, she was surprised that her grandparents had been married in Quebec. "No one ever talked much about the relationship between George and Edith," she said. "My mother and my aunts both agreed that their parents made a fine looking couple on the rare occasions they were together He had blond curly hair while she had jet black hair. They made a striking couple."[1]

George was studying for his Ph.D. and playing and coaching sports as often as he could. How he found the time to do anything else is a mystery. Yet on April 22, 1900, the couple welcomed their first child into the world. Constance Orton was born in Philadelphia.

For George, fatherhood would have to wait; he had committed to racing overseas in the English championships, the Paris Olympics, and the European championships in Belgium. He would be away from his wife and baby for three months. It wouldn't be the last time George was off to the races. On June 20, he set sail from New York aboard the *Southwark* for the 10-day voyage to England.

Edith and Constance stayed in the house on South 43rd Street, surrounded by her family. She was going to have to get used to George being an absentee husband and father.

Daughter number two, Eleanor, was born on July 31, 1904, in York County, Ontario, also known as Toronto. How George and Edith came to have the baby in Toronto is unknown, although George usually visited his parents and siblings at that time of the year. Connie Meaney was aware that her Aunt Eleanor had been born in Canada, but she never asked and was never told why. It may have been a coincidence or they might've planned things that way. Universal health care was not available in Canada at that time, so having the baby there wouldn't have been advantageous. For some reason, George didn't want the folks at the U.S. Naturalization office to know about his daughter's birth country, so he lied on his application for U.S. citizenship in 1920 when, under place of birth for Eleanor, he wrote "Philadelphia."

On October 30, 1909, Edith and George had their third child, a daughter, also named Edith. She was born in Philadelphia, and Connie Meaney does not recall being told why her grandmother, Edith Wayne Martin Orton, decided to name her baby, Connie's mother, Edith W. Orton. It might've been George's idea. He seemed to have had a thing for the name Edith.

Orton always seemed to have a lot on his plate. After earning his Ph.D. in philosophy in 1896, "Doc" Orton went into teaching and coaching. He was the director of physical education and taught languages at the Eastburn Academy, a private school in Philadelphia, from 1897 to 1900. George

Eastburn, who founded the school, was a big proponent of basketball and, along with Orton's help, introduced the sport to Philadelphians around 1897, six years after Dr. James Naismith had invented the sport at the Springfield, Massachusetts, YMCA.

In addition to his duties at Eastburn, Orton was busy with hockey all winter as a player, a coach, and an administrator. He was also a graduate assistant coach on the Penn track team. In 1900, besides travelling all over Europe as a competitor, he wrote several long stories for the *Philadelphia Inquirer*. It was very rare to see a byline attached to a newspaper story in those days, but Orton had star power, and the *Inquirer* knew his views on sport would attract more readers and sell more newspapers. When you are referred to as "George Orton, the famous University of Pennsylvania athlete," people want to hear what you have to say.

These were exclusive, inside stories from a world champion athlete who was still very much active. The perspectives offered by Orton were, in most cases, more interesting and insightful than the stories put out by most reporters. Upon his return from Europe, Orton covered college football for the *Inquirer* in the fall of 1900, writing game stories about Penn, Harvard, Yale, Princeton, Army, Navy, Columbia, Cornell, and Lafayette. The Quakers finished the 1900 season with a 12–1 record, losing only at Cambridge, Massachusetts, to Harvard.

The Penn football coach was George Washington Woodruff, who, in 10 years with the Quakers, won nearly 89 percent of his games! His namesake, George Washington Orton, conducted many interviews with Woodruff in order to gain insight. Orton not only reported on the games but also championed fair play and wasn't afraid to editorialize when it came to the unsavoury aspects of the "win at all costs" attitude that seemed to permeate the college ranks. He wrote in the December 24, 1900, edition of the *Inquirer*: "An amateur is one who strives / Fair as a knight to gain the day; / But does it not for love of gain. / But for sport's sake and love of play."[2]

Orton was a lover of all sports and made it clear in the same article that his alma mater, despite its success in football and track, needed to raise its level of play in other sports if it wanted to compete with the other Ivy League schools:

Athletic activity at Penn this year will be greater and more diversified than ever. Not only will all the old games be pushed, but several new ones have been making a name for themselves. Of these, the basket ball and hockey teams are the most important. Pennsylvania has made two or three abortive efforts to put out a basket ball team, but on each occasion the lack of a suitable gymnasium has made these efforts to no avail. Despite this great handicap, one that is as disgraceful as it is lamentable, the Red and Blue colors are again seen upon the floor. This time the team has made a good start and though they cannot be expected to play a star game their first season they are doing fairly well. Hockey is another game that has been revived. Two years ago, Penn had a very good team, but last year there was no ice and therefore no team. This meant that a completely new start had to be made this season and the team is as yet in such an embryonic state that it is difficult to say whether it can be developed into a winner or not.[3]

Throughout the fall of 1900, Orton's reportage of college football was extensive. He would compose a detailed game story, a sidebar piece that might profile a coach or player, and an editorial. In one instance, he informed the reader that "West Point (Army) was penalized ten yards for coaching from the sideline." I never knew that rule existed in college football at that time. It made sense. Aiding and abetting was against the spirit of amateur athletics.

At season's end, Orton was asked to make his All-American football selections for the *Inquirer*; he wrote a lengthy piece detailing each selection and the reasons that player was chosen. Orton's picks were then used to help determine the consensus All-American selections, which always showed an eastern bias. The major newspapers of the day were in New York, Philadelphia, Baltimore, Boston, Buffalo, and Washington. Because the two official selectors, Walter Camp and Caspar Whitney, along with Orton and other influential writers, were from the east, they saw only games in their region. This was well before the days of the Wright brothers at Kitty Hawk, and even prior to Henry Ford's mass-produced Model T. A train trip could easily take 24 hours each way to a western or southern outpost. That's why the University of Chicago, Notre Dame, Minnesota, Michigan, Georgia Tech, and so on rarely had football players who were first-or second-team All-Americans. With the exception of Chicago, the nation's second most populated city, and St. Louis, its sixth, the top teams offering the best competition were based in the northeast.

Writing, teaching, competing, and coaching took up all of Orton's time. After the Eastburn Academy, he accepted a position with the Blight School in 1901 as their director of physical education. He also taught languages and history. In January of 1901, the *Toronto Star*, under the headline "George Orton Is a Busy Man," printed an interview with Orton, asking him what he was up to in Philadelphia.

> While at the University of Pennsylvania, I did a great deal of newspaper writing, and in the course of time I have come to be considered a Solon on Track Athletics and a good general athletic writer. On this account, I was given charge of college sport on the *Inquirer*. This is an important department down here, where college sport is so prominent. I made a good record last fall on football, and have kept all the other Philadelphia writers on the jump. Besides my newspaper work, I still teach school two hours per day, as the principal did not want me to leave. I also have charge of the amusements and press notices of the Ice Palace here. I find time to play Association football once a week and to captain the best hockey team in Philadelphia, and to act as grandfather to all the other hockey teams in town, collegiate, amateur and scholastic.… and if we can only keep the Ice Palace open our Philadelphia teams will soon be good. My own team, the Quaker City, is in the American amateur championship series, but we have lost our first two games. I hope to do better, as I now know what is the matter.
>
> I am married and have a sweet little baby girl, nearly a year old, so the full dinner pail is also a necessity with me.[4]

In 1902, Orton was offered a position at the prestigious Episcopal Academy, where he taught languages and coached the track and field and baseball teams. The *Philadelphia Ledger* praised Orton's efforts in 1905, saying he "lifted the city's interscholastic sports up to the standard of any section in the country."[5]

Three years at the Episcopal Academy led to the headmaster's job at Banks Business College in Philadelphia in June of 1905. Orton had an entrepreneurial spirit and a love of business. In November 1905, he was appointed athletic commissioner for the City of Philadelphia. His number one priority would be the formation of a playground association similar to the one in New York City, which was formed in 1897. There, the Small Parks Advisory Committee was created to build proper playgrounds with equipment. They trained recreation specialists to show parents and children how to safely use the monkey bars, slides, and swing sets.

Social Reformers such as New York governor (and former NYC mayor) Theodore Roosevelt felt that playgrounds should be designed to be a "healthful influence upon morals and conduct … for the physical energies of youth, which, if not directed to good ends, will surely manifest themselves in evil tendencies." Roosevelt soon became the 26th president of the United States. Not long after, he was named honorary president of the newly formed Playground Association of America. Roosevelt believed that children at play would benefit greatly from adult organization and supervision. Some of the structured activities undertaken during this era included marching, singing, a salute to the flag, organized free play, drills, folk dancing, apparatus work, and basketball.[6]

With the nation becoming more attuned to the benefits of physical fitness, Orton sprang into action. As the athletic commissioner, he developed the Philadelphia Children's Playground Association with the help of his friend R. Tait McKenzie, the director of the physical education department at Penn. As well, AAU president James E. Sullivan appointed Orton to be the first association president of the Mid-Atlantic States. With his knowledge of Philadelphia sports, along with his connections and good name, Orton was the perfect choice. He was a superstar athlete who had always adhered to the healthy body–healthy mind philosophy. As a doctor of philosophy and an Olympic and world champion athlete, Orton had a platform to pass along his expertise to a wider audience. His main target was young people:

Not only should exercises be taken to develop the body, but care should be observed that nothing is done that will nullify such exercise. For the scholastic athlete, I have no hesitation in saying emphatically CUT OUT TOBACCO. It can do no good and in ninety-nine cases out of a hundred it has a deterrent effect, both on the mind and body of the growing youth. If smoking must be done, wait until man's estate is reached. Many a promising athlete is spoiled through the use of tobacco, though every other natural quality has been present and reinforced by good training and developing exercises. A boy cannot do himself justice, either in class room or in athletics, when his brain is beclouded with nicotine. Therefore CUT IT OUT. Eat plenty of good, healthy food. Do not diet too severely, for the growing body needs all sorts of nourishment. But there are so many kinds of healthy food that is palatable, that it seems unnecessary for the boy to eat rich pastries and highly seasoned food. Good meat, vegetables, bread, butter, tapioca and rice pudding, an occasional piece of pie, ice cream and plenty of fruit form a menu good enough for anyone. Get plenty of sleep. This is necessary for physical development, especially when the body is still growing. Late hours, too much society, with its many excitements, should thus be relegated to the background as much as possible. Lastly, keep the body pure. Do not practice any forms of self abuse. This is fatal, and I am happy to say, that instances of it are rare among our athletic youth, for everything in the athletic atmosphere tends to eradicate such pernicious habits. Finally, play fair; run straight, and avoid all underhand and ungentlemanly conduct when competing in athletics or training for a contest. Be a sportsman in the true sense of the term.[7]

Now that he was athletic commissioner, Orton also pushed for more municipal swimming pools to be built. He felt that Rotary, Kiwanis, and Lions clubs and American Legion posts should help finance these pools if public funds weren't available. He urged philanthropists to help fund these commendable and humanitarian enterprises, especially during the sweltering summer months.

> In selecting a site for an outdoor pool a location should be chosen where natural drainage is good. The site should be centrally located as real estate prices, local ordinances and other conditions permit, so that it may be reached with a minimum of time and effort by the greatest number of people. The natural beauty and central location of public parks frequently offer attractive locations for municipal pools.... The pool should be built near a car line or on a paved highway as near to the city as possible.[8]

It's impossible to quantify Orton's contribution to athletics and its positive effects on society. His push for cultural initiatives and his unwavering support for athletic competition of all kinds made him an important figure in the development of 20th-century sports.

AUTHOR, AUTHOR

Orton's command of the English language and ability to communicate with the masses were never more apparent than in his instructional books. He chose his words carefully and thoughtfully and utilized his coaching and teaching skills to write *Distance and Cross Country Running*, published in 1903, and *Athletic Training for School Boys*, in 1905.

The former was the first of its kind, a manual with, literally, step-by-step instructions and photographs demonstrating proper running form and technique. Orton used himself as the model. He wore dark track spikes, no socks, and a white T-shirt with light-coloured shorts. There is snow on the ground, and a walkway has been cleared for his demonstrative poses: head back, forward lean, short stride. He had a poised, relaxed look on the track, similar to the one Joe DiMaggio would display in a New York Yankees uniform three decades later. I could picture Orton gliding past his opponents in perfect form. One writer described him as "elegant."

The book also offered tips on nutrition and interval training, along with biographical sketches and photos of the top performers of the day.

The book was received by the U.S. Library of Congress on May 15, 1903, and was considered by scholars to be "culturally important." Orton was a well-respected author, as evidenced by his work with the *Philadelphia Inquirer* and previously his detailed hardcover book, *A History of Athletics at Pennsylvania, 1873–1898*, which has been updated many times and is a treasured work within the Penn community.

In *Distance and Cross Country Running*, Orton also revealed his position on the importance of nationality and the Canadian-American question:

> Mile running is now in a higher state of development than at any time in the history of American sport. Indeed, judged from the strictly national standpoint, there is very little for the athletic enthusiast of this country to crow over in surveying the championship tables of mile runners. If, however, we take the term "American" to include Canada, as it properly does, we shall not make so very bad a showing.[1]

Here is where Orton reveals his true affection for Canada and admiration for her champion runners: "In 1879, Pellatt of Toronto gave an indication of what Canada was to do later by winning the mile championship in New York at the age of 20."[2]

That name sounded familiar. There was a Henry Pellatt, a wealthy financier who became Sir Henry Pellatt. He was the man who built Casa Loma, the spectacular 98-room Gothic Revival mansion that became a Toronto landmark. Could he have been a world-class miler?

Indeed, it was the same guy.

Working in his father's brokerage firm as a clerk in 1877, the 18-year-old had the habit of leaving work an hour early. When asked about it, he told his father he was training for the world record in the mile run and would concentrate on business once that goal was reached. He almost did it, too. Pellatt won the Canadian championship mile in 1878 in four minutes, 52 and three-quarters seconds in front of an enthusiastic Montreal crowd. The *New York Herald* noted the "courtesy and kindness" shown by the public and that the American athletes "had the sympathy of the spectators, and they had the fairest treatment imaginable."[3]

The following year, Pellatt returned the favour for Canada. Representing the Toronto Lacrosse Club, he battled the undefeated W.J. Duffy of the Harlem Athletic Club in the U.S. championships.

The race was run at Mott Haven, on the grounds of the New York Athletic Club. It was one of the few times Pellatt had run on a cinder track. Duffy, along with a couple of teammates, tried to tie up the "boy from the north," but Pellatt shot out to an early lead. Every time Duffy tried to close the gap, Pellatt, with his long strides, pulled farther ahead. In the last 100 yards, Duffy made a final bid, but Pellatt held him off, winning by just two feet. The time was four minutes, 43 and two-fifths seconds. It was not a world record, as Pellatt had promised, but it was enough to hang up his spikes as the U.S. and Canadian amateur champion and return to his father's firm. Eventually, Pellatt would introduce hydroelectricity to Toronto and establish the Toronto Electric Light Company (TELCO).

In 1893, TELCO installed electric lights at Rosedale Grounds, and on June 28, before 1,200 spectators, the Toronto Lacrosse Club hosted the first nighttime track meet. Pellatt was present as George Orton won the mile and two-mile races, for the first time under the lights.

Pellatt became the president of Toronto's first indoor ice rink, the Arena Gardens, in 1912, but by then his appearance had changed dramatically. He had put on a significant amount of weight since his running career had ended.

Like Orton, Pellatt was a dreamer. He would go on to become famous as the man who built and lost the most recognizable castle in North America. According to his grandnephew, John Pellatt, the family motto was "First or foremost if possible." That seemed to be appropriate given Pellatt's mile-run record and his foresight when it came to the importance of hydroelectricity and the extravagant nature of castle building.

Orton was the foremost authority on running in the early 1900s. He especially appreciated the efforts of the fine Canadian runners who had preceded him. It's quite possible that, as a small boy while recovering from his blood clot, he had read accounts of Pellatt's victories, and perhaps had even seen a picture of him in action. Many great champions had seen their accomplishments go unrecognized. Orton, as an adult historian, felt it imperative that these great champions be singled out. He wrote proudly of these Canadian stars. One, in particular, had his promising career cut short:

In 1888, [George M.] Gibbs of Toronto again startled New
Yorkers by beating not only the Americans, but E.C. Carter,
A.B. George and Tommy Conneff, who had been brought
out by the old Manhattan Athletic Club for the purpose of
putting a stop to Carter's winning course. Gibbs defeated
them decisively and had it not been for most unfortunate
family troubles, Gibbs would, in succeeding years, have
become a very famous runner. In 1890, in his training, he
beat 4 minutes 20 seconds in a trial, only to be forced by
a death in his family not to compete for athletic honors.[4]

George Gibbs was not from Canada, but he called it home. He was born
in 1863 in New York State and eventually settled in Guelph, Ontario. (The
same Guelph where Orton had supposedly attended school.) At five foot
nine and three-quarters and weighing 150 pounds, Gibbs was considerably
bigger than most middle-distance runners. He was as dominant in the late
1880s as Orton was during his prime. Gibbs's battles with Tommy Conneff
were legendary. After beating the crack field referred to in the previous
passage, Gibbs became "an object of considerable interest to the amateur
athletes of the country," wrote the *Buffalo Evening News*.[5]

At the Canadian championships of 1888, at Montreal, Gibbs had the
misfortune of breaking his belt at the start of the mile. He ran the entire
race with one hand holding up his tights but still managed to grab second
place, just two yards behind Conneff. Gibbs went on to win the Canadian
championship three straight years and was "destined to be heard from in the
future in amateur athletics."[6] Gibbs had to give up racing by the age of 27,
however. Having never heard of George Gibbs (big surprise), I wondered
how many other great Canadian athletes had slipped through the cracks and
not made it into the history books. Orton was certainly the biggest name
from that time period, and he recognized himself as such, even though it
was in the third person:

In 1892, another Canadian carried off the honors in the
person of George W. Orton and for five years he won both
the Canadian and American mile championships. We have
already spoken of Conneff's wonderful running in '95. In

'97, J.F. Cregan won. Cregan was the first native of this country to win the mile for eleven years. He repeated the trick the next year. The succeeding season, another Canadian star loomed up and Alec Grant became champion. Thus, in the last seventeen years, the United States mile championship has been won only twice by a native of the country. This should furnish food for thought. But, as noted above, there are more good milers in the country to-day than ever before and all that it needs to make this country as feared in this branch of track and field sport as she is in all others is persistent and careful encouragement.[7]

Orton did not feel nationality should play a part in the new sporting republic that was in the midst of taking shape. Canadians and Americans were the same, in his opinion. When *Distance and Cross Country Running* was first published in 1903, Orton was the holder of the North American mile record: four minutes 21 and four-fifths seconds. One of his rivals was Alexander Grant, who also happened to be his best friend and future business partner.

In Grant, Orton saw a lot of himself, and he mentored his friend on the finer points of distance running. Orton showed Grant how to change his gait over the last quarter of a mile. "By doing so," Orton wrote, "the athlete uses muscles that have not as yet been brought into play and even those which he has been using are set at a different angle of tension and thus made to react more strongly and quickly." Grant, according to Orton, went from "a good distance runner into one of the fastest men we have ever had in this country. He has now mastered the principle and it accounts for the speed which he gets up the last 300 yards of his races."[8]

Orton's book is extensive in its simplicity. He teaches the reader how to train for every discipline from the quarter-mile to the marathon. There are 66 pages of instruction along with 31 photos. The remainder of the book is a catalogue featuring all the sporting equipment sold by A.G. Spalding and Brothers.

Albert Spalding was a legendary baseball pitcher in the 1870s, winning 252 games in six years and pitching and managing the Chicago White Stockings to their first National League pennant in 1876. That year, Albert and his brother Walter obtained the rights to produce the official National

League baseball and opened their first sporting goods store in Chicago. The chain would grow to 13 stores, and in 1899 the company began allowing retailers to order directly from their catalogue, which happened to be included in every one of their Spalding athletic books. Spalding manufactured everything from track shoes to basketballs to boxing gloves to medicine balls. The Spalding Shamrock hockey stick sold for 75 cents and was endorsed by the Stanley Cup–winning Winnipeg Victorias and Montreal Shamrocks. One could buy a Spalding Regulation stick for 50 cents, while the youth stick went for a quarter.

Spalding's Athletic Library began in 1892 and consisted of instructional and statistical books on just about every sport. There were also publications with simple how-to-play rules for parlour games such as dominoes, checkers, euchre, billiards, cribbage, baccarat, hearts, pinochle, and children's games.

Albert Spalding grew his sporting goods and publishing empire by leaps and bounds in the early part of the 20th century. He did his best to reform baseball, getting rid of the gambling and collusion among players and banning alcohol. He also became a one-man crusader, debunking the myth that Abner Doubleday had invented the sport of baseball in Cooperstown, New York, in 1839. It was actually Alexander Cartwright, as part of the Knickerbocker Rules committee in New York, who helped invent the sport in 1845. Cartwright is now widely known as "the father of baseball."

Orton was a major contributor to Spalding's Athletic Library for a number of years, thanks in part to his friend James E. Sullivan. Sullivan was Spalding's right-hand man, having founded the *Spalding Official Athletic Almanac* in 1892. The almanac was recognized as the one reliable authority on athletic records at that time and was considered the bible of sports. Previously, Sullivan had been a sportswriter and published the *Athletics News* in the early 1880s. He was one of the founders of the Amateur Athletic Union in 1888 and later wielded considerable power as its president. As secretary of the American Olympic Committee, he was a key figure in the early Olympic movement, despite his up-and-down relationship with IOC president Pierre de Coubertin.

Regretfully, James E. Sullivan managed to set the women's movement back several decades. He was the dominant adversary of America's female athletes, refusing to allow women to compete in any AAU-sanctioned event. He and the American Olympic Committee went so far as to oppose the participation of American women in the Olympics or any other competition performed in the presence of men. In 1912, the Swedish Olympic Committee admitted women swimmers and divers in what was considered to be the first real female competition allowed at the Olympics. However, Sullivan, a defender of modesty, would not allow American females to compete in bathing suits and refused to sanction their participation in Sweden, even though other nations were allowing women to compete at the Olympics.[9]

Only one woman who had any clout seemed to take up the cause. One of the divers who had been barred from competing, 24-year-old New Yorker Ida Schnall, was a star pitcher for the New York Female Giants baseball team. (She learned how to throw a curve from the great Christy Mathewson of the major league's New York Giants.) Schnall, who boasted of being the "Champion Female Athlete of America," eventually held records in baseball, tennis, wrestling, gymnastics, bicycling, rowing, swimming, diving, running, bowling, ice skating, roller skating, high jumping, broad jumping, and bag punching.[10] She was also a Vaudeville star and a Broadway sensation. Outraged at the decision to ban female athletes from the Olympics, she wrote a letter to the mayor of New York, William Jay Gaynor:

> I am keenly interested in the movement to allow the female element to compete during the future games to be held at Stockholm, Sweden. May I count on your help in bringing the subject to the attention of J.E. Sullivan, secretary of the committee in charge of the American athletes who are to compete in these games? I am sure a word from you to that gentleman will at least get for us a hearing on the subject and may be the means of resulting in a victory for the cause.

The mayor responded almost immediately:

> Dear Miss Schnall: Yes, indeed, it would be a great injustice. Here you are, the champion female athlete of America, and yet they won't allow you to compete in the Olympic Games in Sweden on the 29th of June. If I were you, I would write

to the King of Sweden, protesting loudly, and I do not care how stridulent [*sic*] your voice may sound in his ears. He deserves it all. If he were under my jurisdiction I would make him come to his senses very quick and allow you to compete with the men. Lots of women, nowadays think they can do everything that a man can do, although there may be some doubt about it.[11]

The mayor apparently misunderstood Schnall's request to have females compete, not against men, but rather against *each other*. His tone was condescending and flippant. For his part, Sullivan never did respond, and the United States went to the Olympics without any female representation. Sweden, Great Britain, Australia, Germany, and Austria sent female athletes to compete in three events: 100-metre freestyle, 400-metre relay, and 10-metre platform diving, at which seven of the eight competitors were Swedes. Schnall, however, wasn't done yet. She took on Sullivan and the AAU once again, this time with a wonderful letter to the editor of the *New York Times*:

> This is not from a suffragette standpoint, but a feeling which I had for a long time wished to express. I read in the newspapers wherein James E. Sullivan is again objecting to girls competing with the boys in a swimming contest. He is always objecting, and never doing anything to help the cause along for a girls' AAU. He has objected to my competing in diving at the Olympic games in Sweden because I am a girl. He objects to a mild game of ball or any kind of athletics for girls. He objects to girls wearing a comfortable bathing suit. He objects to so many things that it gives me cause to think he must be very narrow-minded and that we are in the last century. It's the athletic girl that takes the front seat today, and no one can deny it. I only wish that some of our rich sisters would consider the good they can do with only a small part of their wealth and start something like an AAU for girls that will make healthy mothers.[12]

Two months after that letter was published, Schnall's nemesis, Mayor
Gaynor, died of a heart attack at the age of 64. Incredibly, the women's
movement received another boost when its main adversary, James E.
Sullivan, died a year later at age 51. American women suddenly had more
opportunities to compete athletically. Schnall had been the catalyst, daring
to take on Sullivan and the mayor in print. She would go on to become the
captain of the Feminine Baseball Club of Los Angeles, as well as a film actress
and lecturer. She was dubbed "The Most Beautifully Formed Woman in the
World" at the 1915 Pan-American exhibit in San Francisco. She showed off
her form on movie posters for her role as a diving Venus in the 1916 silent
film *Undine*, based on the classic French legend of the sea. In the film, she
appeared in a very comfortable bathing suit that did not seem to bother
moviegoers, especially when she dove 130 feet off a Santa Cruz Island cliff.
Wrote one reviewer: "No one really cared much about the plot of *Undine*:
It was enough that the sylphlike Ida Schnall showed up from time to time
in various states of near-nudity."[13]

Schnall died in Los Angeles in 1973 at the age of 84. The previous
June, U.S. president Richard Nixon had signed Title IX into law. It was a
by-product of the Civil Rights Act of 1964 and would change the course of
women's athletics forever:

> No person in the United States shall, on the basis of sex,
> be excluded from participation in, be denied the benefits
> of, or be subjected to discrimination under any education
> program or activity receiving Federal financial assistance.[14]

When Title IX was signed into law, it meant that all athletic scholarships offered by schools that received federal funding would have to be split
equally along gender lines. The opportunities now available for female athletes would be substantial, and participation in all sports surged dramatically.

The women's movement owes a debt of gratitude to Ida Schnall for her
role as an advocate for female athletics. The Olympics finally allowed women
to compete in track and field in the 1928 Games, 16 years after Schnall
brought the female athlete's plight to the public. Today, the Sullivan Award
is presented to the top amateur athlete in the United States, as it has been
since 1930. However, the ghost of James E. Sullivan continued to cast a

shadow on the female athlete. Fourteen years went by until swimmer Ann Curtis, an 18-year-old from San Francisco, became the first female to win the Sullivan Award. Curtis would go on to win two gold medals and one silver at the 1948 London Olympics. Upon her return to San Francisco, she was given a tickertape parade.

Orton was a vigorous defender of women's rights, especially when it came to athletics. Unlike Sullivan, he encouraged females to be fit and active, to play competitive sports and test themselves against the best. When he was sports director of Philadelphia's sesquicentennial games in 1926, swimmer Ethel Lackie was one of the main attractions. Lackie was a two-time gold medallist at the 1924 Paris Olympics and the world record holder in the 100-metre freestyle and 100-yard freestyle. "Miss Lackie today is one of the greatest swimmers in the world," Orton told the *Pittsburgh Daily Post* in 1926. "Her records show she is better than many men. There is a fine possibility she will soon do the 100 yards freestyle in less than one minute."[15]

The world record at the time was 1:03.3, and Orton was pretty good when it came to making predictions, but not quite this time. Lackie never did break a minute, but in 1927 she notched a 1:00.9. That mark lasted seven years before Holland's Willy den Ouden swam 100 yards in 59.8 seconds in 1934.

It was rare for anyone, especially a man of Orton's stature, to publicly compare the two sexes when it came to head-to-head competition. It wasn't until September of 1973, when 29-year-old Billie Jean King beat 55-year-old Bobby Riggs in tennis, that women athletes were looked at differently. The event, which took place at the Houston Astrodome before a worldwide audience of 90 million TV viewers, was dubbed "the Battle of the Sexes II." Its predecessor, in May of '73, saw Riggs stomp Margaret Court in straight sets after taunting her and all other female athletes, telling them that men were superior. King's victory was a seminal moment in the women's movement.

Early in his career, when women were forbidden to compete in the Olympic Games or other championship events, Orton had studied the great track and field athletes of the day. Since they were all men, he produced a manual showing young men and their parents how to properly train for vigorous activities like competitive sports. At five foot six and 120 pounds,

Orton was in remarkable condition owing to a healthy lifestyle. He stressed the importance of proper training to the reader:

> Very many of our schools now have coaches or gymnasium instructors qualified to examine a boy as to the condition of the vital organs, especially the lungs and heart. Whenever possible, the boy should be examined prior to beginning athletic training. This may be doubly beneficial in that it may indicate what kind of sport is best fitted for the upbuilding of the body.... But the boy should not despair merely because the examination shows him to be in poor condition. This is the very kind of boy needing exercise, only it should be taken under capable supervision and in moderation. In this way the weak heart will become strengthened or the weak lungs permanently cured. Then the cured youth may enter the very sports which previously had been too trying for him.[16]

Although he never refers to his dead arm or the paralysis he suffered as a child, this was clearly written by someone who knew how to strengthen a weakness through exercise. Orton's book had many pictures of top athletes illustrating the proper form and technique for hurdling, broad jumping, pole vaulting, shot putting, high jumping, discus throwing, and the like. He was an early proponent of non-specialization in sport. Orton could run various distances and do hurdles and steeplechase, not to mention play non-Olympic sports (at the time) such as hockey, lacrosse, and soccer at an elite level. Had he concentrated solely on the mile, he likely could've broken four minutes and 12 seconds, his personal best. Today's athletes are specialists and are always challenging a world record. Orton tried everything; he went from being the best miler in the world to winning two Olympic medals at two totally different disciplines — the 2,500-metre steeplechase and the 400-metre hurdles.

Orton, the teacher and coach, felt that many runners especially depended too much on their legs and not enough on the upper body. Sit-ups, push-ups, and deep knee bends combined with dumbbell and club swinging were the basis for a solid training regimen. And, of course, one had to have the right equipment for these activities. The back pages of every Spalding book featured the Spalding Sporting Goods catalogue. Here you could buy just about any item of athletic equipment. In 1916, a decent pair of track shoes would set you back six dollars; a Spalding basketball was eight dollars. The most expensive item in the catalogue was a combination chronometer/stopwatch for $15, available only by special order. Orton's book cost 10 cents.

10

NORTH AMERICA'S
ATHLETIC MISSIONARIES

The biggest year in Orton's life was 1900. He experienced fatherhood for the first time. He was the graduate track coach and volunteer lacrosse coach at his alma mater, Penn. He was attempting to form a hockey team that was strong enough to play in the highly competitive American Amateur Hockey League. He would spend the summer in Europe, running, jumping, and hurdling at the English championships, Olympic Games, and European championships.

The question, early in 1900, was "Who is Orton going to represent?"

It was a fair point. Even though one ran as an individual, it was hard not to be attached to a club or school as a representative. In Canada, Orton had run for the University of Toronto for intercollegiate competitions and represented the Toronto Lacrosse Club in other meets. In the United States, he competed as a member of the Penn squad and, beginning in 1895, represented the powerful New York Athletic Club, known for its elite athletes and iconic "winged foot" logo. Orton never represented the United States or Canada in any competitions.

Since 1908, the International Olympic Committee has identified each competitor with the nation they represent. At the first three modern Olympic Games (Athens in 1896, Paris in 1900, and St. Louis in 1904), competitors were listed as individuals or as representatives of an athletic club or university delegation. National teams did not exist.

In 1908, the IOC retroactively added the name of a country to each competitor. For George Orton's 1900 Olympic performances, that country was the USA. By the time the United States had been officially changed to Canada in the Olympic record books, Orton had long since passed away.

According to Dr. Bruce Kidd, "Prior to 1908, and really, prior to the 1920s, the idea that, as an athlete in the Olympic Games you are representing a whole country, you're symbolizing a whole country, you carry the weight of expectation and pride of that whole country, that was not widely understood in Orton's day."[1]

Although they are referred to as the Paris Olympics, the Games of 1900 were in no way similar to those of today. Medal presentations with the top three athletes stepping onto the Olympic podium had not yet been introduced. There was none of the fanfare that today's Olympic Games provide. Certainly, there were no national anthems played to honour the medal winners. As Dr. Robert Barney explains,

> In 1900 there was none of that. Yes, the athletes came from particular places. Great Britain, Ireland, Czechoslovakia, Canada, and so on, but there was no Opening Ceremony, no Closing Ceremony, no victory ceremony. And the Games, in the newspapers, were almost always referred to as "Exposition contests" and "intercollegiate track and field championships." … and even the medals themselves never said anything about the Olympics on them.[2]

Orton was invited to join a delegation from Penn that would travel to England and then on to the Olympics in Paris. Penn had by far the finest group of athletes out of the entire American contingent. Groups from Chicago, Boston, and New York sent representatives. Athletes representing schools such as Harvard, Yale, Princeton, Georgetown, Syracuse, and Michigan would compete. The New York Athletic Club sent along some crack athletes, as well. Despite travelling together, none were representing a United States team. The American Olympic Committee, however, was quick to adopt every North American athlete as a member of the U.S. team, regardless of their place of birth.

According to Orton, Canadians were supposed to have been well represented. Orton and Alexander Grant were part of the Penn delegation, but there was also a flock of talented Canadian marathoners who had been invited to compete. Ronald McDonald, from Antigonish County, Nova Scotia, was one of the favourites for the Olympic marathon. He had won the 1898 Boston Marathon and was in top form. But a real mystery surrounded the top three finishers in the 1900 Boston Marathon from a few months earlier. All were from Hamilton, Ontario, and veterans of the Around the Bay Race held there. The Hamilton race was notorious for bookmaking, as gamblers bet openly and heavily on the outcome. Those gamblers who won big ended up paying the way for Jack Caffery of the St. Patrick's Athletic Association, plus Billy Sherring and Frank Hughson of the Hamilton YMCA, to travel to Boston, where the trio finished 1-2-3. (Caffery would win again in Boston in 1901.) It was hoped that the three would be able to raise enough money to make the ocean voyage to the Olympics.[3]

Hailing from St. Marys, Ontario, Alexander Grant had just graduated from Penn as the top intercollegiate miler in the country. Grant had beaten Orton a month earlier at Franklin Field, setting a world record in the 1,500 metres that would last for a decade. The *Toronto Star* would refer to Grant as being from Canada but not Orton. Why would the *Star* not mention Orton's Canadian heritage? Was it an omission or an exclusion?

Grant's older brother, Dick, was the runner-up in the 1899 Boston Marathon while a student at Harvard Medical School. He and Orton had been teammates at the University of Toronto and the Toronto Lacrosse Club. Both were scholarly, but Dick Grant's education was self-funded, and he frequently had to leave school because he could not keep up with tuition payments and other fees. Fortunately, Grant was already an established star with the Knickerbocker Athletic Club and therefore had his expenses looked after when competing for them.

Although Orton was no longer a student at Penn, he considered himself to be a Penn athlete and ran with the *P* on his jersey, as he had during his collegiate days. He was also Penn's volunteer graduate track coach. The Penn delegation consisted of 13 athletes, coach Mike Murphy, manager Frank Ellis, and a "rubber," Dave Brown, so named because of his expertise in massage therapy. Whenever an athlete required a rubdown, Dave was the man with the magic hands.

The group left New York at noon on June 20, 1900, on the ocean steamer *Southwark*. Rather than even attempt to train during the 10-day trip, Murphy had put the men through intense workouts in America, allowing them plenty of time to rest up and get their sea legs during the voyage. However, many had gotten seasick, especially during two days of gale-force winds that caused the vessel to rock dizzyingly from port to starboard. Orton, a seasoned ocean traveller, joined many of his teammates in sick bay, although his readers in the *Inquirer* were blissfully unaware of his discomfort: "The trip has been a very pleasant one, and as the grandfather athlete of the team I must say they have conducted themselves in a most gentlemanly manner. They had as much fun as one could desire, but no horse play at all has been indulged in."[4]

Shuffleboard, ring-toss, and skipping were the most popular games on board. Training consisted of running up and down the steps once in a while and the occasional sprint along a 40-yard stretch of clear deck. The shot putters and hammer throwers, Orton pointed out, had no place to practise on board.

The group landed in Southampton, England, on June 30 and took a train to the south coast city of Brighton, 55 miles south of London, to set up training camp. Many of the athletes needed several days to get the feel of the ground beneath their feet. Orton was not at his best. He was still too ill to start in the 1,500 metres and finished a wobbly fourth in the steeplechase. Alex Grant had to drop out of the four-mile run and finished a distant third in the 1,500 metres, his specialty. After the race, he became sick.

The weather didn't help matters: Rain and wind were ubiquitous in London, whereas during training in Brighton, it had been warm and dry. For distance runners in particular, it takes a long time to become acclimated to new surroundings after a rough sea voyage. By the time the English championships were over, however, Americans had won eight of the 12 events. Had it not been for the weak stomachs of the American distance runners, the margin of victory likely would have been greater.

Things were looking up after the event, but Orton had a busy schedule ahead. He was entered in six Olympic events: 400-metre flat, 400-metre hurdles, 800-metre flat, 1,500-metre flat, 2,500-metre steeplechase, and 4,000-metre steeplechase. He was also expected to run in several handicap events that were not part of the Olympic competition. Paris awaited, and with it, plenty of problems. Little did the North American contingent know that the French were about to try to pull a fast one on them.[5]

11

BONJOUR, PARIS!

My earliest Olympic memory is from the 1968 Mexico City Games. Two black sprinters, Tommie Smith and John Carlos of the United States, who finished first and third in the 200 metres, took a stand on the podium for civil rights. While "The Star-Spangled Banner" was being played, they held their black-gloved fists high and stood protesting, wearing black socks. Both were banned by the IOC from competing in future Olympic Games. It's interesting to note that South Africa had been banned from competing in Mexico City because of its racial policy of apartheid. This is when I first became aware of the history of race relations in various parts of the world.

Earlier in the Mexico City Games there was a wonderful moment: A young black man named Bob Beamon shocked everyone by setting a new world record in the long jump — 29 feet, two and a half inches. That shattered the old mark by an astounding 22 inches, and when it was announced, Beamon broke down and wept, covering his face with his hands in disbelief.

The gold medal in the high jump was won by American Dick Fosbury, who introduced a new way of jumping; he went over the bar bending backward. He called it the Fosbury Flop.

For a Canadian, there wasn't much to cheer about during those games. With the exception of a gold medal in equestrian on the final day of competition, no Canadians reached the top of the podium. Watching the games on TV, my family naturally cheered for the Canadian athletes, but if none were competing in an event, we'd choose a different rooting interest. My mom was always a fan of the underdog, and in the 5,000-metre final, she was certain that this one fellow, number 781, was from Israel. Being Jewish and aware of the struggles for Israel to keep its tiny homeland, she started cheering loudly, "Come on number 781! Come on Israel!" She was having such a good time, I didn't have the heart to tell her that number 781 was Mohammed Gammoudi of Tunisia.

As the runners came down the stretch, Gammoudi was about to overtake the leader, Kip Keino of Kenya. I had never heard my mother yell so loud. And that's saying a lot. When Gammoudi hit the tape first, she burst into joyous tears. When I told her the truth about the guy, the colour drained from her face. Tunisia was one of Israel's enemies in the bloody Six-Day War in 1967. Tunisia had supported the Arab forces, led by Egypt, by supplying troops and weapons. Even though Gammoudi was just an athlete, he represented a belligerent, anti-Semitic nation in my mother's mind. These were the first Olympics where the mixing of politics and sports had an effect on me. I was 12 years old.

The Games of the Second Olympiad in Paris would contain plenty of politically charged moments during their run from April until November 1900. Few noticed, however, as the Games took a back seat to the immense World's Fair known as the Paris Exposition. Unfortunately, the size and scope of *L'Exposition Universelle* completely suffocated the Olympic Games. World's Fairs had been wildly popular since the mid-1800s, and they had taken place in London, Chicago, New York, Brussels, and Paris (where the Eiffel Tower was introduced to the world in 1889). These massive expositions carried heavy political and cultural weight, whereas an athletic competition known as "The International Championships" did not. Baron Pierre de Coubertin, the founder of the modern Olympics, admitted years later that the 1900 games were the strangest of them all. They were so disorganized;

half the athletes weren't even aware they were competing in the Olympics. With so many bizarre events taking place, they appeared to be more of a circus than a legitimate athletic competition.

A prime example involved the pistol and rifle shooting competitions. The 1900 Games were the first and last to use live pigeons as targets. Seriously. The ensuing carnage combined with the sound of wounded birds must've been sickening. Clay pigeons replaced their live selves in all future Olympic competitions. Other Olympic events in 1900 included tug of war, motorcycle racing, motorboat racing, polo, golf, cricket, and croquet. One could understand how spectators and participants might've been confused as to what kind of competition they were witnessing. To many, these Olympics were no more than a sideshow to the main attraction. The Paris Exposition was to be a great celebration of mechanics and material progress, showcasing new inventions that would change the world: escalators, talking films, and the diesel engine. Russian nesting dolls and the Ferris wheel were first introduced in Paris.

The cultural focus centred on art nouveau and modern architecture. Every country was there to present the finest they had to offer. Several Canadian exhibits showcased the country as a competitive nation and a place where immigrants would find opportunity. In order to compete in an industrialized world, Canada spent $206,000 on the Paris Exposition of 1900.[1] That was $206,000 more than they spent supporting their Canadian athletes at the Olympics, which were held concurrently with the World's Fair.

Canadian sporting authorities never seriously considered sending a team to Paris or supporting Canadian athletes in 1900. In a letter to the editor of the Toronto *Mail and Empire*, the writer is proud of Canada's athletic talent, yet disappointed that so many Canadians had left to perform in the United States because of the lack of support and encouragement at home: "That we have material in our midst out of which champions are made is proven by the success of George Orton, the Grant brothers, George Gray and others, who in receiving encouragement from foreign clubs, have beaten the world."[2] Gray, the world champion shot putter from Coldwater, Ontario, was supposed to compete in Paris but did not attend. The cost was prohibitive, and no government money from Canada was going toward Gray's expenses.

The Grant brothers had a problem of greater importance. The French organizing committee had scheduled some events for Sunday, July 15 — the

Sabbath. Dick and Alexander Grant were brought up in a strict Presbyterian home. Their father was the Reverend Alexander Grant, of the Knox Presbyterian Church in St. Marys, Ontario. St. Marys is about an hour east of Orton's birthplace, Strathroy, Ontario. It's the home of the Canadian Baseball Hall of Fame. Like many small towns, St. Marys was closed on Sundays. Praying, resting, and reading were the only activities allowed. There was no card playing, no dancing, no games, no running, and certainly no alcoholic beverages or tobacco allowed.[3]

The Grants weren't the only ones who protested Sunday competition. Many in the American contingent said they would not compete on the Christian Sabbath. It was generally known that many working-class clubs in America *did* hold sporting events on Sundays, as there was no other leisure day, but as Caspar Whitney pointed out in *Outing* magazine, "Whatever

Alexander Grant (left) with Orton in 1904. They were teammates at Penn, and later business partners at Camp Tecumseh. Grant was from a strict Presbyterian family and refused to compete on the Sabbath. It cost him a gold medal, as the 1,500-metre race, which he was favoured to win, was run on Sunday, July 15, 1900.

they may do in France, there is no section of the United States where clubs of the first class hold organized sports, track athletics, baseball, football golf or rowing, on Sunday."[4] In Europe Sunday participation was commonplace, and many did not subscribe to the Americans' position on the Sabbath issue. Nevertheless, the Americans went so far as to threaten a boycott of any events that would take place on Sunday after what they felt was a sneak attack by the French officials.

Before leaving for Europe, the U.S. Olympic Committee had been assured by the French that the Games would start on Saturday, July 14, but there would be no Sunday competition. Unfortunately, somebody forgot to mention that July 14 is Bastille Day, a national holiday in France. A huge military parade was scheduled to take place on the grounds where the Games were to be held. When the French realized their mistake, they rescheduled some events for Sunday without informing the Americans. Orton and Penn Relays manager Frank Ellis had left England ahead of the rest of the team in search of accommodations, which they could not secure in Paris. Instead, they booked the team into the Hotel Vatel in Versailles, about an hour from Paris by train.

When the rest of the Americans arrived in France, they were livid upon finding out that some events were scheduled for Sunday. The head of the University of Chicago's contingent, Amos Alonzo Stagg, the famous football coach, complained that "not a single American university would have sent a team had it not definitely been announced that the games would not be held on Sunday." He went on to suggest that all the American athletes would be united and refuse to compete on Sunday. He couldn't have been more naive.[5] Orton was convinced that the French had botched the Olympic enterprise and suggested that "anyone with a blind eye could have seen that the Frenchmen were determined to make the Americans follow the adage 'When in Rome do as the Romans do.'"[6]

Many of the other competitors objected to the Americans having such an advantage. They didn't believe everyone should have to sit out on Sunday just because the Americans were threatening a boycott. There had to be a compromise. The French concession would have the heats and finals of the 110-metre hurdles and the 100-metre dash take place on Saturday afternoon, following the Bastille Day military parade. Qualifying for field events such as the shot put and weight toss would also take place Saturday, while the rest of the events would be moved to Sunday. Had there been a U.S. national team at the time, the Americans would've boycotted the Sunday events en masse. But each club and university was independent and would have to decide on their own. Still, it was believed that all the American athletes would be united in their boycott.

Orton later revealed that Frank Ellis had left the decision to compete on Sunday up to the individuals on his squad. Eight Penn athletes declined to participate on Sunday, while five chose to compete. Orton, along with sprinter-broad jumper Alvin Kraenzlein, sprinter-hurdler Walter Tewksbury, high jumper/pole vaulter Irving Baxter, and pole vaulter Meredith Colket, would carry the colours of Penn. Alexander Grant, who was the favourite in the 1,500 metres on Sunday, declined, as did shot putter Josiah McCracken, another future business partner of Orton's. McCracken would qualify on Saturday but refused to compete on Sunday. Had he done so, he would've won the gold medal. Dick Grant, recently of Harvard, was scheduled to run in the marathon later in the week but fully supported the Sunday boycott. University teams from Syracuse, Michigan, Chicago, and Princeton did not allow their athletes to decide for themselves; they refused to allow them to participate on Sunday. Penn's athletes were not mandated by the faculty.

Instead of competing, the Sunday boycotters attended the events as spectators, and when they saw the Penn and New York Athletic Club athletes put on their track clothes, many "looked longingly at the track … indeed in some cases the managers had a hard time persuading their men not to break through all faculty restrictions by competing."[7] The Penn athletes who did compete were vilified by many Americans. Representatives from Princeton University, in particular, accused Penn of treason. Orton fired back in the *Philadelphia Inquirer*:

> Some are very bitter at Pennsylvania because a few of her athletes ran on Sunday. They say some very harsh things, all of which are unmerited. Cregan, of the Princeton team is a good example. In one breath he states that the Pennsylvania athletes showed a breach of faith in competing and were at least inconsistent after protesting against Sunday games. In the next breath, Cregan admits that if he had been in

a position to do so he would have run. Consistency, thou art is a jewel.[8]

Orton, more than anyone, was aware of what was being written in the newspapers. His ability to understand French, German, and other foreign languages gave him a wealth of knowledge that others did not have. Because of this perspective, Orton felt that an article in the Paris edition of the *New York Times* was uncalled for. The author, whose byline did not appear next to the article, ripped the Penn athletes for competing on Sunday:

> The *Times* reporter must have been as short of news as he was of manners when he published it. It will make no difference whether the facts were so or not, the Paris edition of the *Times* was not the place to air his views.... It was certainly ill-timed for the *Times* to criticise American athletes for showing a little broadmindedness and cosmopolitanism, especially when this saved the day for America.

Orton mentioned that Pennsylvania was the first and last to protest against the Sunday contests, and he and the others decided to run only when it was apparent that the Games would be held whether the Americans competed or not.

> When Cregan and some others tell me that the games would not have been held had Pennsylvania stayed out they are talking nonsense. I know whereof I speak. I talk French, and I was told by the French authorities distinctly and in such a way that there was no misunderstanding it, that the games would be carried out.[9]

On Saturday, Orton easily qualified for the 400-metre hurdles final the next day, surprising the unbeaten French champion and crowd favourite Henri Tauzin by almost nipping him at the wire. However, it was a wasted effort as the French organizers had foolishly set up qualifying heats. Only five men had originally entered the 400-metre hurdles, it being a new event for these championships. The two heats eliminated just one man, while another, American William Lewis, declined to run in the final because it was on Sunday. That meant only three men would start in the final.

The rest of Orton's schedule was full. He would not run in the 400-metre, 800-metre, 1,500-metre or 4,000-metre flat races because of conflicts brought on by the rescheduling of events. He would run in Sunday's 400-metre hurdles final and then try to make good on his prediction in the 2,500-metre steeplechase. On Monday he would participate in the 4,000-metre steeplechase. Tuesday Orton was scheduled to run in the qualifying heats of the 200-metre hurdles. If he qualified, he would run in the finals on Friday. Wednesday he was a late replacement as the scratch in the 100-metre handicap, meaning he had to give head starts to the rest of the field. Thursday he was the scratch in the 2,500-metre steeplechase handicap, and Sunday he was the scratch in the 1,500-metre handicap. That meant he would compete in six finals, three of which were handicap races and not considered official Olympic events.

The 400-metre hurdles final was scheduled to take place at 2:45 p.m. on Sunday, July 15 — a clear and blazing-hot day. Instead, the race wouldn't go off until 4:45 thanks to the incredibly poor management of the Games. According to the program, the events of the day should've ended by 5:00 p.m. To make matters even more uncomfortable, because of the ridiculous qualifying heats, only three competitors — Orton, Tauzin, and American Walter Tewksbury — came to the starting line. At the gun, Tewksbury shot out to the lead and was never headed, winning in 57 and three-fifths seconds. Orton and Tauzin battled it out for the silver medal, but after the final hurdle (a water jump, no less), the Frenchman pulled away to take second place by three metres. Orton ran a 58 and three-fifths for third.

To get a sense of the vast differences between the two disciplines — the 400-metre hurdles and the 2,500-metre steeplechase, the French authorities had scheduled the two races back to back, apparently not thinking or caring that one man was entered in both. This was highly unusual and a good example of how utterly disorganized these Games were. The scheduling screw-up meant Orton would be at a huge disadvantage; he had less than 45 minutes to get ready for the biggest race of his life — the one he had come 4,000 miles to win.

Prior to leaving for Europe, Orton had written a preview of the English championships for the *Philadelphia Inquirer*, predicting he would win the two-mile steeplechase at Stanford Bridge "if in condition." Clearly, he was not in condition that day in London and finished well behind Sidney Robinson. Now, a week later, having once again predicted victory in the newspaper, "if in condition" being the caveat, he was worried. It was 5:30 in the afternoon. He was about to become the fastest of them all. Orton, barely rested, lined up for the 2,500-metre steeplechase alongside Robinson and the rest of the field. His legs were heavy as the starting gun exploded, but he gained his footing, jumped the obstacles without incident, and took to the lead midway through the second of five laps.

The 2,500-metre race was an odd distance — normally the steeplechase was two miles, or about 3,000 metres. The Bois de Bolougne's makeshift oval track was oddly shaped, too, making it an even stranger experience. Orton's pace was too quick, more suited to the 400-metre hurdles, so he backed off. By the fifth and final lap, he had fallen away from the pack, but, as previously reported, his spine-tingling sprint to the finish won him the gold, capping off a day to remember.

Orton's celebration was short-lived, however. He was literally run down, and his stomach was on fire. He needed sleep because the next day he was the favourite to win the 4,000-metre steeplechase, and it was supposed to be even hotter.

Sleep did not come easy that night, but the following afternoon Orton started in the 4,000-metre steeplechase as planned. He was well behind the leaders midway through the race. "Most of the spectators thought that Orton was merely saving himself with the intention of spurting on the last round as he did yesterday," wrote the *New York Times*. "He had not slept during the night and arose this morning with a deranged stomach."

Orton, suffering from an intestinal virus, would finish a distant fifth, but he won the hearts of the fans. "As he ran with set teeth," said the *Times*, "his college comrades cheered him, and when they found that in spite of his pluck he was beaten, they gave him an ovation as rousing as if he had won."[10]

After competing in four races over three blistering days, Orton was again in the blocks on Tuesday afternoon. Unaccustomed to the 200-metre hurdles, and still recovering from his stomach ailment, Orton tried, but he could not adjust to sprinter's mode and failed to qualify for the final.

The American athletes had performed so strongly at these Games that the race handicapper decided to punish them severely. The idea of the handicap system is simple: that all competitors should theoretically cross the finish line at the same time. To achieve that, the handicapper determines what mark or handicap the runner will have according to past performance. In horse racing, the best horses carry the most weight. For human racing, each metre in handicap denotes approximately a tenth of a second in time. In the 100-metre handicap, Orton, who was not a sprinter, replaced world record holder Arthur F. Duffey of the United States, who had pulled a leg muscle in the final of the 100-metre flat race. Orton was the scratch, meaning he had to run the full distance. His opponents would start in front of him, the farthest being six metres ahead. This was an exceedingly difficult handicap to overcome. Orton would have to be six-tenths of a second faster just to get a dead heat. At least Duffey had run 100 yards in nine and four-fifths seconds; Orton wasn't nearly that quick, but the handicapper penalized him nonetheless.

Orton could have opted out, protesting the severe handicap as many other Americans had done, but he was too proud and too competitive. Besides, save for his gold medal in the steeplechase, he hadn't performed particularly well during the week. Thanks to the handicap system, other runners would get sizable head starts over Orton, and 65 entrants had to be whittled down over the course of 15 first-round heats and five semifinal heats. Edmund Minahan, Duffey's teammate at Georgetown University, covered 94 metres in 10 and four-fifths seconds to win. Orton ran the full hundred metres and still managed to finish fourth in the field of eight.[11]

Orton was not impressed with the French track officials at first, especially the starter, who, in his opinion, "would not be allowed to start school-boy sports in America."[12]

Handicap races were not officially recognized as Olympic or championship events, but Orton didn't seem to care. Even though the events were referred to as "Exposition contests" by the newspapers, Orton soldiered on. He was the scratch once again for the 2,500-metre steeplechase handicap. Using Orton's smashing gold medal performance from Sunday against him, the handicapper made it nearly impossible for him to win.

The handicaps were so severe that only 12 runners started, down from 22 who had originally entered. Orton had to concede a ridiculous 230 metres, or 23 seconds, to the eventual winner, Hermann Wraschtil of Austria. The runner-up, Franz Duhne of Germany, had a head start of 24 seconds on Orton. Imagine having to start a race, and before the gun even goes off, your competition is already half a lap ahead. Orton ran gamely but could not overcome the huge gap.

Orton's final race in Paris was the 1,500-metre handicap, run on Sunday, July 22. Few Americans competed that day, and Orton was the only one entered in the field of 17. As the scratch again, he had to give a handicap of 150 yards to the eventual winner, Duhne, and 90 yards to the second-place finisher, Denmark's Christian Christensen. Had all the runners started from the same spot, Orton would've won easily. With the 15-second handicap, however, he could do no better than fourth place.[13]

The other Canadian athletes did not fare well in Paris. Alex Grant, who refused to run in the 1,500 metres on the Sunday, entered the 800 metres but did not qualify for the final. He also started in the 4,000-metre steeplechase but failed to finish, overcome by the heat. Dick Grant and Ronald McDonald ran in the marathon, which was marred by controversy. The winner, Michel Theato, was an unknown Frenchman (later to be declared a citizen of Luxembourg). He, along with France's Emile Champion, finished well ahead of the field. The race was run through the streets of Paris, and there were allegations that some runners had taken a shortcut. The third-place finisher, Sweden's Ernst Fast, finished a staggering 33 minutes behind Champion, the runner-up. Arthur Newton, the 17-year-old American runner, claimed he was never passed after taking the lead late in the race. Many runners took wrong turns on the confusing course. One claimed a Paris gendarme gave him the wrong directions while he was leading. The morning line favourite, Georges Touquet-Daunis, led for the first part of the race but reportedly ducked into a café to escape the afternoon heat, had a couple of beers, and decided it was too hot to continue.

Ronald McDonald claimed that he and Dick Grant were the only ones to finish the proper course. Grant protested the final result, which had him finishing sixth. He told the IOC he was intentionally knocked over by a cyclist as he was about to take the lead. The lawsuit was unsuccessful, and Paris would be his last marathon. He went on to become the director of athletics at the University of Minnesota and in 1916 the University of Havana. He died in 1958 in St. Catharines, Ontario, at the age of 87. Ronald McDonald returned home to Nova Scotia and enrolled in pre-med at St. Francis Xavier University. Later, he graduated from Tufts College Medical School in Boston. He organized several track meets in the Maritimes and was a physician in Port au Port, Newfoundland, for more than 30 years. He died in 1947 at the age of 73. In 1979, he became one of the original inductees into the Nova Scotia Sport Hall of Fame.

★★★

The Olympic Games of 1900 were not well attended. Much of the problem was due to scheduling, but the lack of communication crippled the Games from the very start. French officials not only failed to inform spectators of the changes due to the Sabbath controversy, they neglected to tell some of the American athletes, and several went to the grounds early on Sunday, only to be told their events had been rescheduled for Monday. But of course they hadn't been, and the Americans were incensed. The crowds were disappointing throughout the Games. Were it not for the American spectators, the stands would have been virtually empty.

Of the few thousand Europeans who did attend, many were shocked by the American custom of rhythmic cheering. Led by boisterous college students, many of whom were bedecked in the Stars and Stripes, the American fans kept up a constant barrage, clapping and whistling in perfect synch. These outbursts of American enthusiasm did not go over well, and some spectators were heard to exclaim, "What a bunch of savages!"[14]

Orton had been unable to convince Canadian authorities to put an Olympic team together a few years earlier, yet he fully embraced the ideals of the American sporting republic at these Games. It's ironic that a Canadian would be at the centre of an American controversy: Either observe the Sabbath and be part of a team that will boycott, or compete as a proud individual for the glory of athletic achievement and American superiority. Orton knew that he and the others would be criticized for going against the grain and competing on Sunday, but he was convinced that the decision to compete was the correct one. Had you asked the majority of the American people, they likely would have chosen gold medals over strict observance, especially if it translated into American superiority. Victory, in Orton's mind, was the only way to establish superiority. And the same media that ripped Orton and his teammates for participating on Sunday were now lionizing them as American champions.

Even with many athletes unwilling to compete on Sunday, Americans completely dominated the track events in Paris, as they had in London. Orton, however, was not impressed with the quality of the competition, and he did not hold back in his criticism in his article in *Outing* magazine. "The Europeans run, in general, awkwardly; not using the arms and shoulders to the best advantage. The legs and body do not work together as one piece of mechanism, as in the American sprinter. But even had the English, European and Australian sprinters been able to run as fast, they would have been beaten because of their poor starting."

Orton's close attention to detail made him one of the foremost experts on technical running. Observing the European middle-distance runners, he didn't find them dangerous at all, saying they ran "with the arms drawn up in a cramped position, impeding rather than aiding them." He went on to say, "Their style is unnatural and faulty; either they run on their heels, with too short a stride, or use too long a one." Orton called the English distance runners "mostly plodders, running along with dogged determination, with arms too far up, and faulty stride." He thought that Sidney Robinson, his steeplechase nemesis, ran "flatfooted and just plows along, using his arms the whole time." Orton was also quick to point out that the American distance runners were disappointing, mainly through a lack of condition. Alexander Grant, for example, had fallen ill and didn't recover until late in the week. Even though Orton won America's only medal in a distance race, he admitted to his ill health. About himself, again in the third person, he wrote, "He won through sheer grit rather than condition, as he was not quite up to form."[15]

While Baron Pierre de Coubertin received criticism for the poor organization of the Olympic Games, the Paris Exposition also suffered from a lack of attendance. From a daily average of 230,000 visitors in May, the numbers dipped dramatically to an average of 176,000 by mid-July. Admission tickets, which had a list price of 12 cents and up, were being offered for six cents at the bank. Vendors were selling them for five cents each, while other miscellaneous sellers were offering them for four and even three cents.[16]

It is estimated that close to 50 million people visited the Paris World's Fair over the course of 212 days. Actual attendance figures for the Olympic Games were never released, but, according to the Olympic website, the women's croquet event, featuring French participants only, was witnessed by just one paying customer, an Englishman who had travelled from Nice. He had the best seat on the grounds.

There was no mention of how many spectators viewed the live pigeon shooting event. As Baron de Coubertin would remark years later, "It's a miracle that the Olympic Movement survived that celebration."[17]

By the time the Games had concluded on Monday, all was forgiven and the spirit of goodwill and the Olympic ideal took over. Orton, who had criticized the French for their poor marketing and organization of the Games, had nothing but kind words for his hosts:

> Indeed the American athletes are being entertained largely. The U.S.F.S.A. (Union des Sociétés Françaises de Sports Athlétiques) held a reception at the Hotel de Ville for the visiting athletes. A light lunch and drinks were served. The men were introduced to the high personages present and afterwards shown through the City Hall. It is magnificently decorated. The crystal work, the carving and above all the mural decorations, paintings and tapestry were grand and worthy of the most beautiful city in Christendom. The same evening Baron de Coubertin held a reception. The Baron is the greatest patron of sport in France and his reception was a brilliant affair.[18]

The USFSA proved to be an extremely well-run organization. It had been founded in 1890, with de Coubertin as one of the principles. The group's motto was "*Citius, Altius, Fortius,*" the Latin for "Faster, Higher, Stronger." Their logo at the 1900 Olympics was two interlinking rings, which represented the two groups that had merged to form the USFSA. By 1924, the IOC had adopted the motto and had modified the logo to include five interlinking rings, representing the five continents.[19]

Reports from that concluding banquet suggest that Orton was at his absolute best, soothing the irritation that developed during the Games with a magnificent speech. After the Americans had been praised by the Europeans, Orton stood up and honoured them by offering congratulations in several languages, much to the delight of the French, Germans, Austrians, Danes, Hungarians, Italians, Belgians, Greeks, and Swedes. Those from English-speaking nations Australia, Ireland, and England gave a solid cheer, while the Germans toasted Orton with "*Prosit!*" and the French sang "*Vive les États-Unis!*" As the de facto interpreter for most of the athletes and officials present, Orton translated effortlessly and made friends easily. He was a natural diplomat and could speak and write eloquently. He penned a column for *Outing* magazine in September 1900.

> The Paris games should prove a great object lesson and an encouragement to Continental athletes. All the European countries were represented, and these saw the best athletes of the world in competition, and should benefit from noting their style. In general, the Continental athletes learned much from the Americans as to training. With a better system of training and better models of style, great development should be made throughout Europe the next ten years. For the present, America is far in the lead, and her athletes should have no difficulty in holding that pre-eminence for many years to come.[20]

Orton stayed in Europe after the Olympics and competed in Germany and Belgium. He won the European outdoor mile at Brussels and took the 1,500-metre and 1,800-metre races in Berlin. He also took the time to write about his experiences in France and offered his observations on French athletics:

> The fact that most of the American athletes were students has been observed by the Frenchmen, and the consequence is going to be a system of physical education in the schools. In France no provision is made at all for the physical development of the schoolboys and students. An attempt to introduce sport will be made this year, and the government

is also to be appealed to provide proper places for exercise for the schools in Paris and the departments. This is an immense step in the athletic progress of France, and much good should be the result.[21]

12

HEAVY MEDALS

When it comes to Canada's Olympic history, Orton's story is the first of many. The fact that he was one of the few gold medallists able to overcome serious injury puts him at the forefront of Olympic lore. But there are other stories of Canadian Olympians that deserve mention.

In 1908, the first year Canada sent an actual team to the Olympics, most of the athletes had to pay their own way to get to London, England, and back. One of these was bantamweight freestyle wrestler Aubert Coté, who mortgaged his farm outside of Montreal in order to pay his expenses. Talk about dedication! When he returned home after winning a bronze medal, the Canadian Olympic Committee agreed to reimburse him.

There are others who gave up more to represent Canada at the Olympics. Jimmy Duffy, born in Ireland, had immigrated to Toronto in 1911. He finished fifth in the 1912 Olympic marathon in Stockholm, won the 1914 Boston Marathon with ease, and would've been favoured to win again in 1915. However, when the First World War broke out, Duffy enlisted in the

Canadian Army. He was killed at the second battle of Ypres, Belgium, in April of 1915, just eight days before his 25th birthday.

There are also some bizarre stories involving Canadian Olympic athletes. In 1928, women's athletics and gymnastics were introduced to the Games, and for the first time, females would represent Canada at the Olympics. Seven women were among the 92 athletes who were headed to Amsterdam. At some point during the train trip in Canada, Bobby Robinson, the coach of the men's team, held a special meeting. He chastised the members of the women's 4 × 100-metre relay team: Bobbie Rosenfeld, Myrtle Cook, Ethel Smith, and Jane Bell. Some had been caught drinking soda pop. "You can't win a relay on pop," he told them. "The girls from now on will be in strict training and will be expected to live up to the schedule the same as the men. You can enjoy yourselves after you have won at Amsterdam."[1] The women accounted for four of Canada's 15 medals, including a gold in the first-ever 4 × 100-metre women's relay. After that, they could drink all the soda pop their hearts desired.

At the Tokyo Summer Games of 1964, George Hungerford and Roger Jackson were the Canadian representatives in coxless pairs rowing. They had been together for only six weeks and were not expected to even get out of the heats. So when they crossed the finish line first, there were no Canadian journalists present. To celebrate their gold medal, Hungerford and Jackson drank six Coca-Colas each.

Speaking of drinking, 20-year-old swimmer Alex Baumann needed almost two hours to produce a urine sample after winning the 400-metre individual medley at the 1984 Los Angeles Games. He was in the middle of his third beer when officials realized he was underage and made him switch to soft drinks.

Perhaps the finest example of Olympic sportsmanship involved two friendly rivals in the 1932 Los Angeles Games. Canada's Duncan McNaughton and Bob Van Osdel of the United States were high jumpers and teammates at the University of Southern California. Before their final jump, at 1.97 metres, Van Osdel told McNaughton, "Get your kick working and you will be over." McNaughton cleared the bar, while Van Osdel failed, giving McNaughton the gold medal and Van Osdel the silver. The following year, McNaughton's gold medal was stolen from his car. When Van Osdel, then a dentist, found out, he made a mould of his medal, poured gold into the mould, and sent the replica to his friend.[2]

Speaking of medals, whatever happened to George Orton's Olympic medals? I kept asking myself that question while in the midst of researching the documentary. If the Stanley Cup is considered to be the most prized Canadian sports artifact, where does Orton's 1900 Olympic gold medal rank?

Prior to the 2016 Olympics, where golf was making a comeback for the first time since 1904, a story emerged, telling of an amazing discovery in a farmhouse near Chagrin Falls, Ohio, outside of Cleveland. The gold and silver medals from the golf competition at the 1904 Olympics had been found! Chandler Egan, the runner-up to Canadian George Lyon in the individual competition, had left his silver medal, and the gold medal he had won as part of the team competition, to his daughter, Eleanor Egan Everett. She had passed away in 2012 at the age of 101. While cleaning out the house, her son, Morris Everett, found a metal box on a bookcase shelf. When he and his son opened the box, they found more than 40 medals in near-perfect condition, including the two Olympic medals.

Chandler Egan had died in 1936, a decade after he had redesigned the original Pebble Beach Golf Course in Monterey, California. The medals were thought to have been lost forever. A year after the discovery, Egan's gold medal sold at auction for US$120,000.

There are other stories of Olympic medals having been sold for big money. Some of these stories are very sad. For example, Mark Wells, a member of the U.S. gold-medal-winning hockey team in 1980, sold his medal to help pay for medical treatments related to a rare genetic disease that damaged his spinal cord. A private collector bought the medal in 2010 and then sold it through an auction house for just over US$310,000.

Of course, the more significant the event, the greater the value of the medal. Jesse Owens, the famed black American runner, won four gold medals at the 1936 Berlin Olympics, one of them right in front of the German fuehrer himself. The historical and cultural significance of those victories cannot be overstated, and his medals obviously became extremely desirable. So desirable, in fact, that one sold for US$1.47 million.

When I spoke with George Orton's granddaughter, Connie Meaney, she told me she had definitely seen some medals among her grandfather's things. But was the Olympic gold medal one of them? Did Orton even receive any medals? Some stories suggested no medals were awarded at the

1900 Games. Since there were no Opening or Closing Ceremonies, nor any medal ceremonies, questions arose as to what prizes, if any, had been awarded to the winners. Medals were definitely handed out in 1900, but not for every event.

The website collectors.com shows several 1900 Olympic medals for sale on the cheap. Some are rectangular in shape and were given to administrators, officials, and participants, but not necessarily every event winner. Other medals are round and look more like oversized coins. These were likely given to volunteers, but it's possible that everybody received a commemorative medal of some sort. There were 95 different events contested, and prizes varied wildly. In 1900, Caspar Whitney of the American Olympic Committee wrote that he was disappointed in the supposed "objects of art" that were presented to the winners, calling them "decidedly inartistic bronze birds, silver pins and studs, walking sticks, knives and that sort of thing."[3] There were reports that some winners received expensive French paintings. I had trouble imagining a scene whereby an official handed a Matisse or a Degas original to a sweaty Olympic champion. Perhaps some of the winners had their choice of prizes. Trophies, cups, and even cash prizes were reportedly awarded to some competitors. One report said some winners received 100 francs, which they could use toward the purchase of their Olympic medal, thereby allowing the winner to retain his amateur status.

The 1900 Games were the first to include female competitors, although many didn't even realize they were part of the Olympic Games. Tennis, golf, croquet, sailing, and equestrian events were the five sports they were allowed to compete in. Margaret Abbott of Chicago won the ladies golf competition. Her prize was a gilded porcelain bowl. Abbott thought she was playing in a small, self-contained tournament, held at a course in Compiègne, some 50 miles north of Paris. She had entered simply because she played golf and happened to be in France at the time. (She was studying art with Auguste Rodin and Edgar Degas.) She shot 47 for nine holes and finished first in a field of 10. Ms. Abbott died in 1955 at the age of 76, unaware that she was the first female Olympic champion from the United States. When her family found out, they were shocked.[4]

The Paris Games offered so many different types of prizes, it's impossible to track who won what. Various sources contradict one another. In events where actual medals were awarded, only the winner and the runner-up may have received prizes. We do know there were several different types of medals distributed: solid gold (awarded to automobile racing winners), silver gilded with gold, solid silver, silvered bronze, and solid bronze.

Gold, silver, and bronze medals are supposed to designate the first three Ages of Man in Greek mythology. The Golden Age, when men lived among the gods; the Silver Age, where youth lasted a hundred years; and the Bronze Age, the era of heroes. Oddly enough, when the first modern Olympiad took place in 1896 in Athens, the medals were not distributed that way, even though the IOC has gone back and retroactively awarded gold, silver, and bronze designations to the top three finishers in each event prior to 1908. All the winners in Athens received silver medals because gold was 40 times more expensive than silver at the time. Greek officials awarded bronze medals to the second-place finishers. It may have also been that way in Paris for certain events.

Whether Orton actually received his medals in 1900, or was awarded them retroactively after 1908, or didn't get a medal at all was up for debate. Hopefully, I would find out in San Francisco.

In the meantime, my visit to Philadelphia was paying big dividends. I was meeting people who not only had heard of George Orton and his accomplishments but had stories to tell about him as well.

Mark Frazier Lloyd and Dave Johnson at Penn filled me in with a lot of university-based information, but away from the campus, who else knew about Orton? What did he do when he wasn't winning races and studying for his Ph.D.?

13

"MAKING GOOD BOYS BETTER"

Although Orton had gone against the Sabbath boycott supported by most of his Pennsylvania teammates in Paris, he was still a man of strong moral character. His beliefs were similar to but not as devout as those of Alexander Grant and Josiah McCracken.

The three had met in 1897 thanks to Mike Murphy, the legendary coach who had moved from Yale to Penn to manage the track team and the number one ranked Quaker football team. Murphy had recruited McCracken, a strapping farm boy from Kansas, and Grant, a champion distance runner from the University of Toronto who had to drop out after one year because of financial hardships. Grant was the half-mile, one-mile, and five-mile Canadian champion prior to enrolling at Penn and would soon eclipse Orton as the top miler in the country. Orton, the captain of the track team, was in his final year of eligibility at the university. McCracken played four years of varsity football at Penn, making Walter Camp's 1899 All-American team. He also set a world record for the shot put in 1898 of 43 feet, eight and a half inches. Penn had an incredibly powerful team under Murphy and would eventually send 13 of the school's finest athletes to the Olympics.

Orton, Grant, and McCracken were recruited to be counsellors at Camp Idlewild, a boys' camp on Lake Winnipesaukee near the White Mountains of New Hampshire. The three enjoyed the camp experience so much and bonded so strongly it was decided they should start a camp of their own. On July 16, 1903, the three partners bought 100 acres of land with nearly a mile of lakefront that included a sandy beach. The rundown farmhouse had an attached dormitory and a barn nearby. The price: $1,700. The name: Camp Tecumseh.

Orton was 30 years old at the time; the other two were 29. For several years, on the day after school ended, Orton would leave his wife and family at home for eight weeks and travel 415 miles to the uncivilized wilds of New Hampshire. He and the rest of the Camp Tecumseh travelling party would board a special car attached to the two o'clock train out of Philadelphia's Broad Street Station, bound for New York City. After arriving in Manhattan, they would walk a few blocks to the Fall River Line pier and board a huge steamship for the overnight trip through Long Island Sound and into Rhode Island's Narragansett Bay, finally docking at Fall River, Massachusetts. From there, the group would disembark and board a train headed for Boston, which would arrive at seven o'clock in the morning. After breakfast, the group would take a 9:30 train out of North Station to Weirs Beach, New Hampshire, and then, after lunch, a steamboat ride across the lake to Camp Tecumseh. There was no dock in the early days, so the travelling party had to jump into shallow water about 20 feet from shore and wade in. The entire trip took about 25 hours. The cost for the summer was $200, but if you included train tickets, boat tickets, meals en route, and incidentals, it was closer to $250, or the equivalent of $7,000 in 2018.

Orton's primary role in the early years of Tecumseh was to recruit campers for the summer. Character references were easy to come by as the three owners had impeccable reputations as Olympians and scholars. Orton and McCracken each held Ph.Ds., while Grant had a M.A. The mission statement and a slogan the partners developed was "To make good boys better."

While Grant was teaching at the Berkeley School in New York, and McCracken was busy with his studies at medical school, it was left up to Orton to find the first group of Tecumseh campers for the 1903 season.

The three founders of Camp Tecumseh, Alexander Grant, George Orton, and Josiah McCracken, are immortalized in stone. The camp's motto: Making good boys better.

He put the word out to wealthy Philadelphians with young men in need of maturing. These families could certainly afford the cost, and many had already sent their offspring away for long periods to boarding schools and the like. Through his connections at the Episcopal Academy, and by running advertisements in *Penn Charter* magazine, Orton managed to find nine sets of parents who were comfortable enough to allow their boys to spend the summer in New Hampshire under the watchful eyes of three Olympic athletes.

From the very beginning, Camp Tecumseh was a work in progress, with *work* being the operative word. There was no electricity and no running water. Staff and campers were subjected to difficult yet satisfying labour. They had to build sports facilities, including a backstop for baseball, a gymnastics bar near the beach, and a tennis court.[1] It was thought that hard work was exactly what the boys needed.

Orton, Grant, and McCracken had combined their celebrity and values to create a unique experience according to Mark Luff, who has been associated with Camp Tecumseh in various capacities since 1966. "The three

Orton playing the mandolin at Camp Tecumseh, 1905. When it was time to relax, music was a very popular activity.

most prestigious awards at Camp Tecumseh, the description is 'Courtesy, manliness and a sense of service.' There's nothing about athletic prowess, there's nothing about how fast you run. It's on courtesy, manliness, and a sense of service. Now, if that isn't a well-rounded opinion of a boy growing up in 1903 ... they were ahead of their time."

The Tecumseh experience provided a wonderful creative outlet for Orton, too. This is where he began writing the *Bob Hunt* series of books about camp life for young people. Luff continued:

> So here he starts a camp and then he has the time to sit and write about these experiences that these boys have, as an author. He was an athlete — a star athlete, an Olympic athlete — and yet he was a gentleman. He taught the boys back then how to be a man, how to be a good-hearted person. You've got to remember ... it was a working farm, so these ... boys would come up and get their fingernails dirty. They're planting potatoes, they're haying fields, they're shovelling manure out of a barn, and then they're eating that food that they just planted three or four weeks

ago … it's on their table. So, the whole idea of … boys actually doing a legitimate day's work, I think that's what Orton was after, to teach them that, because those were the values he believed in as a child.

Healthy athletic competition was always front and centre at Tecumseh, and Orton took an active role from the beginning. Baseball, gymnastics, tennis, badminton, tetherball, running, swimming, and various types of boating were available. Overnight trips by canoe and hiking in the nearby White Mountains were regularly scheduled activities. Mount Washington, the highest U.S. peak east of the Mississippi River at nearly 6,300 feet, was the mountain everyone wanted to climb. Luff told me the following story about Orton:

> There was a record, how quick you could climb Washington. So Mr. Orton says, "I could do this." Starts at the bottom, tears up Mount Washington, goes to the summit, goes to the observatory, and says, "I just beat your time, here it is." Apparently somebody says, "I'm sorry you didn't register down below." Orton said, "Okay, thank you." Ran down the mountain, signed in officially, said, "Please, the summit said I needed to sign this, date it, put the time." He took that piece of paper, ran back up Mount Washington, presented it to the observatory, and he not only beat the record, he beat his previous time from the hour before. So that's the kind of story that Tecumseh kids love, and it's indicative of the man. You talk about going after something. He was a little annoyed that he had to do it, and he did it again to prove his point. I mean, that's the kind of man that George Orton was. Give him a task, give him a challenge, and then stand back because he's going to get the job done.[2]

Conquering Mount Washington was extremely difficult, even for the most seasoned climbers. In 1900, another legendary sportsman attempted that very climb. William (Father Bill) Curtis perished during a violent storm on the mountain in late June. His body was found several days later. He was 63 years old at the time and had been a key figure in the development of sport in the late 19th century. Curtis was a champion runner, sculler, and weightlifter as a young man, and later one of the founders of the New York Athletic Club. He helped organize the AAU and was president of the National Skating Association. Curtis had devoted nearly his entire life to all that was good and honest in sport. Orton had similar values, and it's likely he thought fondly of his friend every time he climbed Mount Washington.

Dr. Josiah McCracken sold his share of Camp Tecumseh to Orton and Grant in 1905. A deeply religious man, McCracken's sense of service inspired him to think of others and renounce a life as a well-paid surgeon in Philadelphia. He wanted to make a more significant contribution to society and accepted a challenge to do medical missionary work in China. He moved to Canton (now Guangzhou) and built a medical school there. In 1912, he took a position as professor of surgery at the Medical College of St. John's University in Shanghai. Eventually, he became dean of the college and remained there for 30 years until the Japanese occupation forced his return to the United States. McCracken and his wife, Helen, had six daughters and two sons. The eldest, Josiah Jr., kept the Tecumseh legacy going strong; he was there in the 1930s, and his three sons all spent time at Camp Tecumseh. Josiah McCracken Sr. died on February 15, 1962, at the age of 88.

By 1911, Camp Tecumseh had established itself as a prominent place for young boys to spend their summers, with annual enrollment having reached 100. Alexander Grant, a stern religious type, was a chauvinist in the truest sense of the word. While the two partners struggled financially because of all the improvements made to the camp, Grant would not listen to Orton's suggestions to make the camp co-educational, or at least to have a portion of it used as a girls' camp. As far as Grant was concerned, women and girls had their place, and it wouldn't be at Camp Tecumseh. Even Grant's wife, Mabel, was not allowed to eat in the main dining hall. Mark Luff told me that when he himself began as a camper in the 1960s, ladies were allowed but had to sit at a segregated table known as "the ladies' table."

Orton's business acumen was vital to the financial success of the camp, but he became interested in other projects in addition to his role as secretary-treasurer of Tecumseh. He founded the Saguenay Club, which

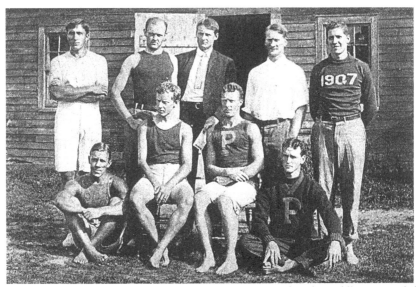

Camp Tecumseh council, 1905. Orton and Grant are seated in the middle, surrounded by elite university athletes who served as camp counsellors and instructors. Several campers at Tecumseh went on to become quite famous.

arranged fishing and hunting trips for businessmen, college men, and Tecumseh boys in the Canadian wilderness. That venture lasted until 1917.

With more and more families wanting to send their daughters to camp, Orton took advantage of an opportunity. He purchased some beachfront property across the lake from Tecumseh and founded Camp Iroquois for families and junior girls. The girls' section was later renamed Singing Eagle Lodge and was run by a surgeon by the name of Dr. Ann Tompkins Gibson.

This was an exciting time for Orton, but it strained the relationship between him and Alexander Grant. While Orton was much more liberal, Grant was very set in his ways. The two remained at odds for a number of years, and in 1924, Orton sold his shares to Grant, ending a 21-year business partnership.[3]

Camp Tecumseh's mission statement of making good boys better drew interesting and talented campers from all walks of life. One of the best baseball players ever seen at camp was pitcher Howard Ehmke, who went on to win 167 major-league games, including one in the World Series for the 1929 champions, the Philadelphia Athletics.

Piano music was also a huge part of the Tecumseh tradition, and young keyboard masters like Philadelphia native Eugene List were invited to attend the camp free of charge in exchange for sharing their musical talents. List made his debut with the Los Angeles Philharmonic at the age of 12 and later played for Winston Churchill, Joseph Stalin, and U.S. president Harry Truman at the Potsdam Conference in 1945. Without a doubt, the best known Tecumseh camper was a fellow they called "Albie." His mother was the legendary screen actress and Philadelphia native Grace Kelly. His father was Prince Rainier of Monaco. Albert Grimaldi was 12 when he first arrived at Camp Tecumseh in 1970. Always nearby that first summer was a Secret Service agent, masquerading as a camp counsellor. American president Richard Nixon was worried that some harm may come to the young prince, and he took every precaution necessary to prevent that from happening. Just before the summer ended, the undercover agent had his cover blown when he opened the trunk of his car, filled with special radio equipment, just as a "real" counsellor walked by. In subsequent years, Albie became a counsellor at Tecumseh, but the Secret Service never appeared again. It was probably just as well.

Here's a fascinating story that Mark Luff told me:

> While Albie was at camp, he fully embraced the joys of being a young man at ease with himself and his cabin mates. At Tecumseh, he could relax and not worry about his princely duties. When Mom and Dad came back, he knew he had to revert back to the young Prince of Monaco, heir to the throne.[4]

Many years later, Albert Grimaldi would follow in the footsteps of the founders of Camp Tecumseh by competing in the Olympic Games. Representing Monaco in the bobsled competition, Prince Albert II was his country's flag bearer at three different Olympics and competed in five Games overall. Albert's maternal grandfather, Grace Kelly's dad, John Kelly Sr., was a three-time Olympic gold medallist in rowing. He would later become the national director of physical fitness under President Franklin D. Roosevelt. His son, John Jr., Grace's older brother, won an Olympic bronze medal in rowing in 1956. Grace Kelly never competed in the

Olympics, but she's the only one in the family to have won an Academy Award. In 1954, she took the Oscar for best actress for her performance as Bing Crosby's wife in *The Country Girl*. Despite its positive influence on many young people, Camp Tecumseh cannot take even the slightest credit for that Oscar statuette.

14

THE PHILLY HALL OF FAME

The 1976 Oscar-winning film *Rocky* introduced moviegoers to the city of Philadelphia and its gritty blue-collar citizens — hard-working, beer-drinking, cheese steak–eating folks who were especially hard hit by the economic crisis of the 1970s. They needed something to boost their collective spirits. Sports can sometimes help with that. Instead of doom and gloom, people start talking about the success of the local team. But the city's professional sports franchises were so bad at the time that Philadelphians either stayed away or booed the teams as mercilessly as they booed the appearance of Santa Claus. Comedian Joe E. Lewis had a famous line that he used for years. "Show me a Philadelphia team and I'll show you a loser."

By the mid-1970s, the Philadelphia Eagles were a perennial laughingstock in the NFL, not having won a title since 1960. The Philadelphia Phillies had never won a World Series in their 90-year history. The NBAs Philadelphia 76ers had plummeted from a championship team featuring Wilt Chamberlain to a record-setting disaster, winning just nine games versus 73 losses in 1973, a mark of futility that stood for 39 seasons. But then there were the Philadelphia Flyers of the National Hockey League, the team George Orton likely wished for when he'd introduced the sport to the city 70 years earlier.

When Ed Snider and his partners went looking to raise the NHL expansion fee of $2,000,000 in 1966, every lender they approached said the same thing they had said to Orton: Hockey will never go over in Philadelphia. Orton had tried his best in the early part of the century, but Philadelphia teams couldn't make a go of it and the fans didn't want to see a loser. The Quakers failed after one NHL season in 1930–31. The University of Pennsylvania hockey program was shut down a number of times because of budget cuts and poor teams. Hockey had no soul in Philadelphia. Even when the expansion Flyers made their NHL debut in 1967, people stayed away in droves. On a good night, 8,000 fans would show up at the Spectrum. Old-time Philly hockey fans must've seen a ghost when the roof blew off their brand new rink on March 1, 1968, during a performance of the Ice Capades. The same hockey rink jinx had torn the canvas roof off the Winter Palace in 1916 and caused the original West Park Ice Palace to burn down in 1901. Perhaps they were right — maybe Philadelphia wasn't a hockey town after all.

The Flyers played the final month of the season on the road, using Quebec City as an alternative home site until the Spectrum's roof could be repaired in time for the playoffs. After getting outmuscled and outscored in their first two playoff series by the St. Louis Blues, the Flyers decided to fight fire with fire and went from the hunted to the hunters.

By using intimidation and other bullying tactics to defeat their opponents, the Flyers became all the rage, much to the chagrin of hockey purists. Philadelphia was public enemy number one. Although Flyers like Bobby Clarke, Rick MacLeish, Bill Barber, and Reggie Leach were fine offensive players, their abilities were overshadowed by a group of thugs dubbed the Broad Street Bullies. As a Toronto Maple Leafs fan, I hated the Flyers like everyone else did, because Dave "the Hammer" Schultz, Don "Big Bird" Saleski, Andre "Moose" Dupont, and Bob "Mad Dog" Kelly would beat up the Toronto players on the ice and on the scoreboard. Even though they were all Canadians, and Bobby Clarke had played for Team Canada against the Russians in 1972, to me they were still a bunch of goons from Philadelphia and a disgrace to hockey. Boston may have had the Big Bad Bruins, a moniker with aggressive alliteration, but the Broad Street Bullies were even more bellicose. Besides, using the street name where the Flyers lived gave it a nice Philly flavour, even though the Spectrum was at 3901 *South* Broad Street. The Flyers won their first of two Stanley Cups in 1974, and two million people packed the streets of Philly to watch the Stanley Cup parade, the largest public gathering in the city's history.

More than 40 years after they won their last Stanley Cup, these Flyers were still godlike figures in Philadelphia. Clarke, Barber, MacLeish, Bernie Parent, and coach Fred Shero had all been inducted into the Philadelphia Sports Hall of Fame, and in 2016, defenceman Jimmy Watson of Smithers, B.C., would be the sixth member of that team to join this exclusive club. When I tracked him down at the reception, I asked if he was aware of the other Canadian being enshrined that night, George Orton. "Well, you know what," he said, "I only discovered this recently, [from] you, by the way. A young man who was a miler at the University of Pennsylvania ... that's where we used to practise, the Flyers, what they call the Class of '23 rink, so there's a connection. We love those fellow Canucks down here."[1]

The other former Flyers present at the Hall of Fame dinner had no idea who Orton was. Not that I was surprised. If I hadn't heard of him before, it's unlikely any of them had. I had to tell them Orton's story and then wait for a reaction. Brad Marsh, the head of the Flyers Alumni Association, grew up in London, Ontario, and is a member of the London Sports Hall of Fame. He wasn't aware that George Orton was in the same Hall of Fame:

> I'm surprised to hear the story around him. It's so unique ... I think it's such a cool story because we always hear, there's always the argument *where did hockey start* and *where was the first game played* and all that, and granted, this isn't part of where the hockey origins were, but, 1896, is that what you said? When I got traded here, our practice facility was at the University of Penn in the Class of '23 rink, and [there are] a couple of old-time Flyers here and we always used to laugh about this old rink that we played in and he was the forefather of it. It's a very unique story. You would think you would've heard about it. You know the Flyers are celebrating 50 years of being in the NHL this year. There's all these stories about hockey in Philadelphia. You'd think somewhere along the line, a story such as that, we would've heard a little bit about Orton.[2]

I also spoke to former Flyer Doug Crossman and told him the story of Orton. He was thrilled at the new connection he had just made:

> I didn't know about him, and you just said that he was from London, Ontario, Strathroy area. Myself and Brad Marsh, we're from there, and it's nice to find out that we had a great athlete there [back then].… Unbelievable. We're always Canadian through and through, and anytime we hear of somebody doing well, and it's a big story, you feel proud.… We have a lot of prestigious Canadians in every walk of life in Philadelphia, and to find out that he's semi-forgotten, it's nice to bring him alive and honour him.[3]

Just about everyone I spoke to that evening felt some sense of regret for not knowing more about George Orton, yet most were fascinated by his story. When Orton had first been selected for induction, I immediately contacted the president of the Hall of Fame, Ken Avallon, and told him about the documentary. The timing couldn't have been better. He asked if I could write the Orton biography for the Hall of Fame dinner program, since I knew all about the man. I said I would. He also wanted to extend an invitation to Orton's granddaughter, Connie Meaney, to attend the dinner and speak.

The Hall is a non-profit organization, and unfortunately, they could only pay for one night in a hotel; Connie would have to look after her own flight from San Francisco if she wanted to attend. She politely declined the invitation but wanted to say a few words about her grandfather and what he meant to her. I made arrangements for those comments to be forwarded to Steve Dolan, the Penn track and field and cross-country coach, who would be making the acceptance speech on Orton's behalf at the dinner.

The event was a lovely affair, and Nick the cameraman and I roamed the hotel ballroom in search of interesting people. When George Orton's name came up, I usually got a blank stare, but one gentleman, Frank Miraglia, wanted to know more. A lifelong Philadelphia sports fan, Miraglia follows all the professional and college sports teams. "When I was looking at the inductees and I saw the name George Orton, I said 'Who the hell is that?'" He suggested that the reason people hadn't heard of Orton was because he wasn't born in Philadelphia. "He doesn't even have the recognition in Canada, so how can you expect the people of Philly to know who George Orton is?" said Miraglia. "Now that I know what he did, I will remember that until I go to the grave, and I will talk about his accomplishments."

I've been told on more than one occasion that of all the professional athletes, hockey players are the nicest and most humble. I happen to agree. Perhaps it's all those long bus rides in junior hockey and the fact that young players have to carry their own equipment that makes them more like you and me and less like entitled superstars. When the Flyers won their two Stanley Cups, every single player on the roster was born in Canada. "Look at what Philadelphia has done with its Canadians," said Miraglia. "We've adopted them. There are millions of fans in this region.... If Jimmy Watson or Joe Watson wound up homeless and destitute, they would take them in [to] live with them ... we love these people."[4]

A two-time Stanley Cup champion with the Flyers, Don Saleski, from Moose Jaw, Saskatchewan, was 67 years old when I spoke to him at the Hall of Fame dinner but could've easily passed for a man in his early 50s. He no longer had the curly locks from his Big Bird days as a member of the Broad Street Bullies, and he looked quite scholarly wearing glasses and a nice suit and tie. We spoke at length about Orton, and Saleski was quite moved by the story of a forgotten Canadian:

> That's pretty amazing, isn't it? A track star running in the Olympics coming from Canada. What's impressive is, in 1892 he ran a four twenty-one, so you know he's running on basically canvas shoes and they had no training or anything, so a guy that was running four twenty back then, that's a heck of an athlete.... If somebody won a gold medal from Canada right now, he'd be celebrated nationwide, right? So I think this is a guy that's worth remembering ... he must've been an amazing athlete. What he did was very significant.[5]

Significant enough that, 60 years after his death, his accomplishments were finally recognized by the Hall of Fame. Ken Avallon explained the process to me:

The Hall of Fame is for all sports at all levels. So it's collegiate, where George would fit, professional, and Olympic, where George would [also] fit. Like most Halls of Fame, there's a nomination process, there's an election committee, and George was nominated. The election committee did their research and he got plenty of votes.... He deserves to be in. [It's] probably a little late, [he] could've gone in a couple of years earlier if you look at his resume. He was one of the top nominees in the Legends category. With George, the fact that he was collegiate, Olympics, plus his administrative work, it was a no-brainer.[6]

When it was time for the induction ceremony, I told Nick that we would both record Orton's acceptance speech, which would be delivered by Steve Dolan. Since Connie Meaney couldn't attend, I wanted to show her what she had missed when I got to San Francisco. The plan was, while she was watching the speech on my phone, the cameraman would record her reaction. This would be a natural ending for the documentary — a woman hears the tributes honouring her late grandfather and reacts (hopefully) with tears of joy, sorrow, regret, pride, or all of the above.

Connie had already emailed some thoughts that she wanted Dolan to include in his speech, and I was looking forward to hearing what both of them had to say. Dolan, like most, knew little about George Orton, other than what he had read in the Penn biographies. Prior to the ceremony, he wanted to know more, so I'd filled him in on a few details I had uncovered. Orton was the first inductee of the evening to be honoured, probably because he was the oldest (he would have been 133 had he lived to see that day). As emcee Dan Baker stepped up to the podium, Nick stood right in front of him, in shooting position, trying not to block anyone's view. As he got up close and personal, I began recording on my phone from my vantage point at the side of the head table. This way, we could cut between the two angles when we went to edit, instead of having to utilize just one camera shot. My recording would be the one Connie would see when we got to San Francisco, so it had to look and sound good.

I met two famous Philadelphia voices that night. The first was Lou Nolan, the longest tenured public address announcer in the NHL. Lou started with the Flyers in 1972 and has been going strong ever since. His voice is deep and rich, with a friendly tinge of his South Philly roots. When the Flyers were winning Stanley Cups, he was the voice who introduced Kate Smith, the team's good luck charm, who would sing "God Bless America" and bring the house down.

The other voice belonged to Dan Baker, whom I had never seen in person before, but whose voice I had heard for many years as the public address announcer for the Eagles (29 years) and Phillies (46 years). Baker's voice was authoritative and commanded attention. As the master of ceremonies, his job was to introduce the nominee, provide a synopsis of his or her accomplishments, and generally move the program along.

The lights went down in the ballroom and the ceremony began with a visual tribute to Orton on the big screen. It showed a few pictures of Orton in action as Baker stepped up to the microphone.

> Our first honoree is George Orton from the University of Pennsylvania. He won a bronze medal in the 400-metre hurdles at the 1900 Olympics. He also, in that same Olympics, won the gold medal in the 2,500-metre steeplechase. A six-time U.S. outdoor champion in the mile. Eight-time U.S. outdoor champion in the two-mile steeplechase. Director of the Penn Relays 1919 to 1925, and inducted to the University of Pennsylvania Athletics Hall of Fame in 1997. Accepting for George Orton, the director of track and field and cross country at the University of Pennsylvania, Steve Dolan.[7]

To a rousing ovation, Dolan walked across the dais, shook hands with Baker, and proceeded to tell the story of George Orton. Nick was recording it; I was recording it. The crowd of about 600 was captivated. Few of them had any idea who Orton was or what he had achieved. Dolan did a beautiful job of capturing the essence of a man who had quietly left a substantial footprint on the Philadelphia sports landscape. I could hardly wait to show the speech to Connie.

Nick and I packed up the gear once Dolan had finished his speech. We were lucky not to have had to wait around for most of the evening as we

Steve Dolan, track and field and cross country coach, University of Pennsylvania. Orton held the same position 100 years earlier, and Dolan spoke eloquently about his predecessor at the 2016 Philadelphia Sports Hall of Fame induction ceremony.

had done all our interviews during the reception. By 8:00 p.m., we were on our way back to the hotel. I had a 7:00 a.m. flight to San Francisco, via Denver, the next day, and I was worried. Nick had shot hours and hours of stuff, yet I hadn't seen even a second of it. There had not been time to see whether it was okay. Since we had shot everything in 4K video, it would take a long time for Nick to render the footage and transfer it from his camera to a memory card that I could take with me. No way was I going to San Francisco without a copy of everything that had been shot on Nick's camera.

As soon as we got back to the hotel, Nick began the transfer process, and we went off to get something to eat.

15

A SAN FRANCISCO
TREAT

had gone to bed around midnight. Nick was still transferring the video, and it wouldn't be ready until the wee hours of the morning. When my alarm went off at 5:15, there was no message from Nick, so I phoned his room. No answer. Shit! I dressed quickly and walked down the hall to the room. *Knock knock*. Nothing. Maybe he had checked out and left it for me. I went to the front desk. Had Nick checked out? No, he was still registered. Panic began to set in.

But as I glanced over at the breakfast buffet, there he was with a big smile on his face. He had the memory card. The transfer had taken ages apparently and wasn't complete until 4:00 a.m. I thanked him and we shared a goodbye hug.

At this point, I had no idea whether he was a good shooter or not. Since I had not brought a laptop with me on the trip, I had no way of viewing the stuff he had shot. I could only pray that he didn't screw anything up.

This phase of the trip had me flying from Philly to Denver on Friday morning, changing planes, and then going on to San Francisco. I had not heard anything from my partner, Mister X, so I gave him a call from the Philadelphia airport to get some details about the cameraperson who would be shooting the Connie Meaney interview Saturday morning in San Francisco. The call went straight to voicemail, so I left a message and got on the plane, thinking no news was good news.

When my plane landed in Denver, there was a message from Mister X to call him. I had a 60-minute layover before my next flight, so I placed the call. After exchanging pleasantries, he laid it on me. "Yeah, Mark, sorry, but your cameraman in San Francisco can't make it. He took a gig in Los Angeles for the weekend."

This can't be happening.

"Have you got another shooter for me?" I asked hopefully.

Silence on the other end of the phone. "Well, I'm working on it," he said. "In the meantime, you've got an iPhone that shoots in 4K, right? I'm sure you can do the interview in a pinch. Just point a camera at any woman and she'll tell you anything."

I knew I was in big trouble. Mister X was a complete screw-up and the documentary was in jeopardy of falling into a deep, dark hole. Here I was, trying to save the production several hundred dollars by staying with relatives instead of at a San Francisco hotel. With those savings, you'd think Mister X could have ensured we had a professional freelance videographer ready for the interview. Instead, his guy had gotten a better deal in L.A., and I didn't know anybody in the Bay Area who was a decent shooter. Could I trust this man to find me another shooter? No chance. Even if I did, it was Friday afternoon and we needed someone for a Saturday morning gig that would last several hours.

I wished Nick could've come with me to San Francisco. I couldn't possibly host, produce, AND shoot the interview with Connie Meaney by myself. What the hell was I going to do?

During the flight to San Francisco my mind was going in a million directions. One thing was for sure: I had to find a shooter. But where? I landed early in the afternoon and my cousin Mona, whom I had planned to stay with that night, sent me a message saying she would pick me up at the bus station in Larkspur, near San Anselmo. So I paid $18 and boarded the Marin Airporter for the one-hour trip through San Francisco, across the Golden Gate Bridge, and into Marin County. It was one of the nicer drives

I had ever been on, despite the fact that Mister X had not called back with news of another shooter. He never did call, and I never spoke to him again. He had screwed me royally. The short-lived partnership was over. I was on my own again.

I hadn't seen Mona in a couple of years, and after a few pleasantries she wanted to know how the documentary was going. When I told her about my dilemma, she suggested that her ex-husband, Mark Steinberg, could do the shooting. Mark was a commercial photographer in a previous life but hadn't worked professionally in that capacity in a number of years. He and I had spent a fair bit of time together in the mid-1990s, especially after I had introduced him to the music of the Tragically Hip, the legendary Canadian rock band. My very good friend Jake Gold had been the manager of the Hip at that time, and he provided us with tickets to the show and a photographer's pass for Mark. This was at the Metro Theatre in Chicago, just a couple of blocks from Wrigley Field. The place was packed, with over a thousand people on the main floor and in the balcony. Mark had his trusty Nikon (cellphone cameras were not popular yet) with him, and even though he wasn't a photojournalist and had never worked a concert before, he was in the pit with the other photographers, right in front of the stage.

The general rule at concerts is that you can shoot all you want from the pit around the stage, but only during the first three songs. Mark was unaware of this rule. Halfway through a wild show, in his excitement to see lead singer Gord Downie up close and personal, Mark climbed up on the stage and started taking pictures. I nearly shit myself. Downie looked bemused, his expression saying, "Who the hell is this guy?" A security guy grabbed Mark and hustled him off the stage. They took his credential and his camera. Jake gave me one of those "your cousin is an idiot" looks and then proceeded to go downstairs.

I thought they were going to kick Mark out, but after explaining the rules, Jake gave the camera back to Mark and even invited him to meet the band backstage after the concert. So that was my lasting memory of Mark Steinberg as a cameraman. Not a real positive vibe, but what choice did I have at this point? He was now my cousin's ex-husband, so he was still my cousin, I guessed.

Mona got on the phone with him and he agreed to help out, even though he didn't have much experience shooting video. "Just make sure we get good sound and the shot is in focus," I told him. "Everything else can be fixed in post-production." I had learned from experience that you could have the most beautiful video in the world, but if the audio is muddy and difficult to decipher, you've got nothing.

I had a fitful sleep in anticipation of an exciting Saturday. During the one-hour drive to San Francisco, I filled Mark in on the Orton story and how I wanted the interview to be shot. I also transferred Steve Dolan's speech over to Mark's phone so we could record Connie's reaction to it on my iPhone. Since Mister X had screwed me out of a professional shooter, we were somewhat limited when it came to equipment, too.

Mark would shoot everything on the iPhone, using a selfie stick that doubled as a tripod. I did not have a remote microphone for the iPhone, but I knew the built-in mic would work as long as the camera was within a few feet and there were no extraneous noises to worry about.

Mark suggested we start shooting as I was walking from the car to the front door of Connie's house, which was located not far from the San Francisco Zoo in a quiet part of the city. As Mark followed along, I spoke to the camera and informed the viewer that I was nervous and excited to be meeting Connie for the first time. I climbed the steps to the front door of her quaint home, with Mark right behind me. I knocked on the door and peered into the window. Mark was ready to capture the moment when she opened the door.

"Hello, nice to finally meet you," said Constance Meaney as she pulled the door wide open. She greeted us with a warm smile and gave me the kind of hug reserved for a long-lost relative. Connie had the slender body of a distance runner, which it turned out she was (must've gotten that from her grandfather). She had long auburn hair and twinkling grey eyes. And she couldn't wait to show and tell us all about George Washington Orton and the memories she had collected.

This is going to be great, I thought.

Constance "Kit" Ulerich was the only child of George Orton's daughter Edith Willis Orton and her husband, William Keener Ulerich, a newspaper publisher and radio station owner. They were from Clearfield, Pennsylvania, not far from the home of the famous groundhog Punxsutawney Phil and about an hour northwest of State College, home of Penn State University.

Constance Ulerich was born on May 14, 1942. She attended Linden Hall, a private girls' school near Lancaster, Pennsylvania, and graduated

The author with George Orton's only living descendent, granddaughter Connie Meaney, at her home in San Francisco. She had kept a few boxes of memorabilia, one of which, I hoped, would contain his Olympic gold medal from 1900.

in 1961. She then attended Penn State and graduated in 1964. She went on to spend a year studying at the University of Salamanca in Spain. In 1965, at St. Francis Church in Clearfield, she married James Rogers, a graduate of Holy Cross University and the Harvard School of Business. They lived in New York City, where Connie was on the editorial staff of the *American Heritage Dictionary* and James worked for International Business Machines (IBM). The two had no children and divorced in the early 1970s, and Constance met and married Frederic Squires in San Diego in 1972. They had no children either and divorced in 1974. She met Ray Meaney and married him in San Francisco in 1982. They've been together ever since.

Connie was an associate professor of Asian studies for many years at Oakland's Mills College, and in 1993 she won a prestigious Hoover Institution national peace fellowship from Stanford University. Higher education certainly ran in the family.

Mark and I had stopped for coffee on the way to Connie's, and I had asked if she wanted anything. She preferred tea, so the two of us enjoyed our hot beverages while getting to know each other. Connie had brought out two boxes filled with memorabilia. Mark began setting up the camera in her somewhat cluttered living room. There was a couch with a big coffee table that would serve as our "set."

Connie and I sat on the couch and chatted away as Mark recorded our conversation without saying, "I am recording." I had found that once a subject knows they are being recorded, their answers become measured. I wanted us to have a real conversation rather than have her answer questions. It was important for all three of us to be comfortable with one another.

Mark had an issue with the lighting, so he asked if Connie could open the drapes to allow the natural sunlight to wash over us. Mark was a still photographer who paid particular attention to things like back-lighting and composition. As I said before, I just wanted the audio to be clear and the video in focus. I would need to trust Mark, as I had trusted Nick, to get the necessary shots. I would also need to direct him to shoot cut-aways, over-the-shoulder shots, reaction shots, and other little tricks that would help provide continuity and make things easier during the editing process.

Connie began by opening one of the boxes she had brought in from the garage. I asked if she was surprised by how much memorabilia there was. "I'm surprised there was any stuff at all," she said. The box contained a number of plastic freezer bags, each filled with pictures and clippings. There was also what appeared to be a jewellery box. "Let's put this aside for now," she said. "We'll get to it later."

It took all of my willpower not to blurt out, "Is the Olympic gold medal in there?"

The first item out of the box was a plaque Connie had received in Montreal in 1996. It was for George Orton's induction to the Canadian Olympic Hall of Fame. It is the only item that acknowledges Orton as a Canadian Olympic medal winner, and the only time anyone from Canada had reached out to Connie. Until now. She was very proud of this award, I could tell.

I wanted to ask about George's Olympic medals right there, but I resisted again because Connie had meticulously arranged everything in advance for this interview. She wanted each item to tell a story, and I was not going to deny her that privilege. Besides, she was a good storyteller and I wanted to know everything about my adopted late great-grandfather and the rest of the family.

The camera was rolling, the documentary was happening, the drama was building. The medals could wait. Over the next few hours, Connie showed us dozens of pictures of the Orton family. "When I see these, it's ancient history and I can't ask my mother or my aunt about them," she said. Connie's mother Edith and Edith's sister Eleanor had a special relationship. Edith, George Orton's youngest daughter, had been divorced from Connie's father, William Ulerich, since 1950, when Connie was just eight. Eleanor, the middle Orton daughter, was five years older than Edith. She had been married to a man named William Bartley. Connie told me she had really loved her Uncle Bill and Aunt Eleanor, that they made a very jolly couple. But Bartley had died in 1960 at the age of 73, leaving Eleanor a widow. The couple had no children. A few years later, soon after Connie had married James Rogers and moved to New York, Eleanor moved into the apartment in the Philadelphia suburb of Wayne with her sister Edith.

Wayne is one of the many communities that dot the Main Line, the affluent western suburbs of Philadelphia along U.S. Route 30, Lancaster Avenue. It was formerly the Pennsylvania Railroad's Main Line and includes such towns as Merion, Wynnewood, Haverford, Ardmore, and Bryn Mawr.

Edith and Eleanor would regularly go for lunch in the area, often out in the country. One July afternoon in 1994, 85-year-old Edith was driving and her 90-year old sister Eleanor was in the passenger seat. Edith forgot to look both ways before pulling into traffic. A Jeep driven by a teenage boy who had just gotten his licence rammed the sisters' car broadside. Both were killed. The boy, inconsolable, was not charged. It was Edith's fault.

After the funeral of her mother and her aunt, Connie Meaney was the only one left on the Orton family tree. She inherited the family's belongings, including those of her grandfather. George Orton's two daughters had kept some memories, and now Connie owned them. Connie had lost her other aunt when she was only 12. Constance Irvine Orton was Connie's "Aunt Toddy," George's eldest daughter. A librarian, she never married or had children and had died of rheumatic heart disease in her hometown of Wayne on February 23, 1954, at the age of 53.

"I'm the only child of my mother and her sisters," said Connie. "I asked my mother once why Uncle Bill and Aunt Eleanor never had any children. 'Because they just didn't' she said." This must have been a familiar refrain in the Orton family. Six children were born to Oliver and Mary Ann Orton: Samuel, Minnie, George, Helena, Irvine, and Maude. Only two had children of their own: George's three daughters and Irvine's two sons (with wife Bertha). But

Irvine Orton Jr. and Earl Orton never fathered any children. Hence, Connie is the last remaining descendant of Oliver and Mary Ann Orton.

It is fascinating to go through someone's life in pictures. Connie had many photos of her grandfather at various stages of his life beginning as a young father. She told me she had never seen any pictures of George as a child or even as a young man. The earliest image I was able to find was a grainy photo of George at the age of 17 or 18 in a runner's pose. "I wonder what he was like as a young man," Connie mused as she revealed a photo of George and Edith with their infant daughter, Constance, taken around 1900. George had the look of a man who would rather be anywhere else than with his wife and baby. "That's the only picture, as far as I know, of George with his family."

Box number two revealed a plastic baggie that contained locks of Orton's blond hair from a hundred or so years ago. There were also pictures from Camp Iroquois, which Connie had visited every summer for two or three weeks at a time starting in 1946. "It started as a camp for girls only, one of the first of its kind," she said. "When I started going to Iroquois, it was more of an adult vacation place where George's friends and family would gather. There was a big lodge and tents and stuff." Camp Iroquois is where Connie first met Doris Bolton. As a little girl, she thought Doris was the manager of Camp Iroquois. Many years later, she found out that Doris Bolton was actually her grandfather George's stepdaughter.

16

LIFE IS A (RELAY) CARNIVAL

Throughout the 1910s and '20s, George Orton was rarely at home with his wife and three daughters. He spent most of his waking hours working. It could have been any number of jobs he held down: teaching, coaching, writing, managing, administration, fundraising, consulting, public relations, and, of course, athletic competition. The more notoriety he attained, the less attention his wife, Edith, and daughters Constance, Eleanor, and Edith received from him. At some point in the late 1920s, George met a woman named (coincidentally) Edith.

Edith M. Bolton was a divorcee with two children. She met George while he was still married to Edith Orton, but that relationship had been deteriorating for decades and divorce was inevitable. Edith Orton filed suit in 1931, claiming not irreconcilable differences or adultery but desertion. George was never home.

He did not contest the suit, and the divorce was granted in 1932. It made all the newspapers for all the wrong reasons. Orton's squeaky-clean image had become tarnished in recent years, and the divorce was another hit to his reputation — and his finances. Throughout the 1920s, Orton was one of the most recognized and influential men in all of Philadelphia. He coached the Penn track team and ran the highly successful Penn Relays. He did a splendid job in promoting the events and the athletes. He was also the racing secretary for the Rose Tree Fox Hunting Club in Media, just west of Philadelphia. Rose Tree held horse racing meets every spring and fall. Orton started doing publicity there in 1914 and remained until 1957.

But it was the Penn Relay Carnival that made George Orton famous in Philadelphia and around the world. Just the mention of his name and the Penn Relays brought out the superlatives. From "The Old Sport's Musings" in the *Philadelphia Inquirer*, April 28, 1924:

> There is one individual who must glow with pride as his eye rests upon those thousands upon thousands of athletes in competition, and the tens of thousands of those who come to witness the achievements of these battlers in abbreviated garb. That man is Dr. George W. Orton, who is the Father of the Penn Relay Carnival. It was in the brain of this man, himself at fifty still an able athlete, not as supple perhaps or as strenuous as in his heyday as a youngster on the track, but still taking his place with a soccer team and playing a game that well might shame some of those one-third his age. It was George W. Orton, known to thousands as "Doc" Orton, who established this athletic festival, and it is to him that the lion's share of its success should always be accorded. He nurtured the child of his brain in his swaddling clothes, and he has seen it reach thirty years of age accepted everywhere as the greatest of all athletic competitions, yielding not even to the Olympics in that respect. It is given to few men in the sphere of sport to achieve what George Orton has done. The Carnival stands as a monument to him, to his indefatigable industry in promoting the festival at all times; to his untiring efforts in seeking to lure overseas the stellar athletes of not only Britain, but of France and even of Italy. It can be stated without the slightest chance of contradiction that

Doc Orton has given the sport lovers of this city greater opportunities to see the stars of their own country and others than any single man who was ever identified with athletics.

For this reason when the success of the Carnival is mentioned, when its accomplishment is broached, the name of one man instantly brings to every mind as the biggest determining factor in such success. And that man is George W. Orton, a hustler of hustlers, himself a great athlete in his younger days and a stage manager par excellence in his present years.[1]

Imagine what it must have been like for George Orton the day that article was published. He was the hottest thing in town. There wasn't anywhere in the city he could go without being recognized. Everything he touched, it seemed, turned to gold. Soon, everybody wanted a piece of him. The committee responsible for the U.S. sesquicentennial celebrations in 1926 approached Orton with a sizable offer. As part of the festivities, Philadelphia would be hosting the World's Exposition, and Orton was the perfect choice to manage the new 75,000-seat stadium, for which the city would break ground in the fall of 1925. He would be in charge of all the extra sporting events, such as the national AAU championships, which would take place during the Exposition.

Unfortunately, the alumni board at Penn, which was responsible for athletics, didn't want Orton working both jobs. In the fall of 1925, they told him he was spreading himself too thin for their liking. Orton assured them he could run the new stadium and continue to manage the Penn Relays. The alumni board disagreed and voted to fire him. He accepted the decision without complaint, even though some in the media were outraged.

"PENN SHOULD BRING GEORGE ORTON BACK TO HANDLE RELAY CARNIVAL," screamed a headline in the *Philadelphia Inquirer* on December 21, 1925. The article read:

Hamlet, without the Melancholy Dane in the title role, is no more incongruous than a Penn Relay Carnival without Dr. George W. Orton conducting the event. The name of "Orton" and "Relay Carnival" are wedded as firmly as "sterling" and "silver," "karat" and "gold." In the realm of athletics they are synonymous, the genial doctor's name being the hallmark of this event throughout the world. To divorce him from the relays and to substitute a nonentity in an athletic sense, is an asinine performance.... Dr. Orton may still plead that his time is too absorbed to handle the affair. But that is only a feeble excuse. The Relay Carnival is in April, the Sesqui events will not start probably until several months afterward. Dr. Orton has built up an excellent staff to handle each affair. Therefore he could easily guide both. He should immediately be recalled to his own post. Athletics demand him, the carnival needs him, and no bias on the part of any athletic source should be allowed to interfere with this greatest athletic event of every spring, one without parallel in the world.[2]

Orton's new position was director of athletics for the Sesqui-Centennial International Exposition and manager of the Philadelphia Municipal Stadium. The pressure was now on to book events for the new stadium, which would be ready in April of 1926. By then, Orton and his team had put together an impressive list of events for the Exposition. Included were national championships in archery, baseball, billiards, bicycle racing, cricket, canoeing, cross country, dog shows, fencing, golf, polo, shooting (using clay pigeons), rowing, swimming, tennis, track and field, lacrosse, motorboat racing, rodeo, and a marathon race from Valley Forge to the Philadelphia Stadium:

The millions of visitors to the Sesqui-Centennial International Exposition will find no greater world exhibit than that which will take place in the new Municipal Stadium and surrounding sport fields in the gigantic program arranged by Dr. George W. Orton.... [He] has successfully completed a sports program which will undoubtedly rival in importance and standards the best Olympic Games ever held. The varied schedule includes

virtually every known sport in this country and abroad....
It is expected that every leading athlete of this country
will compete in one or more of the events arranged for the
Sesqui-Centennial.[3]

Orton had also arranged for the challenge round of the Davis Cup
tennis matches to be played, with the United States taking on France. They
were to feature greats such as Bill Tilden and Henri Lacoste (the man who
made the alligator logo famous). Unfortunately, the matches needed to
be played on a grass surface, and there was not a suitable court for play,
so they were moved to the Germantown Cricket Club. The United States
won, four matches to one, but the championships were not part of the
Sesqui-Centennial events.

In the fall of 1925, Orton had sent a letter to Major League Baseball,
offering the new Municipal Stadium as a venue for the 1926 World Series.
The Philadelphia Athletics had finished second to the Washington Senators
in the American League in 1925, and Orton figured they had a good chance
to take the pennant the following season, especially since the powerful
Yankees had finished eighth. Rather than play home games at Shibe Park,
Orton suggested the Athletics play in the new stadium in South Philly. It
may have worked out, except the 1926 A's were no match for the Yankees
and finished in third place. The World Series would be played in New York
and St. Louis that year, with the Cardinals winning in seven games. The final
out was recorded when Babe Ruth was caught stealing, the only time that
has ever happened in World Series history.

Attempting to get the best black athletes in the country to compete
as part of the Sesqui-Centennial, Orton had arranged for a football game
between two all-black schools — Tuskegee University of Alabama and
Lincoln University of Pennsylvania. Again, he lost out to another venue as
the game ended up being played at Franklin Field: Tuskegee won 20–16.

All the hype surrounding the Sesqui-Centennial did not spur public
enthusiasm. Most Philadelphians felt the city needed housing and new
infrastructure instead of a big party. However, officials were confident that,
with 50 million people living within 500 miles of the new stadium, attendance from May to November would top 30 million, but in the end only
4,600,000 actually paid to attend. It got so bad by the end of June that the

organizers decided to open on Sundays and violate the city's Blue Laws. And so the same issue that had angered Sabbatarians at the 1900 Olympics reared its head again in Philadelphia. Even though the fair was supposed to run until the end of November, organizers were forced to keep the grounds open for all of December so that concessionaires could move their remaining stock.

There were several reasons for the fair's failure. The organizers and local politicians were constantly bickering. Public opposition was fuelled by ongoing construction problems at the venues and bad weather — it rained 107 of the 184 days the fair was open.

Even a great stroke of luck for Orton and company turned out to be a soggy mess. The heavyweight championship fight between Gene Tunney and iconic champion Jack Dempsey was originally scheduled for Chicago, but when Dempsey learned that gangster Al Capone was not a big fan of his, the venue was changed to Yankee Stadium.

Dempsey had not fought in three years, despite public and media pressure to fight a black contender by the name of Harry Wills. Dempsey's last fight had been at the Polo Grounds in New York, where he destroyed Luis Angel Firpo with a second-round knockout before 85,000 fans. New York was once again ready for a massive prizefight, but the state athletic commission refused to issue Dempsey a licence because of his refusal to fight Wills. Hearing of this, Orton and E.L. Austin, the director of the Sesqui-Centennial, offered fight promoter Tex Rickard the Philadelphia Municipal Stadium as an alternative to Yankee Stadium. Rather than fight the authorities in New York, Rickard, along with Dempsey and Tunney, accepted the offer from Philadelphia, and on September 23, 1926, over 120,000 spectators saw Tunney, a four-to-one underdog, completely out-box Dempsey to win the heavyweight title. Dempsey received a staggering $700,000 for the fight; Tunney earned $200,000.

Despite the huge crowd, not everyone approved of the bout's being held in Philadelphia. The *New York Times* claimed the only reason Philadelphia got the fight was to "bolster up deficient receipts" and that it was "disgraceful and humiliating" to the American people.[4]

As the fighters entered the ring, a downpour began that lasted the entire fight. Orton, sensing a tropical storm would wreak havoc, had ensured that a large canvas tent covered the ring so that the fighters would not get wet.

The crowd had to suffer. Even though the Chamber of Commerce had said the fight brought in an extra $3 million in revenue, the Sesqui-Centennial ended up as a huge flop. Four hundred creditors presented bills totaling $5.8 million. It took until May 1929 for the city to pay off the Exposition's tab.[5]

Dempsey and Tunney fought again the following year at Soldier Field in Chicago. Dempsey would've won, but after knocking Tunney down in the seventh round, he failed to go to a neutral corner, as was the new rule at the time. Instead, he stood over the fallen Tunney for up to eight seconds before obeying the rules. This gave Tunney time to shake out the cobwebs, and he recovered sufficiently to win the fight. Experts say Tunney would've been counted out after 10 seconds, but Dempsey's refusal to immediately go to a neutral corner meant that his opponent was on the canvas for 13 seconds. Because of the delay, it became known as the Long Count fight.

After the Sesqui flop, Municipal Stadium became known as a white elephant. Stuck in a swampy region along the Delaware River in the city's southeast section, the stadium would take years to turn a profit, experts said. Orton was named the full-time director of the stadium at a salary of $10,000 annually. His job was to make the stadium profitable, but with no money coming in, he was unable to pay his own salary and that of his staff at city hall. It was a miracle that Orton could persuade any events to come to the scene of such a colossal bust, but he did. By 1929, he had the stadium humming with activity — football games, bicycle races, and boxing and wrestling matches all helped pay the rent, even though Orton had little civic support and no permanent tenant for the huge stadium. The Philadelphia A's played their home games at Shibe Park and weren't going to move to a 75,000-seat monstrosity. They barely averaged 10,000 fans a game and lost money every year.

Orton again made the Municipal Stadium available for the World Series of 1929, featuring the Philadelphia A's and the Chicago Cubs. However, upon further inspection, it was determined that the configuration of the stadium, which was horseshoe-shaped, meant it was 50 feet too narrow in right field, so the idea was scrapped. The Phillies played their home games at the tiny Baker Bowl, which had a capacity of about 18,000. Rarely were there more than a few thousand in attendance for a Phillies game.

The Philadelphia Eagles of the NFL were born in the 1930s and played a few years at the Baker Bowl and then Municipal Stadium before making Shibe Park their permanent home until 1958, when they moved to Franklin Field.

Orton had wooed Villanova University to play its home games at the stadium, but that was only five or six dates a year. He had to find more tenants. He needed a marquee event that would bring thousands of spectators to the Municipal Stadium — or else he wasn't going to have a job for much longer.

17

THE INNOVATOR

In 1895, Orton had lobbied for Philadelphia to be the permanent home of the annual Army-Navy football game. As captain of the Penn track team and a rabid follower of college football, he envisioned two annual sport spectaculars that would be of national interest: the Penn Relays in the spring and the gridiron clash between rival armed forces the Saturday after Thanksgiving.

Army and Navy had played each other just four times before the series was disbanded after a particularly rough game in 1893 at Worden Field on the campus of the U.S. Naval Academy at Annapolis, Maryland. The previous year, the Midshipmen defeated the Cadets at Army's home field, the Plain, at West Point, New York. The rematch was so nasty that fights broke out among spectators, and an admiral from the Navy and an army general threatened to duel at the game's conclusion (won by Navy 6–4). Helmetless players were injured so seriously that U.S. president Grover Cleveland deemed football to be "unsafe" and banned future games between the two teams. Were it not for a letter written by Theodore

Roosevelt, then secretary of the Navy, urging the reinstatement of the rivalry, Orton may not have been able to convince authorities to return to the gridiron.

One of the issues Orton wanted to address was the location of the game. Since it was 270 miles from West Point to Annapolis by train, why not find a neutral site that was about equal distance from the two? Orton suggested Franklin Field in Philadelphia, which is pretty much the halfway point between the two academies. Trains ran regularly from both campuses into Philadelphia's Broad Street Station. Franklin Field would be the ideal venue for the annual Army-Navy clash.

When Franklin Field was built in 1895, it hosted the inaugural Penn Relays, other track meets, and varsity baseball. The Quaker nine beat Lafayette in their Franklin Field debut and went on to lose just once in 10 starts at home that season. One of the stars of the team was outfielder/dental student Zane Grey, who went on to write *Riders of the Purple Sage* and other bestselling books about the American frontier. He began his career as a pitcher from flat ground, but when the pitcher's mound was introduced in 1893 and the distance between the mound and home place was increased from 55 feet to 60 feet, six inches, Grey lost the zip on his fastball and became an outfielder.

When baseball season ended, college football took over at Franklin Field. The Penn Quakers were the top team in the nation and drew large crowds to the new stadium. Eventually, Orton, helped by Theodore Roosevelt's love of football and desire to clean up the game, convinced Army and Navy to resume their rivalry on the gridiron. In 1899, the Army-Navy game returned, this time to Franklin Field, which was its home for 11 of the next 13 years. Football bragging rights among the military were determined by the annual outcome.

In September of 1901, after President William McKinley was assassinated and Vice President Theodore Roosevelt took over, the game had its biggest ally. One of Roosevelt's first trips as president was to Franklin Field for the Army-Navy game. He brought nearly his entire cabinet along, and they marched into Franklin Field wearing top hats, accompanied by the band's rendition of "Hail to the Chief."

Roosevelt's presence lent credibility to the game. He was also responsible for a sporting tradition that we take for granted — switching sides at halftime. Roosevelt left his seat at Franklin Field 10 minutes into that 1901 game and watched the rest of the half from the Navy sideline, with the secretary of defense on the Army sideline. They switched positions for the second half, ensuring at least one leader was on each side during the game. The teams switched sides of the field as well, so there was no advantage to be had. Ironically, as soon as Roosevelt made his way over to the Army side, Cadets quarterback Charles Daly ran the second-half kickoff back 95 yards for a touchdown. Final score: Army 11, Navy 5.

After many years at Franklin Field, the game rotated among stadiums in New York, Baltimore, Chicago, and Pittsburgh. In the late 1920s, Orton revisited Annapolis and West Point, extolling the virtues of Philadelphia's new Municipal Stadium, which he was now managing. Having the matchup in Philadelphia, said Orton, would make the Army-Navy game the greatest annual sporting spectacle in America. By the early thirties, the game had moved back to Franklin Field, and then in 1936, it found its permanent home at Municipal Stadium, later renamed John F. Kennedy Stadium. Orton's persistence had paid off; the stadium hosted the Army-Navy game from 1936 to 1979, except for three years during the Second World War. Today, the annual game is contested most often at Philadelphia's Lincoln Financial Field. The seed planted by George Orton in the 1890s has blossomed into one of the world's most prestigious sporting events.

Orton was always looking for a way to make sports easier to enjoy for the spectator. His idea to put numbers on the backs of college football jerseys in 1914 was revolutionary and gave a nod of recognition to the fan. College football, once a violent, barbaric game, now had specific rules in place thanks to Teddy Roosevelt. The flying wedge, which featured players in a V formation shielding the ball carrier, had resulted in numerous injuries and occasional fatalities. In 1905 alone, 18 football players were killed and 159 seriously injured. Attempts were made to reform the rules by discouraging mass-momentum plays for short yardage gains. Players began wearing headgear and padding. The forward pass became legal in 1906 and made for a wide-open, exciting game. Brute strength alone was no longer enough to win football games. Dexterity, speed, and improvisation became important ingredients, and the fans loved it.

The invention of the centre snap, the huddle, the fake kick, and the man in motion saw football evolve into a sport that rivaled major-league baseball in popularity. Crowds of up to 30,000 regularly watched weekly college football games.

Orton wanted to see track and field reach the same lofty status. He had taken over from Mike Murphy as head coach of Penn's track team after Murphy died suddenly in 1913. Orton was given a five-year contract by the university and was under pressure to produce winning teams. At the same time, he assisted Frank B. Ellis in the running of the annual Penn Relays.

One of the major problems with track and field, according to Orton, was the amount of time it took to complete certain field events. Since there was no clock, spectators quickly lost interest during events such as the running broad jump (now the long jump). If there were 20 competitors and each had three attempts, it would take hours to determine a winner. At the time, a tape was used to measure each jump. The measurement began at the takeoff board, and the tape was pulled until it reached the spot in the sand where the competitor had landed, some 20-odd feet away. This process took a considerable amount of time — too much, according to Orton. So he invented a new system by embedding boards in the ground with the upper edges marked off like a ruler, running from the takeoff to the far end of the landing pit. Each jump would be measured with a square, thereby saving time and ensuring greater accuracy than was possible with a tape measure. Rather than each jump taking a minute or so to measure, the new system would allow judges to get the job done in a matter of seconds. Orton tried this method with his Pennsylvania team in practice, and soon it was accepted and used at all sanctioned meets worldwide.

Orton's invention remains popular today, although many of the top track meets have moved to laser technology to get the most accurate readings. Orton's unique perspective as an athlete and a fan allowed him to devise and implement several rule changes that improved sport greatly. He especially wanted track and field to flourish as a spectator sport, which it did during his time as manager of the Penn Relays, and for many years after. Even though he referred to himself as only a "fair runner" during his record-breaking athletic career, Orton's role as an innovator and administrator cannot be overstated. It was crucial to the growth of North American sports in the 20th century.

18

A TREASURE TROVE

Connie Meaney and I spent several hours looking at pictures and newspaper clippings in her San Francisco home. Every picture had a story to go with it. The earliest photo was from 1900, with George, Edith, and baby Constance sitting between two stone pillars. There was one from around 1915, with George wearing a suit and tie. He looked to be about 20 pounds overweight. "Portly George" is what Connie called him. It's the only picture she had where he appeared to be anything but trim.

As we sifted through the photos, I noticed a shot of George with what appeared to be a cigarette in his mouth. Upon closer inspection, I realized it was a small pencil. Connie mentioned that her grandfather always did the newspaper crossword puzzle, completing it in mere minutes. In this particular photo, he was wearing an undershirt that clearly reveals his shrunken right arm. I asked Connie if she was aware that this was the result of the crippling fall he suffered as a little boy. She answered,

I thought of [that] as something that [was] a part of his boyhood and that he had completely recovered. I know it's hard to believe, but I never noticed that he had a shrunken arm. I never knew that until recently. The story I had heard was that he had fallen out of an apple tree and was gravely injured and the doctors said he would never be able to walk again. And through perseverance and courage and his own spirit he recovered by running through the countryside and became a great steeplechaser. I didn't know there were doctors involved or anything that helped with his recovery. I didn't think that anything carried over into his adult life. I never asked my mother about his arm because I never noticed it.

There were also many pictures taken at Camp Iroquois, where it appeared the Orton family had engaged in some happy times. George's older brother, Samuel, was in a few of the photos. Connie thought he was quite the character. The story she had heard was that "Uncle Sam" had shot a man in the Yukon during the gold rush of the late 1800s and may have been on the lam. Samuel Orton died in New Hampshire in 1947 at the age of 77.

We had looked at just about every item in the two big boxes, yet Connie had yet to reveal any information about the Olympic medals her grandfather had won in 1900. The small wooden jewellery box sat at the edge of the table, and every time Connie reached for a new item to show me, I was hoping she would grab for that and reveal its contents. The suspense was killing me. Did she have the Olympic medal in there?

I think she sensed my anticipation because, out of nowhere, she motioned to the jewellery box. "Oh, I almost forgot," she said. "There's two things I want to show you in here." I could hardly contain myself. I motioned for Mark to get a close-up shot of the box as she lifted its lid.

"There are several things here that I don't know what they are," she told us.

As she opened the box and sifted through its contents, I leaned over and caught a glimpse of something shiny and beautiful. "Is that a gold medal?" I asked, knowing that it was.

"Well, I don't know if it's real gold," she said.

I couldn't help myself. I reached into the box without asking permission and picked up a gold medal on a chain. "Well, it's not an Olympic medal, but it's pretty cool," I blurted out.

I'm sure Connie noticed the disappointment on my face when I first saw it. Ever since she had told me there were some medals stashed away in a box, I had dreamed of this moment. The only Olympic medals that were rectangular and not round in shape were awarded at the 1900 Paris games. This one was gold and round. It was given to Orton for his victory in the 1,000-yard run in 1903 at the Penn Relay Carnival.

Connie wasn't aware that her grandfather was known as "the father of the Penn Relay Carnival." She thought the carnival had something to do with amusement park rides and a circus. Even though there was no Olympic medal in the box, I wondered if Connie had ever seen the rectangular one from 1900. Surely someone in the family had known about it. It would have been made of silver, gilded with gold. Connie reminisced,

> At some point. I'm sitting somewhere with my mother and probably both of my aunts, I think. And I'm not sure why this came up, but they were talking about medals and winning and Daddy and his accomplishments. I don't remember exactly, and I was old enough to know what a gold medal is, so I wasn't a tiny toddler. So I do remember saying where is the gold medal? Where is it? Because there are some lesser ones I haven't found either, like the bronze one, and they just kind of said "We don't know."

Orton's daughters were obviously proud of their father's achievements, but they didn't seem to talk much about them, certainly not to Connie:

> The fact that he won medals was kind of amazing, but they were equally amazed by his scholarly achievements and about how he spoke all those languages and learned Sanskrit and how he could do calculus in his head. That seemed astounding to me. I can imagine running, but I can't imagine doing calculus in my head. I feel they were in awe of him, but they didn't brag a lot either. I think they

came from that Protestant background where you don't toot your own horn and you have to be straitlaced and not self glorifying.

I asked Connie if she ever followed up with her mother and aunt about the medals. Did she ask them straight up about the status of the Olympic gold medal?

Well, not really. Probably because, you know, I didn't see George that much, my grandfather. I have to say he wasn't a huge fixture as a real person in my life. He was this legend person who won gold medals because I didn't see him that often.... The two things that I think of as mostly likely happening, one would be it just got lost somehow. I mean, people in my family are not that organized for a lot of things. I mean, there's all this stuff as you can see [she waves her hand around the room]. I mean, I have piles of stuff, they have piles of stuff, there's all these piles of stuff, so it's possible that it vanished into this maw of things. So that's one possibility. The other one is, maybe he fell on hard times in the Depression and he hawked it. I mean, I just had that thought. It doesn't sound like something he would do, but you never know.

Finances indeed may have been very tight for Orton around that time. He was the manager of the Municipal Stadium from 1928 to 1934, but when he lost that job, and its $10,000 annual salary, things got tight. The Great Depression caused financial ruin for many, and Orton's problems were likely compounded by the alimony payments he had to make to his first wife, Edith. George had married Edith Bolton soon after his divorce in 1932, and with no job to speak of in Philadelphia, he had considered moving to Hamilton, Ontario, so his wife could be closer to her family. He was all set to accept an offer from the Hamilton Olympic Club and McMaster University as director of athletics for the 1935 season when Edith contracted pneumonia in early March of 1935 and passed away in Philadelphia on March 13, at the age of 49. Cause of death was listed as acute cardiac dilatation. She was buried in Hamilton cemetery. Orton never did take the job in Hamilton.

Connie pulled another medal out of the box. "This has a beaver on it," she said.

"So, it's Canadian, for sure," I replied.

She looked at me with a puzzled expression. "Oh, is the beaver the sign of Canada?"

"Yes," I said, trying to stifle a laugh, "it's one of the symbols of Canada."

She then picked up a large magnifying glass in order to read the inscription. "It says Amateur Athletic Association of Canada and it has a beaver on it with a wreath around it."

It is a beautiful medal, made from sterling silver and stamped by a popular jeweller of the time, Richard Hemsley of Montreal. It's about the size of an Oreo cookie. There's no date or name on it, but it's almost a certainty that this was the medal awarded to Orton for his 1892 victory at Montreal. "The Toronto Lacrosse Club held its annual meeting last night," wrote the *Globe* in 1892, "and the feature of the evening was the presentation of a gold medal to Mr. Geo W. Orton of the club, who made a new Canadian record for the mile at the Montreal games."[1]

It's possible that the reporter was mistaken in calling it a gold medal. Gold was 40 times more expensive than silver at the time, and gold medals of any kind were extremely rare. Even at the Olympics, the winners received medals that were gilded with gold or gold-plated. Richard Hennick, who is now in charge of Hemsley's, was unable to find any history on this medal after I had sent him a picture of it. Richard Hemsley was responsible for some lovely custom-made pieces in the late 19th century, and this was certainly one of his most obscure and valuable creations. Since the modern Olympic Games didn't begin until 1896, a medal such as this, in 1892, would've been even more valuable at the time than an Olympic medal.

Dr. Bob Barney, from the Centre for Olympic Studies at Western University, said,

> George Orton's medal, his Olympic medal from 1900, I suspect that the one he got in Canada was greater in terms of looking at it, in terms of its consequence, its

The sterling silver medal won by Orton for capturing the mile run, in record time, at the 1892 Canadian championships in Montreal. His record of 4:21.8 lasted 42 years. Orton kept this precious medal, but his Olympic medal from 1900 has not been found.

physical properties, its lustre, rather than the … Exposition medal.… You showed me that and I had never seen that, but I see the trappings on it. The beaver is interesting because it was certainly a viable icon to the maple leaf at that time. The maple leaf has a deeply etched history in terms of Canadians being aware of it, and loving it and also the beaver.

Once Connie became aware of the significance of the beaver, and how important that 1892 medal must have been to her grandfather, she had a newfound appreciation for it. "I really didn't know the beaver was a national sign," she said. "It makes sense. It's so northern. When you look at the medal under the magnifying glass, it's even more beautiful. You can see the wreath and the beaver and everything."

So Orton's Olympic gold medal is out there somewhere. Were it to be found, it would be impossible to identify. Hundreds of medals would have been awarded in 1900, and with the exception of the event category stamped on the medal (*Jeux d'athletiques* for track and field), there is nothing to distinguish one medal from another. It's possible that the medal Orton received is sitting in a souvenir shop or is part of somebody's coin collection. It could be at the bottom of a box in an attic somewhere. But what if Connie were to find it?

> I mean, I would like to have it, but then the question is, I'm not going to live forever. I'm in my 70s. What would I do with it?… If I knew where it was and it came into my hands, I could … give it back to a Canadian museum or something.… If I had descendants, I would probably have different feelings about it, but there you are.

I mentioned to Connie that, were she amenable, the Canadian Sports Hall of Fame would probably love to have the sterling silver medal that Orton kept from the 1892 Canadian championships. I consider it to be a rare jewel, one of the earliest prizes awarded for excellence in Canadian athletics. I reached out to the hall to see if they were interested, but I never heard back.

Connie had saved the best for last. I was a bit disappointed not to see the Olympic medals, but that Canadian championship medal from 1892 was a real treat. I was not aware a medal like that even existed. Mark shot some video of me holding it in the palm of my hand, and we later took some still photos of the medal. I showed the image to several experts; none had ever seen a medal like it before.

Ever since I had heard Penn track coach Steve Dolan's wonderful speech at the Hall of Fame induction ceremony, I wanted to play it for Connie and record her reaction to it. I thought this would make a great ending to the documentary. But just as I was about to spring it on her, my iPhone battery went dead. We needed about 20 minutes to recharge it, and that gave us an opportunity to relax a bit. Connie had forgotten to mention a few things during the actual interview, including the first time she had met George:

> I don't think I knew I had a grandfather until we went to Camp Iroquois in 1946, when I was four. I guess he and I were supposed to get to know each other, but I was more interested in a litter of kittens that had been born to one of the feral cats on the property. I guess George wasn't used to having children around; he was in his 70s at the time. Anyway, we went for a walk down a dirt road that led to the highway — George, my mother, and me. There was a pond with lily pads. I had never seen lily pads before. That captured my attention much more than my grandfather.

When the battery was charged and Mark had set up the camera for our final interview, I handed Connie the cellphone. I wanted to get her reaction to the Hall of Fame speech, which contained comments about her grandfather she had wanted Steve Dolan to articulate to the audience on her behalf. Mark started recording as I hit "play" on the phone. She watched the introduction by emcee Dan Baker, and then Steve stepped to the microphone.

> It's an honour to be here. It's interesting when I was asked to give this honour tonight and speak on George Orton's behalf, I initially was kind of embarrassed I didn't have more history in my mind on the great George Orton. And then I realized, when George was in his heyday, that was the last time the [Chicago] Cubs won, and I didn't know much about that team either, so here I am. [Audience laughs.] As I dove into George Orton, it was actually fascinating. Frankly, I went from being embarrassed that I didn't know more to thinking I wish I could do more. Because George was incredible in all aspects. First of all from an educational background, George was born in Canada and went to the University of Toronto, where he was an all-star runner and was breaking records in Canada. Then he came to the University of Pennsylvania and did the same thing in the

United States. He set collegiate records in the mile and the steeplechase and was a multiple time national champion. In his time at Penn, he earned his master's and his doctorate in languages; he actually spoke nine languages, so very impressive and a very intelligent man.

When Connie heard that, the corners of her mouth formed a tiny smile and she raised her eyebrows. In editing, I would place that shot in when Dolan mentioned it. Connie kept watching.

While he was in the States, of course, the next thing that was just mentioned was he was an Olympic champion. So he is Canada's first gold medallist in winning the steeplechase. And anybody that debates track and field says [it's] one of the hardest events; well, the steeplechase and the 400 hurdles often come up as two of the hardest events. Well, in one singular day, he won one and was bronze in the other, so I can assure you of this as a track coach: George was a heck of a competitor.

At Penn, he did many things outside of competing. So in his time at Penn he was an all-around athlete — actually, George was an all-star soccer player and an all-star hockey player and played those sports for years and years. Actually [he] started the first college hockey team at Penn and coached it, and then went on to coach track and field at Penn as well. So he made huge contributions at Penn. So he was, as I said, the Penn Relays director, the track coach, and a super athlete at Penn. Also, he's really claimed as one of the authors of the Penn sports history publication, which is something we still cherish here at Penn, and in the city of Philadelphia.

Just to share this, I was very impressed with all the things that he did outside of athletics. So he did something really special: He started the Children's Playground Association in Philadelphia so the kids in the metropolitan area would have great places to play and things to do.

He also was credited with helping bring the Army-Navy football game to Philadelphia when he served as part of the group that was able to pull that off at Municipal Stadium. So George did so much for Philadelphia and he did so much for Penn, it's been a real honour.... His granddaughter asked me to make a few comments because she couldn't attend tonight.

At this point in Dolan's speech, Connie leaned forward and put the phone up to her ear. She had been looking at Dolan speaking from a podium, but now she really needed to *hear* him. She began to squint, just like her grandfather. Then came another tiny smile. This, I thought, will look great. She was listening more intently now.

So his granddaughter wanted me to mention that she had two words for her grandfather. One, that he was a legend.... He actually had an illness and health problems as a youth, to the point where he couldn't walk and couldn't run from a blood clot. He came back from that and they said, "Exercise would be excellent for you," and away he went as a runner, and run he did. He broke all kinds of records. And then secondarily, she talked about how intelligent he was. Not only did he know nine languages ... he was the master of mathematics. He could do calculus in his head.... So she mentioned those things about her grandfather.

She also wanted to give some perspective on what he was as a grandfather, or "grandpa," as she called him. For some perspective, she was 16 when he passed in 1958, and to give you a sense of the time frame, she just wanted you to know that she was a huge Elvis Presley fan; she thought it was important that I noted that. And she said to his passing day, he finished his years in New Hampshire and was a pretty private man at that point, but he said one of his slogans for life was "I'm going to walk a mile every day before breakfast," so the day he passed he was always very athletic. She said he played hockey and soccer until his 50s and 60s at a very high level. So for sure George was a legend in many ways, and it's really an honour to speak to you tonight. She wanted me to close with a comment that both her mother and sisters want to thank the Philadelphia Hall of Fame for honouring the great George Orton. Thank you.

The crowd had given Dolan a rousing ovation as he left the podium and walked back to his seat at the end of the dais. We'd made eye contact and I'd given him a "way to go" smile. He'd smiled back.

Later, seeing Connie's reaction, I remembered how wonderful I felt at that moment — like a proud great-grandson. I was hoping Connie would have similar feelings and we could capture them for the documentary. Mark had been recording her on an extreme close-up shot. Now I motioned for him to pull out to a wide shot of the two of us on the couch. I gently took the cellphone from Connie as the applause from the recording was dying down. She was stoic. Lips pursed. I waited for some kind of reaction. She was still processing, I guessed.

I asked what she thought of it, and she told me she thought it was very nice. I told her I wish she could've been there and she asked how many people had attended the induction ceremony. When I said it was about six hundred, she said, "Really? Great, great. Yeah. That's wonderful."

We then talked about how she was the last in the line of great Ortons. She said she had mixed feelings about it, that it was just the way things worked out for the family. "It just seems too bad," she said, " I feel like I didn't do my duty to the family line or something like that, but there it is."

I told her that, in a way, his legacy was going to live on through the documentary. She agreed, although she still seemed a bit sad. There was nothing more to say.

Mark and I packed up our gear and thanked Connie for allowing us into her home. I said I would keep her in the loop, and she said she would consider what to do with George's medal from 1892. We hugged. The kind of hug you give someone after a day of reminiscing.

★★★

When I began viewing the stuff Mark had shot, most of it was pretty good, although there were some shots that weren't going to work unless we fixed them in post-production. Some were shaky and the lighting was poor in others, but overall the sound was perfect, and that's what was most important. With a professional videographer, these issues likely wouldn't have come up, but Mark was not experienced, and our camera didn't measure up to a pro model. I cursed Mister X again under my breath.

But things were starting to look up as Mark and I drove north across the Golden Gate Bridge to record some on-camera pieces with San Francisco in the background — to show the viewer that I was actually there, rather than standing in front of a green screen pretending I was there.

Being from the area, Mark knew the best spots for capturing the most dramatic views of the city. From the northwest corner of the bridge, there's a view up into the hills that is spectacular and a bit scary (I have an aversion to heights). Mark told me not to look down or behind me, only at the camera as he framed me for the stand-up. I stood on the precipice with the Golden Gate Bridge in the background. We recorded a few takes, with me telling the viewer that I was about to meet George Orton's granddaughter and could hardly wait to see what she had in store for us. In the documentary, this piece would be known as a bridge. It's used to transition from one scene to another, seemingly advancing the story from Philadelphia to San Francisco. Even though I had already interviewed Connie, the stand-up was supposed to make it seem as if I was about to meet her. Shooting out of order is not uncommon, as long as it's in the proper order for the finished product.

The shot was beautiful, but the audio was terrible. A bit of ambient noise is expected when you are recording outdoors, but the combination of the wind and the traffic on the bridge made it tough to understand what I was saying. "You can always fix it in post," said Mark. He was right. I would have to re-record my audio in a studio and try to match it up so the sound would appear authentic. All I needed now was a partner who had access to a studio.

19

"HOWDY, PARTNER"

I said goodbye to Mark Steinberg and thanked him profusely for helping me out. He'd saved my ass. Driving back across the Golden Gate Bridge would have taken him out of his way — he was heading in the other direction, north. He asked if I'd be okay getting back to San Francisco, and I assured him I would. He dropped me off at the north side of the bridge, and I proceeded to take the most glorious walk back toward the city, along the most famous bridge in the world. It's about two miles from one side to the other, and it could not have been a nicer day for a walk.

That night I went to dinner with my cousins Mona, Kathy, and Roy. We had a great time catching up, but I admit I was preoccupied with thoughts of the documentary.

The next morning, Roy drove me to the airport, and on the flight home I watched all the footage Mark had shot and made notes. The next day, I watched 14 hours of footage and the interviews Nick had shot in Philadelphia. It was pretty good — better than I expected, actually. But I needed more. It was November 7, 2016, and I was hoping to have the project completed by the following spring. I needed a partner who wouldn't screw me around.

Brian Gard was the owner of a production company called Visual Rhodes. He wanted to put a weekly sports show together and contacted me in September 2016, asking if I wanted to host the show. I told Brian that my focus was on completing my documentary on George Orton, and I didn't have time to do any other projects. Brian had never heard of Orton before (no surprise), but after he heard the condensed version, he thought it was a great story and that we should stay in touch. A couple of months later, after I had come back from the U.S., I ran into one of Brian's associates, Derek Williams. He wanted to know how things were going, and when I told him I now needed a partner on the documentary, he called Brian up. Brian and I met again and agreed to become partners on the film. Brian would be the executive producer, editor, and cameraman. He had all the necessary equipment plus a full studio at Visual Rhodes. His background was in TV commercials, but this was an exciting opportunity to produce a wonderful story, and he was as enthusiastic about making the documentary as I was.

Brian and I decided on *The American Impostor* as the title. It was catchy, and the film had to have a name anyway, so what the hell. We were open to a title change down the road. I continued to research, write the narrative, and make appointments for interviews while Brian set up a shooting and editing schedule. We got down to business, but it didn't take long before we realized there wasn't enough footage for a feature-length film. More interviews were needed to fill in the gaps and advance the story. We needed plenty of b-roll, which is footage that can be intercut with the main shot and is relevant to the narrative. The viewer doesn't want to see a close-up of someone talking for more than a few seconds, so there has to be b-roll to cover those shots and make them visually appealing. As Brian explains,

> Mark and I realized that the film would be very flat without some action. We devised a plan to hire an actor who could play the part of George Orton. He needed to have blond curly hair, with the lean body of a distance runner. We wanted to do a number of location shots of George Orton running [that] could be incorporated into the film. They would be used as backdrops and for transitions from

one scene to the next. Mark found this amazing young high-school student from Dundas Valley Secondary School named Doug Keen. Doug was a 16-year-old middle-distance runner who could really pass for young George from a distance. When we saw him run, we knew he was the right choice. Like the real George Orton, Doug was a stylish runner who had a long, easy stride. He was slender like George, but a few inches taller. Since nobody alive had ever seen the real George Orton run, we didn't feel we were taking liberties by using Doug in the film. In fact, we nicknamed him "Doug Orton."

We shot several scenes with Doug in December and again in January 2017. We had him running across fields, along muddy pathways, and up and down hills. He wore black shorts, a navy blue crewneck sweatshirt, and black shoes with the white stripes blacked out by magic marker. We shot his scenes in a brownish sepia tone that made it appear to be from the late 19th century. Whenever we shot with Doug, the weather was either cold, damp cold, or bitterly cold.[1]

When I first interviewed Doug Keen, he asked me what kind of runner he was going to portray. I told him that nobody alive had ever seen Orton run, but I had seen pictures of him. He had been described as one who "stepped like a hackney horse." Doug had a similar style, one of high-stepping elegance that made us believe he really *was* George Orton. He was easygoing, took direction well, and was very professional about the whole thing. It was written that Orton's face rarely showed signs of strain or distress when he ran, that it was akin to a walk in the park. Doug was the same. We paid him $20 an hour at first, but he was so good and so believable once we saw the video, we felt guilty, so we doubled his rate.

Before we could begin editing, Brian and I took a trip to western Ontario to spend the day shooting interviews. Brian brought two cameras, two tripods, microphones, lights, and cables. We drove to Strathroy, Orton's birthplace, to interview the mayor and a couple of gentlemen from the Strathroy Historical Society who had previously written about Orton. It was

Doug Keen was a 16-year-old at Dundas Valley Secondary School in Ontario when I recruited him to play the part of George Orton in the documentary The American Impostor. *We took to calling him "Doug Orton" during the shooting of the film.*

the coldest day of the year, and the roads leading to Strathroy were treacherous. What should've been a two-and-a-half-hour drive ended up taking four hours. But it was worth it. After we told the mayor, Joanne Vanderheyden, that the picture associated with George Orton in the Strathroy newspaper was really that of his brother, she couldn't believe it.

> I have a twin, so you could use my twin's picture for me and get away with it, but this was a brother and not even a twin, so yeah, that's crazy.... So a reporter somewhere along the way wrote a story, couldn't find a picture of him, put his brother's picture in, thinking it was him. And all along you've got the wrong person. That's another edge to the story that makes it interesting.[2]

Next door to the Strathroy City Hall is the Library and Historical Society and Museum Strathroy-Caradoc. There we met researchers Bill Groot and Larry Peters. Both have a fondness for Orton because, up until a few years ago, they didn't know Canada's first Olympic champion was from their little corner of the world. There was a nice display in the library honouring Orton, and Brian set up the cameras there so we could do our interviews with the display in the background. Groot had done some deep research into Orton's Strathroy connection. He told us about the 1874 train accident involving Oliver Orton. "He was a real hero that night," said Groot. "He saved three or four lives by dragging those people off the tracks."[3]

I could tell how proud Bill was when he told us the story. It was thought that George Orton would've become famous, considering his athletic achievements, but he was simply a victim of bad timing. "If Orton had run in the Olympics in the 20s," said Larry Peters, "there might've been enough interest that he would've done for running what Bobby Jones did for golf, with those short films and exhibitions. In 1900, the possibility wasn't there."[4]

We thanked the folks in Strathroy, packed up our gear, and headed east, past the snow-blanketed fields of Mount Brydges and Komoka, along the rail line that Oliver Orton used to travel 150 years ago. We were headed to Western University in London to interview Dr. Robert "Bob" Barney, professor emeritus at Western's School of Kinesiology and the founding director of the International Centre for Olympic Studies. He is one of the world's foremost experts on the history of the modern Olympics and was elected Lifetime Honorary Member of the Canadian Olympic Association.

During the interview, Dr. Barney helped us understand the different factions that influenced amateur athletics in Orton's day. He, too, was happy that Orton was finally getting the recognition he deserved as a Canadian Olympian. Dr. Barney told us a great story about the 1908 Olympics in London, the first Games to include actual ceremonies involving the athletes.

> Canada had 32 athletes. They had beautiful dress uniforms with the maple leaf on the chest and a little cap and so on. They were a class act. In those days the parade was not into the stadium before the games but out of the stadium after the ceremony. They sort of shuffled in, lined in the infield, the ceremonies took place, and they went past the King around the stadium as they went out. That's different from today, but it was still a parade, and its uniforms and its contingents and its national symbols.[5]

While at Western, we also interviewed another man who had written about Orton. Mark Kearney co-authored *The Big Book of Canadian Trivia* with Randy Ray in 2009, the book in which the trivia question in question originated. "I had known about Orton being the first Canadian to win a gold medal," Kearney told us, "but when you say it to other people, they say 'never heard of him.' So that was an indication for me that it's a good question to put in the book."[6]

Leave it to the author of a Canadian trivia book to put things in perspective. We left western Ontario with some great stories and drove home through a blinding snowstorm, talking excitedly about creating this wonderful story about an obscure Canadian hero.

Brian and I also interviewed David Langford, the former sports editor of the *Globe and Mail* and *London Free Press*. I wanted his take on why the newspapers of Orton's day ignored this outstanding Canadian. For decades, there were hundreds of stories mentioning Orton, but none referred to him as a Canadian. I asked if that surprised him.

> It does surprise me, and it hurts me. It's shocking. But I one-hundred percent believe what you're saying, and it's very unfortunate. I don't know the reason why — that's the tough part. My initial thought, nobody's communicating. How are you talking to each other? Like the way now we look at Google and get the answers to any questions. Twenty years ago it was different. A hundred years ago, really different.[7]

If there was a newspaper editor who felt it wasn't worth publicizing Orton's achievements in the United States, that would be enough to make Orton *persona non grata*. Perhaps Canadians thought of him as a dirty American professional who would be paid to run. That would've been against their ethics at that time.

Still, how else do you explain that there's never a reference to Orton being Canadian for decades? I asked that question of Paul Berton, editor-in-chief of the *Hamilton Spectator*.

> If the newspaper wasn't writing about the local Olympic hero, then the local Olympic hero didn't matter, as strange as that may seem. But I do think it's sort of odd that no one phoned the editors of the day to say, "Hey, why aren't

you writing about this guy?" Because today we wouldn't get away with that.[8]

Mark Kearney found it very odd that nobody in Canada ever asked whatever happened to Orton. "Somewhere along the line, somebody must've said 'Wait a minute, George Orton, isn't that the guy who used to run around here and won all those big races?'"

The Canadian media had forgotten all about Orton. Even when he made news that was reported around the world, somehow Canadian journalists failed to include the fact that he was one of their own.

In April of 1944, Orton was interviewed by Ed Pollock, sports editor of the *Philadelphia Evening Bulletin*. At the time, it was believed nobody could run a mile in under four minutes. Sweden's Arne Andersson had run a 4:02.6 in Gothenburg, Sweden, in July 1943, but some doctors and scientists insisted it was physically impossible to run a mile in less than four minutes. Not difficult. Not dangerous. Impossible.

Orton had been asked about the four-minute mile in the 1930s and said it would never happen, but a decade later he told a different story. "You will be surprised to know that a runner once beat four minutes for the mile," Orton told Pollock. "His name was W.G. Lang. In 1863, he did a fraction under four minutes on a straightaway course." Apparently, because of the wind, Lang was not credited with the record. Orton insisted, contrary to popular belief, that the four-minute mile would soon be broken. This was big news. "It will take a runner like [Sweden's Gunder] Hagg to do it," said Orton. The first half must be done in 1:58 or better. A mile runner appreciates how fast that is."[9]

That interview made its way around the world. The *Ottawa Journal* ran the story but referred to Orton only as "the former University of Pennsylvania track coach." Nothing about his Canadian roots. The *Globe and Mail* ran the same copyright story on April 13, 1944, and then the next day, future Hall of Fame journalist Jim Coleman chimed in. "You may have noticed on this page yesterday in which Dr. George W. Orton says somebody some day will run a mile in under four minutes." Coleman continued, saying, "Dr. Orton is a Canadian, and many years ago at Varsity Stadium ran a mile in 4:21.4-5."[10]

Coleman had it half right. Orton was Canadian, but he set the mark in Montreal, not Toronto, and certainly not at Varsity. When, as predicted,

Roger Bannister became the first to break the four-minute mile in May of 1954, Orton's name came up as one of the greatest runners of all time. Sort of.

J.V. McAree of the *Globe* wrote:

> The fact that in recent years many great runners have been trying to beat the four-minute mark, and gradually approaching it, meant that sooner or later the goal would be reached. No Canadian sportswriter seems to have mentioned the fact that about the beginning of the century there was a famous mile runner, George Orton. We do not know what records he shattered or how he stood in international competition, but he was the best Canada had seen in many years. He stepped like a hackney horse and was a most stylish performer. We think he later became a medical doctor.[11]

It would have been easy for any reporter to find out what really happened to Orton. All McAree had to do was pick up a telephone and he would've discovered that Orton was *not* a medical doctor and had won all those championships, including an Olympic gold medal. Instead of chastising other scribes for not writing about Orton, McAree could've gotten his facts straight rather han speculate. Had he done so, Orton would've received some hard-earned recognition and not been mistaken for someone else. The fact is, Irvine Orton, George's brother, became a dentist in Rochester and Syracuse, New York. Maybe McAree got his Dr. Ortons mixed up. He wouldn't have been the first.

20

THE FOURTH ESTATE

Newspapers were the primary source of information for hundreds of years, and this book could not have been written without the liberal use of information gleaned from them. Until I became a journalist, I believed everything I read in the newspaper to be true. I was convinced that every story was based on facts obtained by the journalist from credible sources. I was taught that, even though you can't guarantee the absolute truth, a journalist has to strive for accuracy above all else. The relevant facts need to be checked and, if necessary, corroborated. Also, the story has to be balanced and objective and the reporter impartial, uninfluenced by special interests and unencumbered by conflicts of interest.

I learned that, in journalism, you own a story. If it's accurate and balanced, you will get the credit. But if mistakes are made, the reporter must accept responsibility and correct them as well as apologize for the errors.

I have no doubt that McAree, Coleman, and others who wrote about Orton had good intentions, but I am now challenging the accuracy of some of their stories. Fact-checking that should've been done at the time was ignored, and these inaccuracies have lived on and are taken as gospel. The more often they are referenced, the more untruths are perpetuated about Orton.

Not every story was checked thoroughly for accuracy. The principles of journalism were not always followed. Some published stories were not based on information collected and prepared by reporters; often they were press releases or announcements. Public-relations people and entrepreneurs were frequent visitors and callers to newsrooms, hoping to have a favourable story published or broadcast. When I worked in radio, the local wrestling promoter, Frank Tunney, would always drop by with a story about a wrestler, the upcoming fight card, and a bunch of free tickets to Maple Leaf Gardens. Within the hour, his press release was being read on the air, unedited. Occasionally, an advertiser wanted to promote an event they were sponsoring, so they would write something up and present it to the editor, who might publish it without so much as giving it a second look. There was no byline attached to the story, so if somebody complained, it would be difficult to point the finger of blame at an individual.

Imagine reading a great story and then learning later that it was completely fabricated. There's an oft-used expression credited to Mark Twain (although it could be an Irish proverb): *Never let the truth get in the way of a good story.*

For decades, the sportswriters in Canada ignored Orton or fabricated stories about him being a physician or attending school in Guelph or competing as an American. Even after it was discovered in the 1970s that he was Canadian born and raised, he received no accolades. I feel as if he and his accomplishments have been completely ignored and disrespected. The *Dictionary of Canadian Biography* STILL refuses to recognize Orton as a Canadian. The photo associated with George Orton is still the wrong one. One of the deans of Canadian sportswriting, W.A. Hewitt, in his book *Down the Stretch*, wrote that Orton "was a Toronto product who graduated from the University of Toronto in 1893 and later attended University of Pennsylvania." Hewitt did not mention Orton's 1900 gold medal performance at the Paris Olympics, the first by a Canadian. Had he known or cared, he could've written a great story. Instead, his omission helped drive Orton farther into the abyss of Canadian obscurity.

After he had been declared a Canadian, and even after his Olympic medals were officially taken away from the U.S. totals and added to the

Canadian tally, journalists still got it wrong. In 2004, Orton, the track and field star, was referred to as a swimmer by the *Globe and Mail*.[1]

In the June 27, 2017, edition of the *Toronto Star*, a feature on Canada's top summer athletes was published to commemorate Canada's 150th anniversary (the dreaded sesquicentennial). Olympic champions Donovan Bailey, Penny Oleksiak, and Rosie MacLennan were prominently featured, with photographs alongside their stories. George Orton was part of the article, as well, but the picture they used was the wrong one and the text said he competed for the United States at the Olympics.

Since I was in the midst of writing this book when that article was published, and I knew one of the co-authors, I got in touch to give him a heads-up that the story was wrong and that they needed to correct the mistake. This was done as a professional courtesy. Had I published an item or announced something on the air that contained incorrect information, I would certainly appreciate someone pointing it out to me so I could rectify the problem. In this case, no correction was made by the *Star* and I never heard back from the co-author. I also contacted the public editor of the *Star* by email to let her know the situation. I just wanted an acknowledgement that a mistake had been made and that it would be corrected. You've published this misinformation, at least run the right picture of the guy. She replied that she would look into it and get back to me. I never heard back.

Even though George Orton was not my real great-grandfather, I took this as a personal affront. It was disrespectful to the Orton family and, by extension, to me. Maybe someone at the *Star* will read this and publish the correct picture of Canada's first Olympic champion instead of a shot of his brother in future. From a journalistic standpoint, it would be the right thing to do. If you write something and publish it, you've got to own it.

I learned the hard way that if you try to fool someone and get caught, your credibility goes out the window. When I was hosting the radio phone-in show on 590/CKEY, the Toronto Maple Leafs were always the number one topic of conversation. It didn't even matter whether it was hockey season. At one point in 1982, the Leafs were in 21st place in a 21-team NHL. They were so bad, I suggested on the air that fans boycott the upcoming game against Detroit and send a message to owner Harold Ballard that something had to be done. Dozens of callers said they would join me in a boycott, and we organized a group to protest in front of Maple Leaf Gardens that Saturday night. I had made up placards that said "We're Number 21" and "Ballard Must Go." When Saturday night arrived, about a hundred or so listeners, some of whom brought their own signs, congregated on the street as thousands of fans made their way past us and into the Gardens. Someone told TV producer Ralph Mellanby about it (it might have been me), and pretty soon there were cameras recording us for the opening to *Hockey Night in Canada*, the most-watched TV show in the country.

I was in seventh heaven; you couldn't buy publicity like this. I started thinking about all the new listeners we could gain, and my ego got the best of me. The bright TV lights were on and we were protesting for the cameras. The newspapers also had photographers there to capture the moment. One fan had a dummy dressed up as Ballard with a hockey stick inserted into its backside. It was a beautiful protest. Just then, a guy showed up holding a fistful of tickets for the game that night. Eight or ten of them. He must've been really pissed at the Leafs because suddenly, in front of all the cameras, he produced a lighter and LIT THE TICKETS ON FIRE!

I don't know who the guy was, but he turned a really good protest into a great one. We all gathered around the burning tickets while the photographers recorded the moment. The Leafs lost that night, and the next day, Sunday, the picture on the front page of the *Star* was of your humble reporter and his minions holding up placards and burning Maple Leafs hockey tickets. The Sunday *Sun* also had a story and a picture. The *Globe and Mail* did not publish on Sundays, but the next day an article appeared by the fine journalist Allen Abel. He and his photographer had picked up the charred tickets from the sidewalk. They were not Maple Leafs tickets; they were Toronto Marlies junior hockey tickets, which looked exactly the same, with a big Maple Leaf and the colour and section where the seats were (gold, red, blue, green, or grey). I was accused of perpetrating a hoax. The guy who lit them pulled a fast one on everybody, but I was the one who paid for it. My boss suspended me for two weeks for besmirching the reputation of the radio station, even though I had done so unwittingly. Lesson learned.

21

"WE'LL FIX IT IN POST"

Brian Gard and I finished recording our interviews and shooting the other footage, and now it was time to go into the editing suite and put the documentary together.

The editing software Brian used in his studio was terribly underpowered for this task, much to our consternation. We discovered this while transferring the 4K video footage from the camera to the editing software; it was taking far too long. For every minute of video, it took 10 minutes of real time to render and refresh. At this rate, it would take 400 hours before we could even begin editing. When you're trying to tell a story, you need to get into a rhythm, and we couldn't do that. We ended up editing segments in 30-second pieces, and it looked like crap. Brian and I agreed that we would end up killing each other if this pace continued, so we had to buy a new suite. Once that was in, we really started to hum along.

The opening scene is set to banjo music. The camera was placed on train tracks, and the shot looked down the tracks into the distance, with a beautiful blue sky as the backdrop. The silhouette of a runner is heading toward the camera along the train tracks. It's Doug Keene, playing the part of the young George Orton. As he comes closer, you can't quite make out his face; only that he has curly blond hair and runs with an elegant stride. The opening credits roll as he approaches the camera and a few seconds later runs right through the shot. This scene took the most time to get right because we were certain that if the audience didn't connect with George Orton in the first minute or so, we might lose them. So the opening scene had to be special.

Then we went to footage of us posing the trivia question to various people: "Who was the first Canadian to win an Olympic gold medal?"

January, February, and most of March in 2017 were spent in the editing suite. I would write the scenes and find the corresponding visuals, then we'd assemble them with music and effects, if necessary. The story started to take shape and we could soon see the finish line. Meanwhile, I had to keep a full script and transcribe every word spoken, every visual and musical clip used, every name and title. You name it. All items had to be numbered. Every word and sentence had to be double-checked for spelling and punctuation. The result was a 206-page manuscript and a 58-minute documentary. We went through about 40 hours of video and over 600 photos, newspaper articles, documents, screen grabs, and other still shots. When it was finally finished, we agreed to take the weekend off, then come back and look at it with clear heads.

A week later we had changed the beginning, the end, and almost everything in between. Editing can be cruel. The problem was simple: I wasn't telling a story so much as narrating one. Rather than go into a studio and voice-over some footage, I needed to get out there and tell the story on camera, face to face with the audience. Brian and I re-shot nearly every stand-up. The changes made a huge difference, and a few weeks later we had a documentary that was pretty darned good. Brian then took over trying to find a distributor:

> I approached several distributers in Canada and got absolutely no interest in the film. A little bit of a shock and really devastating. Most told us that Canadian-content films were of little interest to the Canadian viewing public. So we went to the U.S. distribution market. A few of them

responded positively and were much more interested in distributing the film. By this time, Mark had been offered a publishing deal after somebody influential saw a rough cut of the documentary and suggested he write a book.

I had actually sent a finished copy of the doc to a few influential people. Some liked it more than others, but everyone thought it had potential. I received some good advice about the publishing business versus the TV and film business. I found out that 90 percent of all books are purchased around Christmas, and in Canada sports books don't sell very well unless they're about hockey. By seeing the story in documentary form, these people got a sense of how the book could turn out rather than guessing what the story was about.

Another problem with the documentary was late-arriving information. Once the film was "in the can," some information I had not been aware of came to light. I couldn't go back and update the film, so the opportunity to write a book would allow me to include some of these late-arriving stories that didn't make into the documentary.

Maddison Oswald is from Pilot Butte, Saskatchewan, a town of 2,000 people just outside of Regina. When she was 12 years old, in 2009, she did a project on George Orton for her grade seven class. Somehow, the project found its way to the internet via YouTube, and that's when I discovered that somebody else in this country once had a keen interest in finding out more about the man I was writing about. When I contacted Maddison in early 2018, she was completing her fourth year at the University of Regina, working toward a degree in human justice with a criminal justice concentration, as well as a degree in psychology and a minor in French.

I asked her how she ended up doing a school project on, of all people, George Orton.

"The reason I chose to direct my focus on George Washington Orton was simply that he was responsible for a remarkable and significant detail in Canadian history — one that went unrecognized for a substantial amount of time," she said. "I can recall searching dozens of web pages for an answer to my question: Who was the first Canadian Olympic medallist? The results were conflicting. Half claimed that Orton was the first and the other half pointed toward another athlete, so I felt that I had to figure out which was accurate." She said that once she discovered that Orton held the title, his story did not disappoint. "I have always been determined to get to the truth, even as a child, so I feel grateful that I came across Orton's story early on in my academic career. I do remember the entire project took, from start to finish, about a month." Not surprisingly, she said the lengthiest part of the project was the research aspect. She found out, as I had, that information about Orton was very difficult to find. "I was wary of committing to a project where the research was so contradictory," she added. "However, after sticking with it, it turned out well and I'm happy to still have the knowledge of Orton today."

I asked if she felt Orton's accomplishments had slipped through the cracks of Canadian history.

"Absolutely," she said. "I recall reading in several accounts that his official records were either never recorded or destroyed, which definitely adds to the confusion that surrounded his achievements. In addition, it strikes me as odd that Orton's name was never mentioned once in my history classes or any class for that matter. I am able to name the first NHL player to score a goal and the first Grey Cup winners, but I had no knowledge of the first Canadian Olympic medallist. So to answer your question, yes, I would argue that Orton and his accomplishments were neglected immensely, not maliciously, but neglected nonetheless."

I asked if she recalled any comments she received from teachers, students, or parents about the project and the subject matter. Maddison told me her teacher was quite excited about her chosen topic. "She and I always got along very well because we were both avid sports fans, so she was excited to see the information I had found. As for other students, I think that the types of projects that were completed kind of clumped together by subject matter." She said her project fell under "Heritage Fair," which happened every second year at the school and for which each student would do a project looking at an aspect of Canadian history. "At this time, I was playing hockey," she explained, "so my other friends and teammates who were also completing these projects took interest in mine as I took interest in theirs, as we all had a tendency to lean toward sports history in Canada."

The visual presentation that I'd seen was quite extensive, and I wondered if it had been an enjoyable experience for her. "To be truthful, throughout my elementary school years we were required to research and present projects that focused on parts of Canadian history every year. While they were all equally interesting and important, this one is the only one that has stuck with me for this long. I think that the enjoyment that I pulled from this specific project comes from the fact that Orton's particular story felt to me as though it was a piece of lost history. The uncertainty of who the medal belonged to and how long it remained unknown to Canadians really created a sense of pride once it was discovered as it was like finding something you didn't know was lost. The talent that he possessed was remarkable and he deserves to be recognized." She added, "I find it quite sad knowing that he likely passed away never knowing the impact that he had on Canadian history or having anything to show for it."[1]

I wondered if there were other students like Maddison who had heard the name George Orton but couldn't find enough information via the internet and abandoned their research. There wasn't much of a story for them to tell. Hopefully, future students will find an abundance of information available should they choose to do a project on a great Canadian.

22

THE LAST MILE

George Orton's golden years were spent mostly in New Hampshire with his stepdaughter, Doris Bolton. Twice a year, however, he went to work in Media, Pennsylvania, just outside Philadelphia. The Rose Tree Fox Hunting Club was located there, and every spring and fall, for four weeks at a time, Orton would work long hours there.

He was 41 years old when he began as the club's publicist and racing secretary in 1914. Rose Tree offered fox hunts and other riding adventures to its members, but its main attraction was horse racing, and in particular, steeplechase or "jump" racing. It's interesting that one of the world's great human steeplechasers would be so deeply involved with the equine version of the sport. Both involve athleticism, strength, speed, endurance, and sure-footedness.

The famous Grand National steeplechase, run at Aintree near Liverpool, England, began in 1839 and is the most prominent of all jump races. The Grand National course is nearly seven kilometres long, with a total of 30 jumps for horse and rider to negotiate. Like the Kentucky Derby in

America, the Grand National is popular in England among those who don't normally watch or bet on horse racing.

Rose Tree was the first American club to offer jump racing, even before the Civil War began (the wealthy DuPont clan and other prominent Philadelphia families were founding members). By the early 20th century, thoroughbred or "flat" racing was the most popular sport to bet on, but an anti-gambling sentiment had begun to sweep the nation. In 1908, the Hart-Agnew Law barred wagering at racetracks. By 1911, the State of New York had fully and completely shut down flat racing.[1] Since steeplechase had a different aesthetic and appealed more to the sporty, outdoors type, it had never been dependent on wagering. Once flat racing began its decline, jumping courses sprouted up at places like Belmont Park and Saratoga, where the Whitneys and Vanderbilts owned the finest horses, many of them top jumpers. Without flat racing to bet on, many city slickers set out for the countryside to watch the jumpers in action. The Meadow Brook Cup was first run in 1883 on Long Island. The Maryland Hunt Cup had its first running in 1894. By the time Orton started at Rose Tree, two more Maryland races had been sanctioned by the National Steeplechase and Hunt Association, the sport's governing body since 1895.

Orton's knowledge of cross country and steeplechase made him, once again, the perfect man for the job. Rose Tree's hiring of Orton would prove to be a shrewd move. His business acumen allowed the club to become profitable very quickly. The wealthy members now had to pay higher annual fees, and those who wished to participate in the fox hunts were assessed a premium. The money went toward improving the facilities and attracting top horses, trainers, and jockeys for the spring and fall meetings.

Orton's name and reputation helped, too. He was constantly sending out press releases trumpeting the upcoming racing cards and profiling the top horses, trainers, owners, and riders. The publicity paid off. Large crowds began attending the races at Rose Tree while Orton looked after tickets, admissions, concessions, parking, and a multitude of other responsibilities. And he loved it, apparently. When asked by a reporter whether he had ever ridden a horse, the kind-faced, bespectacled man admitted that he hadn't, despite his 40 years at Rose Tree. His best year was when the greatest horse not named Secretariat appeared at Rose Tree. "The biggest crowd we ever had was 1928," Orton told a reporter. "That was the year Riddle brought

Man O' War here. Why, you couldn't get all the people in. Now, there was a horse.... Man O' War was the only horse I ever saw about which I couldn't find some fault. From every angle he was perfect."[2]

Riddle was Samuel Riddle, the owner of Man o' War, who was as famous as Babe Ruth and Jack Dempsey in the 1920s. Riddle was an honorary president at Rose Tree and later owned 1937 Triple Crown winner War Admiral. Man o' War was a legendary racehorse, having won 20 out of 21 races. His only loss was to a horse named Upset. What a thrill it must've been that day in 1928 when he appeared at Rose Tree. "I love horses and racing very much," said Orton in 1955, "but my best sports have always been track, ice hockey and soccer. If I hadn't banged my knee so bad from playing soccer and ice hockey in my younger days, I would be very active in pushing for a big arena and big time ice hockey in Philadelphia."[3]

Orton also kept up a lively correspondence with the alumni associations at Penn and the University of Toronto. In January of 1950, he wrote a letter to the head of the University College alumni, enclosing a cheque to cover his annual dues. In it, he wrote, "Though I graduated in 1893, I still take interest in the University. I am 77, but very thankful that I am in very good health and mentally as good as ever, whatever that might mean."

Later that year, while working at Rose Tree, Orton was profiled in the *Chester* (Pennsylvania) *Times*:

> Speaking to Dr. Orton in his crowded office, one is astonished to find that this former scholar of languages was an athlete of note. He was a distance runner, a champion one.... Dr. Orton is a short, thin, wiry man. His right arm is injured and his left eye is poor. In spite of ill health in his childhood, in spite of too many injuries during his life, Dr. Orton persisted in developing himself physically and building himself up. Because of his injuries he does not hunt and of course does not ride.[4]

In March of 1951, Orton wrote to the *Pennsylvania Gazette*, Penn's alumni publication, reporting that he was pretty shaken up after suffering a broken collarbone in an auto accident. The other driver, he wrote, was at fault and had to pay for the car and a doctor. He went on to say he was busy collecting data and writing a history of Rose Tree Fox Hunting Club and was hoping to have it finished in time for the club's 100th anniversary (he missed it by one year).

Meanwhile, Orton's damaged right hand no longer worked properly, and in late 1952 he lost the full use of the hand. In August of 1954, at age 81, he wrote that he was still driving but that the car was in the shop with clutch trouble. Considering he had lost the use of his right hand, one wonders how difficult it must've been to drive a car with standard transmission.

Although he hadn't been part of the Philadelphia sports scene for two decades, the 84-year-old Orton was honoured along with other great athletes on March 28, 1957, at the Penn Alumni Varsity Club dinner, where he was reacquainted with his old teammate and business partner, Dr. Josiah McCracken, whom he had not seen in more than 50 years.

A few weeks later, on May 18, he wrote rather than typed a letter on Rose Tree stationery to a man named Leonard. In it, he says "eighty-four years of age seems to be a special point as I had no trouble until I got to that age…. I've given up driving as I have very little use for a car now." Orton's handwriting is difficult to decipher, but at the end of the letter he writes, "I am probably the only man in the U.S. alive who is a member of the American Academy of Poets, which is wholly undeserved, and has also been elected to the American Track and Field Hall of Fame."

Sadly, the second part of that statement was not true. Orton may have been told he was going to be inducted, but he never was. Not until 1974 did the National Track and Field Hall of Fame begin inducting people. Mind you, he should be in. After all, how can they overlook a record 17 national championships, his success with the Penn Relays, and two Olympic medals on the track?

Orton's final public appearance was in April of 1958 when he fired the starter's pistol to open the Penn Relays at Franklin Field. Sixty-three years earlier, he had won the mile at the inaugural Penn Relays, and now, at the age of 85, he was being honoured for his service. A few days later, barely able to walk, the greatest runner of his generation would enter hospital in New Hampshire. On a Tuesday evening, June 24, 1958, George Washington Orton passed away peacefully.

He would never know how much of an impact he had on the lives of thousands. But I know — he was quite a man.

EPILOGUE

Before sitting down to tackle this book, I read Stephen King's *On Writing: The Memoir of a Craft*. In it, King mentions how important it is for him to stay in good physical and mental shape during the writing process. Spending that many hours a day behind a keyboard without doing some form of physical activity can only lead to problems. I discovered this after a few short days; the more I wrote, the heavier I got. This unhealthy practice had to end, and it was George Orton who was going to help me get in shape.

Inspired by my subject, I took up running. At first, I could run only a few blocks before becoming winded. The more I wrote about Orton, the better I got at running. Soon, I could run a kilometre without stopping. Then two, three, four, and finally up to five kilometres. Each day, I looked forward to two things: writing and running. In that order. I would write for four or five hours and then get the urge to run, like Orton. I followed the instructions from his book: head held high, arms pumping back and forth instead of side to side, breathing through the nose instead of the mouth. If nothing else, I learned how to stay in shape. Thanks for the inspiration, George. Whenever I ran, you were running with me.

ACKNOWLEDGEMENTS

I could not have possibly written this book without the help and support of many people.

At Dundurn, my editors Allison Hirst and Jenny McWha were extremely patient with me, for which I am thankful. As a first-time author, the publishing business was quite foreign to me, and these ladies helped guide me through the process while cleaning up any mess that I had created. Copy editor Patricia MacDonald and publicist Elham Ali should also be recognized here for their fine work. Brian Gard, my partner in the documentary, was extremely supportive and loved the story (almost) as much as I did. From a research standpoint, Mark Frazier Lloyd, Dave Johnson, and Ken Avallon provided an abundance of material for me on Orton's life in Philadelphia, specifically at the University of Pennsylvania. Brad Marsh and the other members of the Philadelphia Flyers alumni were extremely excited to find out about the father of Philadelphia hockey, and encouraged me to tell them more. Dr. Robert K. Barney and Dr. Bruce Kidd were kind enough to share their stories of the early days of track and field in Canada and at the Olympics. Bill Groot and Larry Peters provided solid information on Orton's early days in Strathroy, and Kim McInnis unearthed a good deal of information on his life in Winchester. Mark Luff and the good folks at Camp Tecumseh provided numerous photos and stories about Orton's life at camp.

Connie Meaney was kind enough to invite me to her home in San Francisco and share her grandfather's story for several hours. Her contribution to this book cannot be understated. Mark Steinberg, Brian Salvatore and Nick Mosher shot beautiful pictures and sound for the documentary, and helped craft the story on a visual level.

My very good friend Jake Gold, of the Management Trust, believed in the project from the beginning, and was instrumental in getting a publishing deal done.

My sons, Jake and Dean Hebscher, thought it was pretty cool that their dad was writing a book. Now that it's done, I hope they'll read it.

My parents, Sid and Sylvia, have always encouraged my creativity. My mom was the first to read a copy of the manuscript, and then passed it on to my dad. They both said they enjoyed it immensely. That's good enough for me.

Appendix

ORTON'S ATHLETIC VICTORIES

1900 PARIS OLYMPIC GAMES
2,500-METRE STEEPLECHASE: *GOLD MEDAL*
400-METRE HURDLES: *BRONZE MEDAL*

U.S. NATIONAL CHAMPIONSHIPS (17)
1-MILE RUN: 1892, 1893, 1894, 1895, 1896, 1900
5-MILE RUN:1892
2-MILE STEEPLECHASE: 1893, 1894, 1896, 1897, 1898, 1899, 1901
CROSS COUNTRY: 1897, 1898
10-MILE RUN: 1899

CANADIAN CHAMPIONSHIPS (7)
1-MILE RUN: 1892, 1893, 1894, 1895
2-MILE RUN: 1893, 1894, 1897

EUROPEAN CHAMPIONSHIPS (3)
1-MILE RUN, INDOORS: 1898 (BRUSSELS)
1-MILE RUN, OUTDOORS: 1900 (BRUSSELS)
2-MILE RUN: 1898 (PARIS)

ENGLISH CHAMPIONSHIPS (1)
2-MILE STEEPLECHASE: 1898 (STAMFORD BRIDGE, LONDON)

WORLD CHAMPIONSHIPS (4)
1-MILE RUN: 1893 (CHICAGO)
2-MILE STEEPLECHASE: 1893 (CHICAGO)
1,500-METRE RUN: 1898 (BERLIN)
1,800-METRE RUN: 1898 (BERLIN)

NOTES

Chapter 1: The Biggest Race of His Life

1. Donald W. Hendrickson, "A New Factor in Missouri Valley Athletics" (Wichita: Kansas Magazine Co., 1909), 31.
2. George W. Orton, "America's Chances in To-Day's Paris Games," *Philadelphia Inquirer*, July 14, 1900.
3. George W. Orton, "America Holds Superiority," *Philadelphia Inquirer*, July 31, 1900.
4. George Orton, "The Paris Athletic Games," *Outing* magazine, September 1900, 691.
5. George W. Orton, "America Holds Superiority," *Philadelphia Inquirer*, July 31, 1900.
6. *New York Times*, July 17, 1900.
7. George W. Orton, *Distance and Cross Country Running* (New York: American Sports Publishing Company, 1903), 15.
8. George W. Orton, "Penn's Athletes Shake Their Legs," *Philadelphia Inquirer*, January 7, 1901.

9. "About Various Sports," *Buffalo Courier*, July 7, 1893. Orton wins one- and five-mile AAU titles.

10. "A Famous Victory," *Toronto Daily Star*, July 18, 1900.

11. Gaétan Sanfaçon, "Etienne Desmarteau," *Dictionary of Canadian Biography*, vol. 13 (Toronto and Laval, QC: University of Toronto/Université Laval, 1994).

12. Stephanie Abba (*Dictionary of Canadian Biography*), email to the author, November 14, 2017.

13. *Olympic Review* 193 (November 1983): 781, 782.

Chapter 2: The Documentary

1. *Globe*, February 28, 1874.

2. *An Historical Sketch of the Village of Winchester (Old Home Reunion August 4–8, 1934)*, historical review of Winchester, published in connection with centennial celebrations, June 23, 24, 25, 1967.

3. Bob Finucane, "Bob Tales," *Chester (PA) Times*, May 15, 1942.

Chapter 3: The Boy Who Never Walked

1. Nathan B. Stouffer, "College Track Athletics," *Appleton's Magazine*, January–June 1905, 674.

2. Nathan P. Stouffer, "College Track Athletics," *Appleton's Magazine*, New York, January–June 1905, 674.

3. *Philadelphia Bulletin*, December 19, 1905.

4. "Athletics," *Globe*, September 28, 1891.

5. *Varsity* (University of Toronto), October 6, 1891.

6. *Varsity*, October 6, 1891 to March 22, 1892, 157

7. *Varsity*, October 12, 1892 to March 29, 1893, 144.

8. *Census of Canada, 1851–1921*.

9. "Athletics," *Globe*, October 18, 1892.

10. "Athletics," *Globe*, October 18, 1892.

11. "Athletics," *Globe,* October 21, 1892.

12. "Activity in Athletics," *Philadelphia Inquirer*, December 24, 1900.

13. "Collegiate Athletics," *Globe*, September 3, 1892.

14. "Geo. Orton Marvel of Athletic Ability," *Philadelphia Bulletin*, January 12, 1921.

15. *Chicago Tribune*, August 8, 1893.

16. "Athletics, Canadian Championships," *Globe*, September 19, 1893.

17. *Philadelphia Inquirer*, May 11, 1953.

18. *Akron Daily Herald*, October 14, 1893.

19. "Geo. Orton Marvel of Athletic Ability," *Philadelphia Bulletin*, January 12, 1921.

20. George W. Orton, *Distance and Cross Country Running* (New York: American Sports Publishing Company, 1903), 15.

Chapter 4: A Dirty Pro

1. *Ottawa Evening Journal*, June 10, 1895.

2. Dr. Bruce Kidd (vice-president, University of Toronto), in discussion with the author, December 16, 2016.

3. Kidd, in discussion with the author.

4. *Toronto Star*, September 21, 1895.

5. Dr. Robert Barney (professor emeritus, Western University), in discussion with the author, December 15, 2016.

6. Kidd, in discussion with the author.

7. "For the Purity of Sport," *Globe*, September 6, 1897.

8. Andy Lytle, "Echo of Flying Feet," *Toronto Daily Star*, August 11, 1936.

9. "George Orton Exonerated," *Globe*, December 22, 1897.

10. Ron Flatter, "Thorpe Preceded Deion, Bo," ESPN.com, accessed April 23, 2007.

11. Bert Randolph Sugar, *Hit the Sign* (Chicago: Contemporary Books, 1978), 100.

12. *Winnipeg Tribune*, October 4, 1913.

13. Peter Unwin, "Who Do You Think I Am? The Story of Tom Longboat," CanadasHistory.ca, September 13, 2015.

14. Flatter, "Thorpe Preceded Deion, Bo."

15. Kidd, in discussion with the author.

Chapter 6: Philadelphia Freedom

1. William H. Rocap, "Seventeen Titles for Orton," *Philadelphia Public Ledger*, January 7, 1923.

2. Rocap, "Seventeen Titles for Orton."

3. "Yale Won the Relay," *Philadelphia Times*, May 31, 1895.

4. Letter to University of Pennsylvania Alumni Association from University of Western Ontario, November 26, 1975.

5. "Oxford-Cambridge Four Wins," *New York Times*, May 2, 1920.

6. *Philadelphia Inquirer*, May 28, 1950.

7. Bruce Kidd, *The Struggle for Canadian Sport* (Toronto: University of Toronto Press, 1996), 41.

8. Dave Johnson (director, Penn Relays), in discussion with the author, November 2, 2016.

Chapter 7: The Father of Philly Hockey

1. *Toronto Star*, January 25, 1897.

2. "A Varsity Canadian Club," *Philadelphia Inquirer*, April 4, 1896.

3. *Baltimore American*, December 27, 1894.

4. *Montreal Gazette*, December 17, 1936.

5. *Lincoln Evening Call*, January 11, 1895.

6. W.A. Hewitt, *Down the Stretch* (Toronto: Ryerson Press, 1958), 32, 33.

7. "Mr. Pond Smashed Mr. George Orton," *Philadelphia Inquirer*, February 20, 1897. See also "A Fine Hockey Row," *Baltimore Sun*, February 20, 1897.

8. "A Fine Hockey Row," *Baltimore Sun*, February 20, 1897.

9. "Ice Sports," *Amateur Athlete*, vol. 2, March 4, 1897, 17.

10. *Brooklyn Daily Eagle*, December 18, 1919.

11. *Pittsburgh Press*, July 21, 1917.

12. "Orton Skates in 3:59.1," *Philadelphia Inquirer*, January 20, 1899.

13. *Chicago Tribune*, December 21, 1894.

14. *Providence Sunday Journal*, July 17, 1955.

15. *Brooklyn Daily Eagle*, January 5, 1901.

16. Bob Kitirinos, "A Letter: 115 Years of Ice Hockey at Penn," The Buzz blog, *Daily Pennsylvanian*.

17. "Skating News," *Billboard*, February 7, 1920.

18. "Plan to Number Players …," *New York Tribune*, February 1, 1914.

19. "Plan to Number Players …"

20. Howard Butcher IV, phone conversation with the author, December 11, 2017.

Chapter 8: Family Life

1. Constance Meaney, interview with the author, San Francisco, November 5, 2017.
2. *Philadelphia Inquirer*, December 24, 1900.
3. *Philadelphia Inquirer*, December 24, 1900.
4. "George Orton Is a Busy Man," *Toronto Star*, January 16, 1901.
5. Adam R. Hornbuckle, *American National Biography*, vol. 16 (New York: Oxford University Press, 1999), 775–76.
6. "History of Playgrounds and Parks," nycgovparks.org.
7. George W. Orton, *Athletic Training for School Boys* (New York: American Sports Publishing, 1905), 15, 17.
8. "Now My Idea Is This!" *Philadelphia Evening Ledger*, July 24, 1926.

Chapter 9: Author, Author

1. Orton, *Distance and Cross Country Running*, 9.
2. Orton, *Distance and Cross Country Running*, 11.
3. Carlie Oreskovich, *Sir Henry Pellatt: The King of Casa Loma* (Toronto: McGraw Hill-Ryerson, 1982), 19.
4. Orton, *Distance and Cross Country Running*, 9, 11.
5. "The Fastest Mile Runner," *Buffalo Evening News*, October 28, 1888.
6. "The Fastest Mile Runner," *Buffalo Evening News*.
7. Orton, *Distance and Cross Country Running*, 11, 13.
8. Orton, *Distance and Cross Country Running*, 11, 13.
9. Margaret Costa and Sharon R. Guthrie, *Women and Sport: Interdisciplinary Perspectives* (Champaign, IL: Human Kinetics, 1994), 125.
10. *Ripley's Believe It or Not*, King Features Syndicate, June 25, 1943.
11. *New York Evening World*, June 13, 1912.
12. *New York Times*, July 19, 1913.
13. John Thorn, *Ida Schnall and the New York Female Giants*, Our Game, mlb.com.
14. *Cornell Law School's Legal Information Institute (20 U.S. Code § 1681 — Sex).*
15. *Pittsburgh Daily Post,* March 7, 1926.
16. Orton, *Athletic Training for School Boys*, 7.

Chapter 10: North America's Athletic Missionaries

1. Kidd, in conversation with the author.
2. Kidd, in conversation with the author; Robert Barney, in conversation with the author, December 15, 2016.
3. George Orton, "America's Chances in To-day's Paris Games," *Philadelphia Inquirer*, July 14, 1900.
4. George Orton, "Penn's Athletes Had a Pleasant Sea Voyage," *Philadelphia Inquirer*, July 9, 1900.
5. George Orton, "Penn's Athletes Had a Pleasant Sea Voyage," *Philadelphia Inquirer*, July 9, 1900.

Chapter 11: Bonjour, Paris!

1. Kevin B. Wamsley, "American Boys in Paris: Canadian Participation in the Games of 1900," *Fourth International Symposium for Olympic Research,* 135–39.
2. *Toronto Mail and Empire*, June 26, 1900.
3. Fred G. Clark, *1903–1993 Camp Tecumseh* (West Kennebunk, ME: Phoenix Publishing, 1994), 5.
4. Mark Dyreson, *Making the American Team* (Chicago: University of Illinois Press, 1998), 62.
5. William Oscar Johnson, "The Taking Part," *Sports Illustrated*, July 10, 1972, 38.
6. George Orton, "America Holds Superiority," *Philadelphia Inquirer*, July 31, 1900.
7. George Orton, "Sunday Question Viewed at Paris," *Philadelphia Inquirer*, August 4, 1900.
8. Orton, "Sunday Question Viewed at Paris."
9. Orton, "Sunday Question Viewed at Paris."
10. "Orton Meets Defeat," *New York Times*, July 17, 1900.
11. "Americans Get Big Handicaps," *Pittsburgh Daily Post*, July 20, 1900.
12. Mark Dyreson, *Making the American Team* (Chicago: University of Illinois Press, 1998), 66.
13. Bill Mallon, *The 1900 Olympic Games: Results for All Competitors in All Events, with Commentary* (Jefferson, NC: McFarlane, 1994); *Pittsburgh Press*, July 21, 1900; "Paris Athletic Games Concluded," *Philadelphia Inquirer*, July 23, 1900.

14. *New York Times*, July 15, 1900.

15. George Orton, "The Paris Athletic Games," *Outing* 36 (September 1900): 691–93.

16. "Smaller Crowd at Paris Fair," *Chicago Tribune*, July 21, 1900.

17. Dyreson, *Making the American Team*, 71.

18. *Philadelphia Inquirer*, August 4, 1900.

19. David Miller, *The Official History of the Olympic Games and the IOC — Athens to Beijing, 1894–2008* (Edinburgh: Mainstream Publishing, 2008).

20. George Orton, "The Paris Athletic Games," *Outing* 36 (September 1900): 693.

21. George Orton, "New Power in Athletics Coming," *Philadelphia Inquirer*, August 13, 1900.

Chapter 12: Heavy Medals

1. David Dupuis, "Penetanguishene's First Olympic Star," 2011, Penetanguishene Sports Hall of Fame, pshof.ca.

2. David Wallechinsky and Jaime Loucky, *The Book of Olympic Lists* (London: Aurum Press, 2012), 152.

3. Dyreson, *Making the American Team*, 67.

4. Margolit Fox, *Margaret Abbott: The First American*, pulse.ng; *New York Times*, March 9, 2018.

Chapter 13: "Making Good Boys Better"

1. Clark, *1903–1993 Camp Tecumseh*, 1, 2, 4, 8, 9, 18, 25.

2. Mark Luff, in discussion with the author, Episcopal Academy, Philadelphia, November 3, 2016.

3. Clark, *1903–1993 Camp Tecumseh*, 49.

4. Luff, in discussion with the author.

Chapter 14: The Philly Hall of Fame

1. Jimmy Watson, in discussion with the author, Philadelphia Sports Hall of Fame, November 3, 2016.

2. Brad Marsh, in discussion with the author, Philadelphia Sports Hall of Fame, November 3, 2016.

3. Doug Crossman, in discussion with the author, Philadelphia Sports

Hall of Fame., November 3, 2016.

4. Frank Miraglia, in discussion with the author, Philadelphia Sports Hall of Fame, November 3, 2016.

5. Don Saleski, in discussion with the author, Philadelphia Sports Hall of Fame, November 3, 2016.

6. Ken Avallon (president, Philadelphia Sports Hall of Fame), in discussion with the author, November 3, 2016.

7. Philadelphia Sports Hall of Fame induction ceremony speeches, November 3, 2016.

Chapter 16: Life Is a (Relay) Carnival

1. *Philadelphia Inquirer*, April 28, 1924.

2. *Philadelphia Inquirer*, December 21, 1925.

3. *Pittsburgh Press*, March 28, 1926.

4. Joseph Lewis French, "Disapproval of Sesqui Fight," *New York Times*, September 12, 1926.

5. Martin W. Wilson, "Sesquicentennial International Exposition (1926)," The Encyclopedia of Greater Philadelphia [online].

Chapter 18: A Treasure Trove

1. *Philadelphia Evening Bulletin*, April 13, 1944.

Chapter 19: "Howdy, Partner"

1. Brian Gard (executive producer, *The American Impostor*), in discussion with the author, February 2018.

2. Joanne Vanderheyden (mayor, Strathroy, ON), interview with the author, December 17, 2016.

3. Bill Groot (researcher), interview with the author, December 17, 2016.

4. Larry Peters (researcher), interview with the author, December 17, 2016.

5. Dr. Robert Barney (Western University), interview with the author, December 17, 2016.

6. Mark Kearney (author), interview with the author, December 17, 2016.

7. David Langford (editor), interview with the author, December 17, 2016.

8. Paul Berton (editor-in-chief, *Hamilton Spectator*), interview with the author, March 12, 2017.

9. *Philadelphia Evening Bulletin*, April 13, 1944.

10. Jim Coleman, *Globe and Mail*, April 14, 1944.

11. J.V. McAree, *Globe and Mail*, May 19, 1954.

Chapter 20: The Fourth Estate

1. "Awards Recognize Canada's Finest," *Globe and Mail*, March 17, 2004.

Chapter 21: "We'll Fix It in Post"

1. Maddison Oswald, email interviews with the author, January 11, 2018, and March 7, 2018.

Chapter 22: The Last Mile

1. "History of Jump Racing," National Steeplechase Association, nationalsteeplechase.com/history.

2. Bob Finucane, "Bob Tales," *Chester* (PA) *Times*, May 15, 1942.

3. Matt Zabitka, "82 Year Old …," *Delaware County* (PA) *Times*, April 29, 1955.

4. Galja Barish Votaw, "Venerable Rose Tree," *Chester* (PA) *Times*, April 20, 1950.

BIBLIOGRAPHY

Books

Census of Canada, 1851–1921.

Clark, Fred G. *1903–1993 Camp Tecumseh*. West Kennebunk, ME: Phoenix Publishing, 1994.

Cooper, Pamela. *The American Marathon*. Syracuse, NY: Syracuse University Press, 1998.

Costa, Margaret, and Sharon R. *Guthrie Women and Sport: Interdisciplinary Perspectives*. Champaign, IL: Human Kinetics, 1994.

Dyreson, Mark. *Making the American Team*. Chicago: University of Illinois Press, 1998.

Hewitt, W.A. *Down the Stretch*. Toronto: Ryerson Press, 1958.

An Historical Sketch of the Village of Winchester (Old Home Reunion August 4–8, 1934). Historical Review of Winchester. Published in connection with centennial celebrations, June 23, 24, and 25, 1967.

Kidd, Bruce. *The Struggle for Canadian Sport*. Toronto: University of Toronto Press, 1996.

Mallon, Bill. *The 1900 Olympic Games: Results for All Competitors in All Events, with Commentary*. Jefferson, NC: McFarlane, 1994.

Miller, David. *The Official History of the Olympic Games and the IOC: Athens to Beijing, 1894–2008*. Edinburgh: Mainstream Publishing, 2008.

Oreskovich, Carlie. *Sir Henry Pellatt: The King of Casa Loma*. Toronto: McGraw Hill-Ryerson, 1982.

Orton, George W. *Athletic Training for School Boys*. New York: American Sports Publishing, 1905.

———. *Distance and Cross Country Running*. New York: American Sports Publishing, 1903.

Sugar, Bert Randolph. *Hit the Sign*. Chicago: Contemporary Books, 1978.

Wallechinsky, David, and Jaime Loucky. *The Book of Olympic Lists*. London: Aurum Press, 2012.

Articles

Amateur Athlete, Volume 2. "Ice Sports." March 4, 1897.

Baltimore Sun. "A Fine Hockey Row." February 20, 1897.

Buffalo Courier. "About Various Sports." July 7, 1893.

Buffalo Evening News. "The Fastest Mile Runner." October 28, 1888.

Chicago Tribune. "Smaller Crowd at Paris Fair." July 21, 1900.

Coleman, Jim. *Globe and Mail*. April 14, 1944.

Cornell Law School's Legal Information Institute. 20 U.S. Code § 1681 — Sex.

Finucane, Bob. "Bob Tales." *Chester Times* (Pennsylvania). May 15, 1942.

Flatter, Ron. "Thorpe Preceded Deion, Bo." ESPN.com. April 23, 2007.

Fox, Margolit. "Margaret Abbott: The First American." *New York Times*. March 9, 2018.

French, Joseph Lewis. "Disapproval of Sesqui Fight." *New York Times*. September 12, 1926.

Globe. "Athletics." September 28, 1891; October 18, 1892.

———. "Athletics. Canadian Championships." September 19, 1893.

———. "Collegiate Athletics." September 3, 1892.

———. "For the Purity of Sport." September 6, 1897.

————. "George Orton Exonerated." December 22, 1897.

Globe and Mail. "Awards Recognize Canada's Finest." March 17, 2004.

Hendrickson, Donald W. "A New Factor in Missouri Valley Athletics." Wichita: Kansas Magazine Co., 1909.

"History of Jump Racing." National Steeplechase Association. www.nationalsteeplechase.com/history.

"History of Playgrounds and Parks." nycgovparks.org.

Johnson, William Oscar. "The Taking Part." *Sports Illustrated.* July 10, 1972.

Kitirinos, Bob. "A Letter: 115 Years of Ice Hockey at Penn." The Buzz blog. *Daily Pennsylvanian.*

Letter to University of Pennsylvania Alumni Relations from University of Western Ontario. November 26, 1975.

Lytle, Andy. "Echo of Flying Feet." *Toronto Daily Star.* August 11, 1936.

Marsh, Lou. "Longboat Runs Dorando." *Toronto Daily Star.* January 4, 1909.

McAree, J.V. *Globe and Mail.* May 19, 1954.

New York Times. "Orton Meets Defeat." July 17, 1900.

New York Tribune. "Plan to Number Players …" February 1, 1914.

Orton, George W. "America Holds Superiority." *Philadelphia Inquirer.* July 31, 1900.

————. "America's Chances in To-Day's Paris Games." *Philadelphia Inquirer.* July 14, 1900.

————. "New Power in Athletics Coming." Philadelphia Inquirer. August 13, 1900.

————. "Penn's Athletes Shake Their Legs." *Philadelphia Inquirer.* January 7, 1901.

Philadelphia Bulletin. "Current Sports." December 18, 1905.

————. "Geo. Orton Marvel of Athletic Ability." January 12, 1921.

Philadelphia Evening Ledger. "Now My Idea Is This!" July 24, 1926.

Philadelphia Inquirer. "A Varsity Canadian Club." April 4, 1896.

————. "Activity in Athletics." December 24, 1900.

————. "Mr. Pond Smashed Mr. George Orton." February 20, 1897.

————. "Orton Skates in 3:59.1." January 20, 1899.

————. "Paris Athletic Games Concluded." July 23, 1900.

————. "A Varsity Canadian Club." April 4, 1896.

Philadelphia Times. "Yale Won the Relay." May 31, 1895.

Pittsburgh Daily Post. "Americans Get Big Handicaps." July 20, 1900.

Presse, Michelle. "Last Call Is Over for the Hard-Drinking Journalist." *The Signal.* Kings College Review. December 11, 2015. www.signalhfx.ca.

Ripley's Believe It Or Not. King Features Syndicate. June 25, 1943.

Rocap, William H. "Seventeen Titles for Orton." *Philadelphia Public Ledger.* January 7, 1923.

Sanfaçon, Gaétan. "Etienne Desmarteau." *Dictionary of Canadian Biography Vol. XIII.* University of Toronto/Université Laval, 1994.

Stouffer, Nathan P. "College Track Athletics." *Appleton's Magazine.* January–June, 1905.

Thorne, John. "Ida Schnall and the New York Female Giants." Our Game. mlb.com.

Toronto Daily Star. "A Famous Victory." July 18, 1900.

Toronto Star. "George Orton Is a Busy Man." January 16, 1901.

Unwin, Peter. "Who Do You Think I Am: The Story of Tom Longboat." Canada's History. Accessed September 13, 2015.

Votaw, Galja Barish. "Venerable Rose Tree." *Chester* (PA) *Times.* April 20, 1950.

Wamsley, Kevin B. "American Boys in Paris: Canadian Participation in the Games of 1900." Fourth International Symposium for Olympic Research.

Wilson, Martin W. "Sesquicentennial International Exposition (1926)." The Encyclopedia of Greater Philadelphia [online].

Zabitka, Matt. "82-Year-Old …" *Delaware County* (PA) *Times.* April 29, 1955.

Interviews

Abba, Stephanie, *Dictionary of Canadian Biography.* Email message to author, November 14, 2017.

Barney, Dr. Robert, professor emeritus, Western University. Discussion with the author, December 15, 2016.

Butcher, Howard. Phone conversation with IV, December 11, 2017.

Johnson, Dave, director, Penn Relays. Discussion with the author, November 2, 2016.

Kidd, Dr. Bruce, vice-president, University of Toronto. Discussion with the author, December 16, 2016.

Luff, Mark, Episcopal Academy, Philadelphia. Discussion with the author, November 3, 2016.

Marsh, Brad. Interview with the author, Philadelphia Sports Hall of Fame, November 3, 2016.

Meaney, Constance. Interview with the author, San Francisco, November 5, 2017.

Philadelphia Sports Hall of Fame induction ceremony speeches. November 3, 2016.

Saleski, Don. Interview with the author, Philadelphia Sports Hall of Fame, November 3, 2016.

Watson, Jim. Interview with the author, Philadelphia Sports Hall of Fame, November 3, 2016.

IMAGE CREDITS

INDEX

Book Credits

Developmental Editor: Allison Hirst
Project Editor: Jenny McWha
Copy Editor: Patricia MacDonald
Proofreader: Dawn Hunter
Indexer: Siusan Moffat

Cover Designer: Laura Boyle
Interior Designer: Sophie Paas-Lang

Publicist: Elham Ali

Dundurn

Publisher: J. Kirk Howard
Vice-President: Carl A. Brand
Editorial Director: Kathryn Lane
Artistic Director: Laura Boyle
Production Manager: Rudi Garcia
Publicity Manager: Michelle Melski
Manager, Accounting and Technical Services:
Livio Copetti

Editorial: Allison Hirst, Dominic Farrell, Jenny McWha,
Rachel Spence, Elena Radic, Melissa Kawaguchi
Marketing and Publicity: Kendra Martin, Elham Ali,
Tabassum Siddiqui, Heather McLeod

dundurn.com   dundurnpress
@dundurnpress   dundurnpress
dundurnpress   info@dundurn.com

FIND US ON NETGALLEY & GOODREADS TOO!

DUNDURN